Lush & Efficient

Gardening in the Coachella Valley

Eric A. Johnson, desert landscape consultant
David Harbison, CVWD water management specialist
Dennis C. Mahr, CVWD communications director

Coachella Valley Water District

Coachella Valley Water District, CVWD, is a local government agency controlled by five directors elected by the registered voters within its 1,000 square mile service area. That area in the southeastern California desert extends from west of Palm Springs to the communities along the Salton Sea. It is located primarily in Riverside County but extends into Imperial and San Diego Counties.

John W. McFadden, president
Russell Kitahara, vice president
Tellis Codekas, director
Patricia A. Larson, director
Peter Nelson, director
Tom Levy, general manager-chief engineer
Dennis C. Mahr, communications and legislative director

The information in this book is true and accurate to the best of our knowledge. It is offered without guarantees on the part of the authors and the publisher, who disclaim any liability in connection with the use of this information.

Published to promote wise water use as a public service by Coachella Valley Water District.

Address inquiries to:

**Coachella Valley Water District
PO Box 1058
Coachella, CA 92236**

A version of this publication appears on the internet at http://www.cvwd.org

Photography

Cover photo
by Scott Millard
Additional photography
Robert Keeran / CVWD: page 8, 12 (left), 24 (top), 30, 41, 44, 45 (left), 46, 47 (left), 48 (left), 52 (left), 57 (right), 58 (top center), 63, 64 (right), 66, 68 (right), 69 (left), 74 (left), 77 (left), 81 (left), 84, 87 (bottom), 93, 96 (left), 97 (right), 98 (left), 99 (right), 100 (right), 107 (left), 109 (top right), 117 (left), 121 (left), 125 (left, right), 127 (left), 129 (left), 131 (left), 132 (left).

Scott Millard: © page 1, 6, 7, 9, 10, 11, 12 (right), 13, 15, 16, 17, 19, 20, 21, 22, 24 (left and bottom), 25, 26, 27, 28, 29, 37, 40, 42, 43, 45 (right), 47 (right), 48 (right), 49, 50, 51, 52 (right), 53, 54, 56, 57 (left and center), 58 (left, right, bottom), 59, 60, 61, 62, 64 (left), 65, 67, 68 (left), 69 (right), 70, 71, 72, 73, 74 (right), 75, 76, 77 (right), 78, 79, 80, 81 (right), 82, 83, 85, 86, 87 (top), 88, 89, 90, 92, 94, 95, 96 (right), 97 (left), 98 (right), 99 (left), 100 (left), 102, 103, 104, 105, 106, 107 (right), 108, 109 (left, bottom right), 110, 111, 112, 113, 114, 115, 116, 117 (right), 118, 119, 120, 121 (right), 122, 123, 124, 125 (center), 126, 127 (right), 128, 129 (right), 130, 131 (right), 132 (right), 133, 134, 135, 136, 137, 138, 139, 140, 141, 143, 144, 145, 147, 148, 149, 150, 151.

Acknowledgements

Directors and staff of the Coachella Valley Water District extend their gratitude to Scott Millard of Ironwood Press in Tucson, Ariz., for bringing this revised book to fruition. Scott and primary author Eric A. Johnson were partners at Ironwood Press and published several excellent desert landscaping books together. It appeared that the best way to do Eric's final work justice was to have Scott package it. He did more than package it, he lent his photo collection to provide many needed pictures.

CVWD directors and staff also extend their gratitude to the staff of The Living Desert in Palm Desert for maintaining healthy examples of most of the plants found in this book and for allowing the water district to use Living Desert facilities to conduct its annual homeowners' landscape workshops.

A special thank you goes to Ann Copeland, now retired from CVWD. An educational specialist who taught water science to the children of Coachella Valley, she took on the additional responsibility of working closely with Eric Johnson, reading his text and identifying photos to illustrate it. She also worked closely with co-author Dave Harbison in developing and improving the district's landscape workshops that supplement this publication.

Additional CVWD staff who contributed to the success of this publication include Jim Weston who worked closely with co-author Dave Harbison, and members of the CVWD communications staff—Kathy Papan, Bob Keeran, Tom Voss and Frank Orlando—who helped prepare the pieces for Scott Millard to assemble.

Thanks, too, to Jacqueline A. Soule, PhD, Tucson, Arizona, for her assistance in reviewing the text for accuracy.

Library of Congress Cataloging-in-Publication Data

Johnson, Eric A

Lush & efficient: a guide to gardening in the Coachella Valley / written by Eric A. Johnson, David Harbison, Dennis C. Mahr.--Rev. and expanded ed.

p. cm.

First published as a booklet in 1988.

Includes bibliographical references (p.   )

ISBN 0-9628236-6-X (pbk.)

1. Desert gardening--California--Coachella Valley. 2. Desert plants--California--Coachella Valley.   I. Title: Lush and efficient. II. Harbison, David, 1943-2001. III. Mahr, Dennis, 1942-   . IV. Title.

SB427.5 .J632001

635.9'525'0979497--dc21

2001028710

David Harbison and Eric A. Johnson

This book is dedicated to David Harbison and Eric A. Johnson, its primary authors, who passed away prior to its publication.

David Harbison was urban water management specialist for Coachella Valley Water District for more than 14 years, and was a popular speaker locally on water-conservation topics. He was honored as "Irrigation Person of the Year" by the California Irrigation Institute shortly before his passing. Harbison was deeply involved with landscaping and water conservation throughout his career, and garnered 20 years of experience in designing agricultural, commercial and residential irrigation systems in the San Joaquin Valley and the southwestern United States before coming to the desert in 1976. He became known for his annual water-conservation seminars that educated homeowners as to how desert gardens could be water-efficient, lush and and beautiful.

Harbison was a leader in establishing CIMIS stations in the Coachella Valley, which supply vital evapotranspiration information to farmers and large domestic irrigators, instrumental in setting standards for water use in urban areas, working with state and city governments. He was also a member of the Department of Water Resources Agricultural Water Management Council, and appeared in legislative hearings to support what would become the Water Conservation Landscaping Act of 1992. This then became the standard for water-efficient landscape guidelines for communities throughout the state of California.

Eric A. Johnson was recognized as an expert horticulturist and landscape designer throughout California and the Southwest. He was a generous teacher and mentor to many. His work, and the way he lived, gave all who knew him inspiration. Johnson was commonly referred to as the "Landscape Guru" of the Coachella Valley in recognition for his pioneering work in promoting the benefits of using lush, colorful, water-efficient plants. One of his specialties was developing maintenance programs for area golf courses and large housing developments. He served as landscape specialist for the City of Palm Desert, designing and consulting on projects throughout the city. Landscapes that were given the Johnson touch include the Desert Willow golf resort and Civic Center Park. Even the landscaped medians throughout the city were designed by Johnson. Other high-profile Johnson projects included the Vintage Club Golf Course in Indian Wells, the Springs Country Club Golf Course and area golf courses designed by Pete Dye, Jack Nicholas and Arnold Palmer.

Johnson was equally prolific as a writer, helping establish Ironwood Press, a book-publishing company. Eric authored the respected *Johnson's Guide to Gardening: Pruning, Planting & Care*, and co-authored *Beautiful Gardens: Guide to Over 80 Botanical Gardens, Arboretums and More in Southern California and the Southwest;* as well as *How To Grow The Wildflowers* and *The Low-Water Flower Gardener.* Other published works included *Landscaping to Save Water in the Desert, Landscaping in the Coachella Valley*, and this volume, *Lush & Efficient*, first published as a booklet in 1988. He also contributed to many well-known magazines and journals, including *Arizona Highways, Palm Springs Life* and *Los Angles Times Home* magazine.

The Coachella Valley Water District extends its appreciation to these men. Their dedication and effort have made the Coachella Valley a better place to live.

Contents

A guide to selecting and growing over 300 species of landscape plants for the Coachella Valley, including annuals, perennials, wildflowers, vines, ground covers, shrubs and trees.

The Desert Gardening Difference

$\mathcal{D}$ESERT GARDENS *CAN* BE LUSH AND EFFICIENT. Contrary to the image of a desert garden consisting only of cacti, boulders and gravel, there are many native and introduced dry-climate trees, shrubs, vines, ground covers and perennials that are unusually attractive with lush foliage, distinctive form and showy flowers. Many Southwest desert plants provide as much or more color over longer periods than introduced tropical or subtropical plants.

The permanent resident can plant for year-round enjoyment while the seasonal visitor can plant for three or four months of spring color. Garden style is up to individual tastes, time and funds.

This book offers alternatives to a *high-maintenance garden* with tall oleanders for screening and wind protection with formal trimmed hedges, thirsty canopy trees, large lawns and expanses of spring annuals. You'll discover ideas for *transitional gardens* that provide a harmonious blend of subtropical plants in a mini-oasis or private patio garden. Add a small lawn for close-up viewing and enjoyment, and allow the remaining garden to gradually blend, or make a transition into, more water-efficient landscaping.

Gardeners who prefer the easy life may join the desert by planting native and introduced low-water use trees, shrubs and ground covers, with cacti, succulents and yuccas for accents. Creating earthen mounds and dry creek beds and add well-placed clusters of boulders and gravel provide a natural look that requires little water and maintenance.

Left: Lush, colorful and water-efficient: Planting low-water use trees, shrubs and ground covers with cacti and succulents for accents can yield spectacular results.

Above: Agave and bougainvillea make a simple yet striking plant combination.

High-water use plants such as hibiscus, azaleas, philodendron, cape honeysuckle and gardenias typically have soft tissues that require regular moisture to survive. Many subtropicals and tropical plants (nurserymen call them "the green stuff") are native to regions receiving 50 to 150 inches of rainfall annually. In the high temperatures and often low humidity of Coachella Valley summers, few introduced plants of this kind can survive without regular applications of water and shelter from sun, wind and cold.

Water-efficient natives and many introduced plants indigenous to low rainfall areas of the United States, Australia, Africa and the Mediterranean region can be grown successfully in the Coachella Valley. They have the ability to survive on little moisture after they are established for a year or two in the garden. Their physical makeup allows them to develop leaves, branches and roots that conserve what water is available. Some adjust to dry spells by going dormant until the next rain or water application is made. Olives, mesquites, palo verde, African sumac, cassias, Texas ranger, oleanders, crepe myrtle and Mexican bird-of-paradise are in this group. Subtropical bougainvilleas, strangely, flower better when plants are stressed for water.

Overwatering often creates serious problems. There is a fine line between the correct amount and excessive moisture. Keeping plants on the dry side, and encouraging deep and well established roots with deep irrigations, helps make plants more self-reliant and conditioned to extreme heat, drying winds and cold.

The Economics of Landscape Water Use

Most of a homeowner's water consumption can be traced to uses *outdoors* rather than *indoors*. In fact, it is estimated that 80 percent of urban water consumption in the Coachella Valley takes place outside the house.

To reduce water bills, many have opted for "natural" landscaping—a few cacti sprouting through decorative gravel. Others, recognizing the physical and psychological cooling affects of lush landscaping have planted tropical paradises. Unfortunately, they require huge volumes of water just to keep them alive through Coachella Valley's scorching summers.

However, home gardeners can have the best of both worlds—low water bills and lush plantings. The formula includes selecting water-efficient plants, grouping plants of similar water needs, and installing an efficient irrigation system.

Water-efficient natives and plants indigenous to low rainfall areas can be grown successfully in the Coachella Valley. This planting is at the Coachella Valley Water District's Palm Desert office.

The Ingredients of a Desert Garden

Heat

When summer temperatures reach 90°F to 125°F and humidity is low, the toll on young plants can be severe in a number of ways.

Increased soil temperatures in the shallow root zone of annuals and perennials can quickly kill new roots. Signs are brown leaf edges and wilting of new growth.

In areas of sandy, rapid-draining soils, plants suffer from too rapid drainage of moisture.

High heat is most stressful on plants grown in nurseries located in more temperate climates of the coast, and brought inland into the desert. The sun's intensity due to reflected heat from walls and windows add to the stress, especially in a west exposure June through September. Details on how to develop a landscape that creates shade to reduce energy costs is described on pages 11 to 13.

Cold Temperatures

Coachella Valley frost patterns, generally occur more frequently in lower elevations on clear and windless nights. Dry air temperatures drop about one degree for every 350 feet decrease in elevation. Cold air draining down mountain slopes usually settles in washes and in low pockets.

Signs of frost potential are indicated when temperatures drop to 50 degrees before 9 p.m. when there's no wind and a clear sky. Average date for the first killing frost is Nov. 21, with the last frost around March 15.

During periods of low temperatures, roots of tender plants can be protected by covering root areas with 2 to 3 inches of mulch, such as bark or composted manures. Tender container plants should be moved under the shelter of a wide overhang or patio overhead.

Plant selection should be determined on their inherent hardiness to frost. Tropical and subtropical plants are more likely to escape frost damage in highest elevations. One of the best methods of learning which plants to use in any landscape is by examining older, well-established gardens in the area.

Wind

The flow of winds and accompanying sand is one of the most trying experiences for gardeners in the Coachella Valley. Plants can help curtail the bite of wind and sand in the form of dense windbreaks (see page 12 to 14). They must be tall enough to reduce the wind's force.

Wind patterns coming through San Gorgonio Pass fluctuate with westerly storms and coastal fogs. They are most prevalent during late winter and spring months. Dust and sand begin to move when the wind reaches 15 miles per hour (mph) or more. A mild dust storm may develop at 20 mph. A severe sand storm can create havoc with windshields, paint and plants; usually develops at 30 mph.

Local winds contrary to the westerly flow often are stirred by the development of low-pressure areas in the lower desert or are brought in by tropical *chubascos,* storms originating off the west coast of Mexico or southwest of San Diego.

If winds are common in your area, locate plants in the garden with the wind factor in mind. Fortunately, the flow of sand decreases yearly as new developments anchor sand dunes. Walls, fences, hedges, lawns, gravel and ground covers also help reducing the problem.

Coachella Valley Soils

Experienced dry-climate gardeners realize the importance of managing soil, water and plants successfully. Fortunately, valley soils can be made productive. In upland and eroded areas, soils are shallow and require more work to become acceptable for plant growth.

Soils in the Coachella Valley fall into definite categories. Areas west of Palm Canyon Drive and south of Highway 111 in Palm Desert are sandy to rocky due to the area's alluvial structure. In some coves, wind-blown

The mild climate of the Coachella Valley allows a wide range of plants to be grown successfully. Tropical and subtropical plants are more likely to escape frost damage in the valley's highest elevations.

sand covers much of the ground. East of Palm Canyon Drive and north of Highway 111, most soils are predominantly sandy. In all cases, drainage is usually good.

Layers of *caliche,* also called *hardpan,* is a cementlike layer of calcium carbonate that accumulates below the soil surface. It can be a few inches to several feet thick, and is often encountered on slopes or flat areas. If the gardener's shovel bounces back at him, he can test the hard area by pouring vinegar or acid onto the area. If it bubbles, it's caliche.

Slow-draining soil can be found in La Quinta and points south. Here, gardeners must break through layers of silt or clay before water can drain. Silty sand builds up a crust that practically seals itself when water is applied. Commercially available soil penetrants made of sulfur compounds can be effective in combatting this problem. Wide planting holes, setting plants a bit higher to allow crown drainage of plants and other provisions are necessary in La Quinta and some lower elevation regions.

Organic Materials: Mulches and Additives

The addition of organic materials such as ground bark, composted manures and planter mix aids desert soils. Mixed into the soil, these materials retain moisture and provide roots with a better growing environment.

Mulching and additives can prevent soil crusting; reduce weed growth, need for cultivation, water use and even lower soil temperatures. Materials generally available include packaged composted ground bark, cotton seed hulls and composted sawdust. In windy areas, a layer of gravel helps to hold the mulch in place.

Working soil additives into planting areas make sand and loam soils more water retentive. Soil around new plants should be blended well with existing soil. Be aware that you must add enough material to substantially change the soil's composition. The small chart on page 17 will give you a guide as to how much a 2-cubic foot bag will cover. Prepare soil a few weeks before planting will allow additives to better incorporate into existing soils.

Soils in the desert are often alkaline, caused by an

In many parts of the Coachella Valley the soils are almost pure sand. Such conditions require that plants be given frequent irrigations due to the rapid drainage.

accumulation of sodium and calcium. Due to low rainfall, these two elements don't adequately leach out if soils are heavy. Fertilizer, such as ammonium sulfate or soil sulfur, worked into the soil thoroughly, helps lower the pH to an optimum 7.2. Deep watering in soil that has good drainage help alleviate the problem.

Salinity, or salts, is a problem in tight soils if there is not enough rainfall to leach, or move the salts down and away from plant roots. Farmers flood fields to leach salts into underground drains. Adding iron sulfate or soil sulfur to planting areas can help the residential gardener combat salt buildup.

Many desert areas on *alluvial slopes,* areas of young, rocky soils at the base of mountains, have deep strata of decomposed granite, commonly called *D.G.* These soils have been created by extreme water action caused by storms and the resulting runoff. Drainage is rapid. Plant roots grow well in such soils if given adequate moisture. However, when dry, alluvial soil is difficult to work. Mixing in soil additives and adding water to soil before digging and planting can help.

Landscaping for Climate Control

When you live in a hot desert climate such as that of the Coachella Valley, you probably spend more money to cool your home than to heat it. And as mentioned in the introduction, outdoor water use can be as much as 80% of a home's water consumption. Energy and water prices have been increasing and are likely to continue, prompting residents throughout the Southwest to find ways to conserve them both. The following supplies some ideas on how to conserve energy by using water-efficient plants in combination with appropriate landscape and irrigation system design.

How Plants Modify Climate

It's easy to feel the drop in temperature on a hot day when you walk beneath the shade of a dense tree, even if winds are blowing. Trees, shrubs and ground covers can greatly reduce cooling loads of buildings in hot arid climates by modifying air temperatures, solar heat gain, long-wave heat gain and heat loss by convection.

You can design or retrofit landscaping to keep cooling

You'll feel a definite drop in temperature on a hot day when you walk beneath the shade of a dense tree, even when breezes are flowing. Many plants appreciate the cooler conditions as well.

Research has shown that irrigated trees and shrubs around buildings dramatically reduces cooling costs.

Shading air-conditioning units can reduce their workload, making them more energy-efficient.

costs reasonable. Locating trees, shrubs and vines to shade homes can effectively lower the number of hours and amount of energy needed to cool a home.

Plants also cool air around homes through the process of *evapotranspiration* The evaporation of moisture at the leaf surface cools the air around the leaf. Research has shown that irrigated shrubs around a home can reduce cooling requirements by up to 24 percent. A mature, wide-canopy shade tree can cut cooling costs by 42 percent.

It is necessary to know where the sun is in the sky when temperatures are at their hottest so that plants can be positioned to block the sun's rays. The path of the sun during summer is much higher in the day than it is in winter. This means that summer sunshine tends to warm the east and west walls and the roof. Most sunlight in winter strikes south-facing walls.

Trees—Trees provide direct shade for outdoor spaces, walls, windows and the roof area of a home. The choice of tree types for summer shade could be either *evergreen*, where trees remain in leaf all year, or *deciduous*, when leaves drop and branches are bare in winter. In colder areas, it's a benefit to use deciduous trees, which allow warming sunlight to reach walls and windows.

Keep in mind that many trees take as long as five years to provide any degree of shade. Some deciduous trees provide a shade canopy cover twice as fast as some evergreens.

Ground covers—Ground covers decrease heat around a structure and on walls and windows, thereby reducing cooling costs. In place of a sea of gravel, a landscape composed of ground covers, a small lawn and shrubs can greatly reduce the heat around a home. The benefits of this cooling outweigh the additional cost of water to establish and maintain the plants.

Windbreaks and Hedges Help Control Climate

Windbreaks have long been a part of the history of the Coachella Valley. In the past several decades, thousands of acres of orchards, date groves, vineyards, vegetable crops and small villages were developed from Salton Sea to Palm Springs. Windbreaks of many kinds were planted to reduce the impact of wind and blowing sand.

Without the blow-sand control offered by the rows of tamarisk windbreaks planted by Southern Pacific, railroad tracks would be quickly covered by sand dunes.

Development in the Coachella Valley continues to claim large acreages of sand dunes up to and across

Oleander is a common windbreak in the Coachella Valley, but a viral infection has caused many stands to decline and die. The chart on page 14 lists other suitable windbreak plants.

Interstate 10. The need for controlling blowing sand and dust becomes even more important as government laws for clean air controls are placed to reduce the impact of blowing sand and dust.

Hedges and windbreaks helped control the burning and desiccating effects of the intense summer sun by creating cooler, sheltered *microclimates*. Microclimates are created with shade trees, fencing, walls and dense windbreaks. The single, double- or triple-hedge design continues to help create a kind of climate control that allows more fragile plants to grow and thrive.

Windbreak Basics

Consider the intensity of the afternoon sun, heat and wind when you locate trees and hedges for windbreaks, hedges and screens. It is well known that tree leaves can block 80 percent of solar radiation.

Divert wind with height and density. Tall trees can reduce wind velocity as much as 50 to 200 yards down wind. Study existing windbreaks. Look for for wind-created shaping of plants that were developed by prevailing wind patterns before you plant.

Multiple-trunk trees maintain better vertical growth under the stress of wind. Even with dense foliage, pines and cypress withstand heavy or constant winds with a rugged persistence.

All windbreak trees must have deep irrigation to survive. Drip irrigation has proven to be ideal to help trees develop deep roots.

A triangulated pattern with 12- to 18-foot spacing of trees, with lower ground level 10-to 12-foot shrubs (see chart, page 14), and conifers with great density, can create a strong barrier.

Trees for Windbreaks

Brachychiton populneus, bottle tree
Casuarina cunninghamiana, river she-oak
Ceratonia siliqua, carob
Cupressus arizonica, Arizona cypress
Cupressus glabra 'Gareei'
Eucalyptus microtheca, coolibah tree
Eucalyptus spathulata, narrow-leafed gimlet
Juniperus scopulorum 'Blue Heaven'
Nerium oleander, oleander
Pinus eldarica, Afghan pine
Pinus pinea, Italian stone pine
Populus species, poplars
Rhus lancea, African sumac
Tamarix aphylla, tamarisk

The photos above are the same *Casuarina* species windbreak near Indio, taken 7-1/2 years apart. Screening was used the first years after planting to protect citrus until trees attained sufficient size.

Alternatives for Oleander Windbreaks

Plant	Size (feet)	Density	Bloom Color & Season	Water	Foliage*	Growth
Baccharis sarothroides Desert broom	8x12	medium	none	low	green	rapid
Calliandra californica Baja fairy duster	5x5	fine	red, spring	low	refined green	rapid
Calliandra eriophylla	4x6	fine	pink, spring	low	refined green	rapid
Callistemon viminalis Bottle brush tree	15x20	medium	spring & summer	moderate	green	rapid
Cassia species	6x6	medium	yellow, winter-spring	low	gray	rapid
Condalia warnockii	8x10	security	white to green, Oct.- Nov.	low	green, decid.	rapid
Coursetia glandulosa	8x12	fine	white, yellow, pink; spring	low	green, decid.	rapid
Cupressus arizonica Arizona cypress	20x20	dense	none	low	gray green	slow
Dodonaea viscosa Hop bush	10-12x8	dense	spring	low	bright green	rapid
Elaeagnus pungens Silver berry	10x15	heavy	yellow, fall	moderate	olive	slow
Eucalyptus spathulata	20x20	dense	white, spring	moderate	green	rapid
Feijoa sellowiana Pineapple guava	15x15	dense	white, May & June	low-mod.	glossy green	moderate
Forestiera neomexicana New Mexican privet	6x8	dense	negligible	low	med. green	rapid
Fraxinus greggii	15x10	medium	spring	low	bright green	rapid
Ligustrum japonicum Japanese privet	10x12	dense	white, spring	moderate	glossy green	rapid
Leucophyllum frutescens Texas ranger	6-8x10	medium	rose purple, summer & fall	low	gray green	rapid
Myrtus communis Myrtle	10x12	dense	white, spring	moderate	glossy, bark green	rapid
Photinia X fraseri	6x6	dense	white, spring	high	dark green	moderate
Prunus caroliniana Carolina laurel cherry	10x8	dense	white, spring	high	dark green	moderate
Pyracantha fortuneana	10x12	dense	white, spring	moderate	dark green	rapid
Rhamnus californica Coffeeberry	3-15		white	moderate	gray to green	moderate
Rhus lancea African sumac	25x30	dense	fruit, female tree messy	low	dark green	rapid
Rhus ovata	2-1/2x10	dense	pink	moderate	glossy green	slow
Simmondsia chinensis	6x10	dense	spring	low	gray green	slow
Sophora secundiflora	12x10	full	lavender, spring	low	gray	slow
Tecomaria capensis Cape honeysuckle	10x15	open	orange, winter & fall	moderate	light green	rapid
Tecoma stans Yellow trumpet flower	12x20	open	spring & summer	low	green	moderate
Vauquelinia augustifolia	15x10	open	white, spring	low	green	moderate
Vauquelinia californica	14x10	open	white, spring	low	green	moderate
Viburnum tinus laurustinus	8x12	dense	white, spring	high	dark green	moderate
Vitex agnus-castus Chaste tree	15x25	medium	lavender, summer & fall	moderate	green	deciduous
Xylosma congestum	8x12	dense	none	moderate	yellow green	semi-dec.

Evergreen unless indicated otherwise.

Microclimates, the small climates around your home, can be used to your advantage. This protected spot is an ideal location for cold-tender plants.

Shade cast by trees or buildings create cooler, more protected planting sites. Eastern exposures are well-suited for plants that wilt in full sun.

Grouping Plants by Sun and Water Need

Plants that are efficient users of water employ many tricks to stay alive. Some go dormant in the summer. Others have leaves modified to conserve available moisture. They may have small surface areas; be thick, waxy or leathery; or fuzzy or hairy. Others have green trunk and branches. Still others have well developed, deep root systems designed to grab available moisture. Deciduous plants may require more water in summer, but survive on decreased water in winter.

Often, thirsty young plants become water-efficient adults. Many fast-growing young plants require a lot of water the first few years, but as growth slows with age and a deep root system develops, they may require only occasional deep watering.

Not all *native* plants use less water than introduced plants. Some plants native to dry wash areas, such as poplars, are high water users with aggressive roots.

Matching the Plant with the Exposure, and the Exposure with the Plant

Plants have natural light and heat tolerances. When you have a location at your home that you want to plant, get to know the exposure—north, south east or west—and select a plant that will grow there without stress.

South and West—The west location with afternoon sun is by far the most difficult growing area during the searing heat of the summer months. A south location has the benefit of winter warmth, and all season sun. Only sun and heat-loving vegetation perform best planted in a south or west exposure. These include the best of interior desert natives.

East—The east side of a building or wall is perhaps the most ideal situation for most sun-loving plants. Plants may be heat tolerant, yet are easily burned by direct exposure to the hot afternoon sun. They will thrive along the east side of a structure. Plants tolerating some shade also belong in this group.

North—The north side must be used for shade plants, but during summer months may receive sun. Plants in this north exposure may need protection from the afternoon or morning sun during this period. Shade-loving plants and those with limited heat tolerance belong on the north side of structures or trees. When working with this group, be aware of reflected heat from adjacent sidewalks, driveways, streets or masonry walls.

Planting areas for the more-sensitive plants can be expanded by taking advantage of shade from trees and structures. The filtered shade of an acacia or palo verde tree is a perfect place for plants prone to sunburn. This is especially true if they are in containers, which pre-

Planting areas for more cold- or heat-sensitive plants may exist in many unexpected locations. The filtered shade beneath this palo verde is a perfect place for a selection of potted plants.

vents root competition for water. Extremely sensitive plants should be potted so they can be moved to appropriate protection as seasons change. These plants must be located carefully, considering the variables in their exposure, spacing, water needs and cold tolerances. Not all are thirsty!

Hydrozoning Plants

Grouping plants according to their moisture needs is is called *hydrozoning*. This helps in the design and application of drip irrigation systems, which are just as valid for low-water use natives and other dry climate plants as for high-water subtropicals.

Highest water use plants should be closest to the water supply, such as planting areas within patios and along walls. This zone is the location for annuals and luxuriant, water -thirsty subtropicals.

Vigorous plants, such as cassias, Texas rangers and mesquites, are planted in the moderate water zone.

In dry climates, the low water zone in a home landscape is usually farthest from the house and water supply. Drought tolerant trees and shrubs are planted here.

Selecting and Buying Plants

When buying nursery stock, remember extremely large plants such as boxed trees take longer to become established than a plant set out from a 5-gallon container. Unless extremely slow-growing by nature, a smaller plant can establish itself faster than a large one, and may even outgrow it. The smaller plant has the added advantage of reduced cost, and usually react more favorably to transplanting than larger plants of the same species.

Mail-order plants—These are often shipped from suppliers in the Midwest or East, and generally arrive too late for the Coachella Valley. Order only if the shipper will guarantee delivery for planting in January or February.

Bare-root plants—Roses, grapes, fruit and shade trees are generally in nurseries December through February. They are graded by trunk diameter and height. Medium-sized plants are preferred for planting.

Flats, pots, packs and quarts—Nurseries usually supply annuals, perennials and ground covers in these types of containers. Avoid plants heavy with mature flowers,

How Many Plants do you Need?

100 plants . . .

Spaced 4 inches apart will cover 11 square feet.

Spaced 6 inches apart will cover 25 square feet.

Spaced 8 inches apart will cover 44 square feet.

Spaced 10 inches apart will cover 70 square feet.

Spaced 12 inches apart will cover 100 square feet.

Spaced 15 inches apart will cover 156 square feet.

Spaced 18 inches apart will cover 225 square feet.

How Much Soil Amendment do you Need?

2-cubic foot bags . . .

1 bag covers 175 square feet 1/6 inch deep.

1 bag covers 54 square feet 1/2 inch deep.

1 bag covers 27 square feet 1 inch deep.

overgrown or too succulent. Select plants with fresh growth and with buds ready to bloom.

Gallon, 5-gallon, 7-gallon and 15-gallon containers— Plants with heavy pruning cuts, oversized or root bound conditions should be avoided. If containers are filled with roots, plants are probably stunted and seldom develop normal growth. Trees often become overgrown in containers. Also avoid plants with sunburned trunks, cracked or woody trunks, severely trimmed branches and binding tree ties. To select the right specimen, look for fresh, new, vigorous growth.

24- to 60-inch boxed trees—These are often field grown and transplanted into boxes to establish and regrow.

When shopping for plants, consider the following important aspects of knowing and understanding plant performance.

❏ Size and width at 5 years, 10 years, maturity

❏ Rate of growth: slow, moderate, rapid

❏ Flowering habit, bloom period, foliage type

❏ Water requirement: low, moderate, high

❏ Nutrient needs; native plants minimum

❏ Soil type, drainage requirements

❏ Exposure: shade, sun, filtered shade

❏ Hardiness to cold, heat, wind

❏ Relationship to other plants' moisture needs

❏ Ideal planting season

When shopping for plants, keep in mind that smaller plants generally establish faster and transplant easier than larger plants of the same species. Look for uniform, healthy growth, and avoid plants that are root bound.

Planting Step by Step

1. Plant as soon as possible after purchasing to prevent drying out of the rootball. Best idea is to dig planting holes before buying plants. Prior to planting, water the container well to ensure the rootball soil is moist. Remove the plant from the container. If plastic, turn upside down and knock the edge against a hard surface to gently slip the rootball out. Handle plant carefully by its rootball—not by the stem—this helps prevents root injury.

2. Dig holes for plants that are at least two times wider than the rootball. It helps root growth if the ground is loosened beyond a plant's *dripline,* the area near the perimeter where rainfall would naturally drip off the plant to the ground. Fill hole with water to moisten the surrounding soil before planting. If water does not drain in an hour or two, dig deeper for more adequate drainage or select another planting site.

3. Place rootball in planting hole and add soil mixture, firming it around the rootball. Water plant and add soil mixture around the sides to eliminate air pockets. After soil settles, add more soil so that it reaches the top of rootball.

4. Use soil to build a basin around the perimeter of the rootball. It should extend to at least twice the size of the rootball. Make the height of the basin so it will hold at least 3 inches of water. If planting a tree that needs support to stand on its own, supply two stakes, and tie them loosely to tree as shown above.

Pruning by the Seasons

When you prune, you are directing plant growth. It is important to keep some key rules in mind that will help in maintaining or modifying the plant's structure.

Through all seasons in Coachella Valley, plants have a great vitality when given reasonable care and supplied with adequate moisture. Pruning, shaping, thinning and dead-heading flowers become important regular aspects of plant maintenance—more important than many gardeners realize.

There is a lack of understanding by many concerning how to maintain water-efficient plants in dry climate areas. Proper and creative pruning thinning and trimming promotes attractive growth, maintains a natural form and reduces garden work and debris.

Some Pruning Basics

Good pruning and shaping techniques start with plant selection. The gardener must consider rate of growth and mature size; plant form and texture; location related to sun, shade and soil type; flowering habit and spacing for width, height and proximity to structures, walks and pedestrian traffic areas.

Poor pruning practices are often perpetuated by a lack of knowledge about plant growing habits and flowering periods. Contributing to the problem is the over-planting of many new gardens, done to achieve an immediate mature effect.

Follow these guidelines to help you gain an understanding of this most misunderstood gardening practice.

❏ Generally, cold-hardy plants can be pruned in the fall. Subtropical and tropical plants respond better in late spring and early summer.

❏ Always remove injured, diseased, or dead wood out of trees and shrubs.

❏ Removing crowded stems and weak growth helps plants develop better structure and form.

❏ Naturalistic pruning, light, selective removal of branches and limbs, gives plants an opportunity to grow in their own form. Hedge-sheared plants are robbed of their individuality, flowers and natural beauty.

❏ Cut stem stubs close to a main stem to aid healing.

❏ Nip tips of new growth to increase bushiness.

❏ Fast-growing trees such as the many acacias, elm, silk oak, eucalyptus, mesquite, palo verde, and bottle brush need thinning to reduce chances of wind damage.

❏ Remove sucker growth on trees to prevent branch growth in the wrong area.

❏ Pruning roses requires a specialized approach. It is described on page 145. The same is true when pruning citrus trees. See page 147.

❏ Pruning tools work much better when you keep them sharp, and use the right size pruning tool that is in scale with the job.

❏ Better plant shape and regrowth develops when

Renewal: Many landscape grasses such as *Muhlenbergia rigens* benefit from being cut back severely in late winter to early spring.

Grooming: To improve plant appearance, remove spent flowers and stems after bloom. This is *Salvia clevelandii,* chaparral sage.

plants are pruned gradually over a period of time in contrast to once-a-year heavy pruning. As a rule, remove no more than 20 percent of the plant's foliage at any one time to avoid stress and sunburn of trunk and branches.

It is never too late to correct past pruning errors. Plants have great ability to recover from poor pruning and you can improve their appearance with time and adequate moisture.

Tree Topping

Tree topping, also called *heading,* refers to the removal of major portions of the tree's crown by cutting branches to stubs or to the trunk. This type of negative pruning is most conspicuous on eucalyptus and mulberry trees.

This mutilation results in clusters of stems emerging below the stub cuts, creating excessive, small weak branches vulnerable to breakage. The new growth can increase wind resistance, as the mass of branches become a "sail" in the wind, often causing extensive damage or loss of the tree. On a small scale, topping creates openings for invasion of rotting organisms. Stubbing also upsets the entire growth pattern of the tree. Over a period of time, the tree will generally decline in effectiveness and its monetary value can actually depreciate by 20 to 50 percent.

The Irrigation and Pruning Connection

The relationship of irrigation and pruning is a close one. The amount of water usually determines the amount of pruning needed. Overwater, and growth can be too lush, and succulent. Underwater, and plants become stressed, reducing healthy growth and inviting attacks from pests and diseases.

Proper irrigation is one of the most important elements to growing healthy trees. Deep watering with drip irrigation that places moisture deep in the root zone can be provided by irrigation schedules that takes into account the size of a tree and its root system. Trees in turf areas without drips or bubblers often have problems related to surface roots and a lack of deep roots to help stability and resistance to heavy winds. For more information, refer to the section about micro-conversions on pages 12 to 14.

Fertilizing

In many parts of the Coachella Valley, sandy soils and rock and sand soil combinations are common. They have excellent drainage qualities, but tremendous amount of water must be applied to keep plants alive when temperatures are high. Rapid soil drainage and frequent irrigation *leaches* plant nutrients down and away from plant roots. The result is a need to replenish these nutrients more frequently.

Because of the rapid leaching of nutrients from the root zone, you get far better results by applying fertilizers more often and in smaller doses. Adding soil amendments in the form of organic type materials are also useful to counter the rapid loss from leaching. Adding

Avoid topping trees. It ruins the tree's form, shortens its life and may cause it to become a hazard.

Baccharis 'Centennial' should be cut back every few years to prevent dead stems from mounding. Plant at left shows fresh new growth; plants at right shows build up of dead stems and branches.

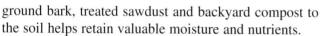

Compost makes one of the best mulches available, plus adds nutrients and organic matter to the soil. This simple compost pile was easy to make with cinder blocks.

Even if your lawn is small, it will respond with vigorous growth when given high nitrogen fertilizer. A healthy lawn also prevents weeds from becoming established.

ground bark, treated sawdust and backyard compost to the soil helps retain valuable moisture and nutrients.

The availability of fertilizers packaged for specific plant types and uses reduces the need to do your own mixing of nutrients. Commercially available azalea and camellia food, citrus food, rose food, and lawn fertilizer make a fertilization program simple.

After many years of testing in commercial projects and in nursery growing operations, slow-release fertilizers have become useful products for the home gardener. They can be added safely to the soil mix at planting time around plants roots, and provide nutrients over many months, reducing costs while improving plant growth.

New shrub and tree plantings can take a well-balanced application of organic plant food by the second or third month after planting.

Azaleas, camellias and gardenias generally need acid-type nutrients when plants complete their bloom cycle. Continue applications monthly through summer. Citrus trees maintain a good growth pattern when fertilizers are applied regularly from February to the first part of September. Roses need a steady diet from early spring into late fall, based on the bloom cycle. As roses complete a bloom period, apply a balanced rose food.

Lawns respond with vigorous growth when given high nitrogen fertilizers. Provide a monthly application from early spring through late winter. A healthy lawn prevents weeds from becoming established, and color retention is far better.

Deep-rooted trees often require deep applications of nutrients. This can be achieved by placing three or four slow-release tablets into 12- to 18-inch-deep holes dug into the soil around the drip line. Deep watering is

essential at all times.

Annuals, perennials, and ground covers often have shallow roots so pelletized types of fertilizer are safest to apply. Neglecting fertilizer applications can slow growth to the point where plants are actually stunted.

Liquid organic fertilizers are easy to use. The reaction period is fast and safe, and they can be applied more often. Dichondra lawns, ground cover plantings, newly planted annuals and perennials respond readily and favorably to liquid fertilizers.

As mentioned, continuous leaching can cause problems in availability of nutrients in the soil. Plants show a need by a yellowing of leaves. *Chlorosis,* for example, is caused by the lack of available iron or other elements in the soil. In such cases it can easily be identified: Leaf veins remain green while the rest of the leaf turns yellow. Apply iron chelates as soon as it is noticed.

Fertilizers are continually changing, and becoming more specialized for various kinds of plants. For this reason it's wise to seek current advice from your nursery on which fertilizers may be best suited for the special plants you are growing.

Mulching to Save Water

Covering the soil with a layer of organic material prevents soil crusting, reduces cultivating and watering, improves soil structure and lowers soil temperatures. Mulch layers should be about 3 inches thick. In large open areas, mulches help reduce weed problems and can add a decorative covering.

Mulches cool the upper layers of soil. The sun can bake the top inches of soil, damaging tender roots near the surface. Soil temperatures in mulched areas can be

Ladybird beetles (ladybugs) are beneficial insects, preying on insect pests such as aphids.

Be on the lookout for aphids in early spring. They love to attack tender new growth.

8 to 10 degrees cooler compared to soils without mulch.

Mulches maintain uniformity of soil moisture more readily. In areas where a silty covering effects the flow of water into the lower soil, a mulch reduces the airtight silt layering and permits moisture to flow.

Materials that are generally available include such organic matter as ground bark, composted redwood sawdust and compost. Gravel or rock are merely coverings. They does not improve soil structure. Bark chips and chucks can be used, but they turn gray in one season when kept moist, and can be blown about in strong winds. Animal manures are not always satisfactory due to problems with salt accumulation.

As mulches decompose and combine with the soil, it is necessary to replenish them. Mulches that remain too soggy should be pulled back from stems and trunks of plants to prevent fungus and disease problems.

Controlling Insect Pests

In many cases you can identify insect culprits by the damage they inflict on leaves and other plant parts. Fortunately, the number of pests in the Coachella Valley are seasonal and the majority of native shrubs, trees and ground covers are bothered by few, if any, insect invaders.

Sucking Types of Pests

Aphids leave their mark with curled leaves, distorted new growth and damaged flower buds. Their first arrival coincides with the burst of new growth in the spring, their most vigorous period of activity. Aphids come in many colors—black, green and yellow—and can literally cover lush tips of new leaves and stems.

Because injury is caused by their sucking of vital juices, you can control them by applying contact sprays, either systemic or those that create a fuming action.

To avoid killing their natural predators, such as ladybird beetles (ladybugs), with an insecticide meant for aphids, you can wash off the pests with water from a garden hose. Spray as soon as you see evidence of their activity and repeat weekly while they are active.

Aphids prefer roses, some annuals, new growth on pyracanthas, oleander and even citrus. Vigorous-growing plants such as oleanders usually have no problem outgrowing their damage.

Spider mite activity causes leaves to be mottled, stippled, and even yellow in color. Most damage occurs with arrival of hot weather. Shaking suspect leaves over a clean sheet of white paper will readily indicate presence of spider mites. They are so tiny that a magnifying glass must be used to see them.

Mites attack citrus, and are common pests on conifers such as Italian cypress and prostrate junipers. Follow the same controls as with aphids. If infestations are severe, treat with a miticide.

Chewing Types of Insects

Thrips are practically invisible pests, but leave their marks on the surface of leaves and fruit, causing them to form streaky and distorted scar tissue. Their most active period begins during the warming trend in early summer and again in early fall.

Controls are the same as with aphids and spider mites.

Beetles, caterpillars and grasshoppers leave behind ragged chewed-out areas on leaves and flower buds. Some critters even roll up leaves; others cut off stems of succulent annuals below the soil line.

Many *systemic* controls are available, which means that they are absorbed by the plant, and kill the pests when they tap into the sap of the plant. Other controls are sprayed on the foliage of leaves and stems.

Lawn moths and their caterpillars are only evident when you see the moths flying around at dusk over the grass preparing to lay eggs. The caterpillars that hatch do the actual damage. Apply controls onto the grass. In severe or questionable situations, contact a local nursery to determine the most current control materials to apply. Improvements are being made continually on sprays and dusts.

The incorrect use of pest control chemicals can be extremely dangerous and hazardous. Read all product labels and follow instructions carefully.

Disease Prevention and Control

A preventive control program is probably the best method for reduce the problem of fungi or other plant diseases on certain susceptible plants. Major plant diseases in Coachella Valley often involve citrus, oleander, roses and annuals such as petunias, vincas, and zinnias.

Poor soil drainage, with excessive soil piled high around the crown around the base of trees and sunburn damage on stems can bring on gummosis on citrus. Indications of this disease are the formation of lesions in the bark area near the base of the stem. Discolored sap may flow from the infected area. For controls, see Citrus, page 148.

Overhead watering of roses in the evening hours during periods of high humidity can bring on mildew. You'll see it as a gray powdery covering on new foliage and buds. Apply sprays or dust to treat at first sight. Avoid by watering at ground level and early in the morning, rather than evening. Zinnias and grapes are also susceptible to mildew. It may be helpful to grow plants or varieties that are less susceptible. Contact your nursery for recommendations.

Oleander leaf scorch deserves special mention. It's a recently discovered bacterial disease believed to be spread by glass-winged sharpshooter, a native leafhopper insect. Symptoms are brown leaf tips, with dieback spreading to branches, then to the entire plant. The bacteria shuts down the plant's water-conducting system, eventually killing the plant. Currently, older plants, 20 to 30 years old, are most affected. In addition to oleanders, other plants may be susceptible. At this time there is no cure. Contact your local cooperative extension service for help with this disease.

Weed Control

When you are engaged in a constant struggle to control weeds, you need to evaluate the costs, methods and effectiveness of using chemicals and their impact on the environment (local and world).

It's important to control weeds in gardens and landscapes to reduce aggressive competition for water, garden space and nutrients. A weed-free garden is more attractive and more healthy. Several options are available to control weeds. They include hoeing and cultivating, mulching to make them easier to remove, pulling by hand, applying chemicals or using the solarization method.

Using the Sun for Weed Control

Solarization, using the sun to kill weed seeds, is an important but simple weed control method used by commercial vegetable growers in the Southwest. Similar applications apply to the home garden as well.

The process begins after the weather heats up—late spring to early fall. Soak the area to be treated so moisture reaches to 6 to 12 inches deep. Cultivate soil to 4 to 6 inches deep. Lay clear plastic over the area. Shovel soil over edges of the plastic covering to seal in heat. Allow seeds time to germinate (2 to 4 weeks). The heat build up under the plastic quickly kills weed seedlings. After seedlings have been killed, remove the plastic and dead growth. Work the soil well before planting your wildflowers, vegetables, or annuals and perennials.

As for methods that require chemicals, seek the advice at your nursery for control products and application instructions. Monocots or grassy type weeds such as Bermuda grass, nut grass or Delhi grass require a material that kills weeds into the root zone. Broadleaf weeds such as Russian thistle, spurge and others have spray materials formulated for their control. In all cases chemical applications must be applied carefully. Follow all directions on the product label.

Month-by-Month Gardening Calendar for the Coachella Valley

January

Usually, the coldest month, days are pleasant and nights are cool. There's even a chance for frost.

Lawns overseeded with annual ryegrass need regular moisture and mowing. If yellowing occurs, apply high nitrogen fertilizer.

Last chance to plant bare-root roses and deciduous fruit trees. Prune roses and deciduous fruit trees.

Plant cool-season vegetables and herbs.

January is the ideal month to make additions or changes in the garden while cool temperatures prevail. It is a good month to retrofit your garden.

Now's the time to transplant cold-hardy plants, including perennials.

Check tree stakes and ties for support against strong winds in the spring months.

January: protect citrus fruit.

February

Warming trends this month set the stage to fertilize citrus trees. Water annuals and perennials diligently. Control winter weeds.

Complete pruning of roses and deciduous fruit trees.

February is prime planting time for shallow-rooted ground covers, native plants and other low-water use plants. Hold off planting frost-tender plants such as citrus and bougainvillaea until next month, due to the potential for late frosts.

Continue to plant winter vegetables. (See page 145.)

Check plants for aphids or other pests and control as soon as you notice them.

Begin deep root watering of trees in anticipation of spring growth surge.

March

The warm, mild weather of March prompts rapid and excessive growth of plants and, unfortunately, insect pests. Roses, citrus and hibiscus are most susceptible. For aphids, wash them off with a strong jet of water. If this does not work, check with your nursery for a safe product. When thrips attacks citrus, they cause leaves to curl, scar fruit rind, but control is difficult. Take some comfort in the fact they will be gone soon. White flies

Animal pests will want their share in spring.

are attracted to the color bright yellow. Place a sheet of yellow cardboard covered with petroleum jelly near susceptible plants to capture them.

Spray olive trees with a flower control spray and again when two-thirds of blossoms are open to reduce fruit set on olives.

The color tempo of fall-planted annuals reach peak bloom. Thin crowded plants, such as petunias. Tip back snapdragons to create new flowering stems.

Apply crabgrass control to lawns.

Water requirements increase on all lush plantings. Reset irrigation system clocks for more time.

Fertilize citrus, lawns, perennials and vegetables.

As flowering bulbs complete their bloom, remove old flower stems, fold and tie leaves with a rubber band for a neater look while bulbs develop.

Plant landscape plants to get them a start on becoming established before summer heat arrives. Most Southwest desert native trees and shrubs adapt better without fertilization.

March: Add mulch around cool-season vegetables.

April

A great garden month when the color season peaks.

April is the ideal planting month for tropicals such as bougainvillaea, hibiscus, lantana, cape honeysuckle and citrus. Begin preparing soil in sunny beds to plant lisianthus, calliopsis, marigold, periwinkle and zinnias in May.

If periwinkle plants wilt and die, they likely have periwinkle wilt. Remove and discard plants.

Bermudagrass needs to be "encouraged" this month. If lawn was overseeded with winter ryegrass, cut rye low, which slows its growth, giving Bermuda the opportunity to regrow. Apply high-nitrogen fertilizer and water in thoroughly.

As temperatures increase in the latter part of April, winter annuals will begin to look tired. Remove as plants fade or begin to die out.

Prune and thin cassias and Texas rangers in a natural form after flowering to control growth when plants reach 4 to 5 feet high. This increases spread and creates additional flowering wood for the following season.

Review irrigation schedules and increase water along with increase in temperatures.

Remove dead flowers and fertilize roses after each bloom period for a final crop before hot weather.

Control weeds and Bermudagrass in flowerbeds.

May: Extend watering basins for summer irrigations.

May

The first touch of summer begins to affect plants in many ways. Human activity in the garden also begins to be affected by the heat this month.

Review drip irrigation systems and flush out lines to eliminate debris that could clog lines or emitters. Increase watering schedules to twice the amount you were watering last winter.

Apply organic mulches beneath the root areas of citrus, roses and perennials while it is still temperate enough to work in the garden.

Winter and spring annuals are fading, while many perennials such as coreopsis, gaillardia and rudbeckia are developing vigorously and beginning their color season.

Clean up dead leaves and faded flower stalks on day-lilies. Depending on your garden's elevation, it may be

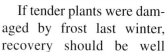

June: water regularly.

time to remove spent yucca flower stalks.

Apply acid fertilizer to azaleas, camellias and gardenias. With the watering schedules increasing, observe plants for chlorosis problems (yellowing of leaves) that might indicate lack of available iron. Use iron chelates if this occurs.

If tender plants were damaged by frost last winter, recovery should be well underway. Prune dead stems and branches to live tissue to clean up plants.

June

Summer has arrived with a vengeance. Time to stay tuned to a demanding irrigation program.

Prune to control rampant growth of oleanders, citrus, lantana, bougainvillaea and hibiscus. Thin excess interior growth of mesquites. Remove crisscrossing branches of palo verde trees.

Control tough, invasive Bermudagrass as soon as you notice it in planters and flowers beds before it can take over.

July: Check plant ties.

Roses, shrubs and young trees will enjoy a 2- to 3-inch thick mulch to keep roots cool and slow evaporation of moisture from the soil.

Palms transplant most readily in hot weather. When moved early in the warm season, plants recover with good growth, responding to heat and deep irrigations in well-drained soil.

Provide shade to protect sago palms from direct sun.

July

With highs of 105°F to 125°F, gardening activity practically comes to a standstill. Gardeners who are early risers find ways to take care of specific jobs despite the heat and, often, high humidity. Regular weed control is important.

Trim off spent roses that keep trying to flower despite the heat. Provide adequate mulches to help plants survive high temperatures. Continue to monitor irrigation systems. Any gardening task seems to become a gigantic obstacle in summer.

In the shelter of air conditioning begin thinking about some plans for fall planting or retrofitting the garden to become more water efficient. Use the traditional technique of using graph paper to lay out existing garden elements. After July, it is only two months until fall planting season, a time for renewal.

July: Vines need support.

Deep water trees. Palms need special deep watering. soaker hoses can be helpful. A good time to plant or transplant palms.

When chlorosis shows on eucalyptus and other trees, treat with chelates. Ask your nursery for product details.

August

A near repeat of July, only high temperatures seem to extend longer and higher humidity plays more of a role. Rains may or may not appear.

Remove dead basal foliage of perennials. Deadhead spent flowers of coreopsis and rudbeckia.

Trim away dead flowering stems of *Salvia greggii,* red

August: Trim *Salvia greggii* for more flowers in fall.

salvia. This stimulates creation of new flowering stems for the fall and winter season. Likewise, lightly cut back

old, tired stems of *Salvia farinacea,* blue salvia, to encourage new basal growth.

Time to make plans to plant annual and perennials. Order seeds of adapted wildflowers for planting of wildflowers in October. If weather is not too hot, prepare fall planting beds by digging organic materials into top 8 to 10 inches of soil.

Rebuild basins on plants, especially on slopes, to hold in irrigation water. Check drip systems for performance.

Control invasions of Bermudagrass. Hold off on lawn fertilization. Renovation and reseeding is a mere two months ahead.

Green scum on the soil surface the garden indicates excessive moisture. Check irrigation lines and hose bibs for leaks.

Hold off extensive shearing or pruning plants for another month. Pruning now may expose formerly shaded stems and foliage to sunburn.

September

As the sun drops lower to the south, irrigation can begin to taper off, however, deep watering of trees continues.

Beginning the 15th of this month, prepare for the most important planting season of the year. Planting reaches

September: prime time to plant.

its peak by Oct. 15, when winter and spring annual color such as petunias, snapdragons and pansies must be in the soil. This narrow window of time allows new plants to develop roots when the soil is warm before cooler late fall and winter air temperatures come on. Plant wildflowers, trees, shrubs and perennials. Plant bulbs and bulb cover such as sweet alyssum.

If renovating and reseeding lawn with annual or perennial ryegrass, it's time to slow down Bermudagrass growth by reducing irrigation and applications of fertilizer.

As part of soil preparation in flower and vegetable beds, add organic mulches and slow-release pelletized fertilizers.

If petunias, snapdragons and pansies were planted

continuously in the same soil for a number of years, apply a fungicide to prevent die-off problems with new plantings.

October

This is a month of sunny days yet it's usually comfortable to work in the garden. Plants are thriving as well. For information on planting step by step, see page 18. Hold off planting cold-tender tropical and subtropical plants such as citrus until spring, unless you have a mini-oasis area where plants are protected from wind, cold and direct sun.

October: sow wildflower seed for flowers in spring.

This is the month to turn your home into a showplace. Everything is in your favor: Nurseries are loaded with fresh plants in containers, flats, small pots and 4 inch pots. Well-rooted seedlings react readily to transplanting during this season. Pre-moisten soil prior to planting. Water plants in gently after planting and continue to water as they begin to become established. Avoid excessive moisture. Dig down into the soil with a trowel to 6 inches to make sure moisture penetration is adequate.

Overseed Bermudagrass lawns until mid-October. Wildflower seeding period is most ideal from Oct. 15 to Nov. 15. Pre-moisten soil before sowing seeds.

November

Continue fall planting programs if you missed the October period. Plants will establish slower with cooler temperatures.

Apply high-nitrogen fertilizer to ryegrass-seeded lawns to spur green color as days shorten and colder nights temper growth.

Bring tender container plants under shelter to protect from cold temperatures.

By November, many established perennials such as rudbeckia and gaillardia that flower from summer into fall have completed their bloom cycle. Cut back to basal growth and clean up leaf debris.

Chrysanthemums are in their prime. Cut flowers to use for bouquets. This helps flowering branches from drooping excessively.

At various times during October, November and into December, Texas rangers are in bloom. It's a good time to select by flower color at your nursery. This water efficient plant has many garden uses. More than a dozen selections are now available.

Roses in most areas will enter winter dormancy, although they may continue to bloom until severe frost. Keep beds moist. Wait to prune in late January or early February.

By now, red bird of paradise have gone dormant. Cut back stems to 18 inches above ground.

Hold off pruning or thinning citrus until spring.

December

This is a great month to take advantage of this delightfully mild winter weather, and tackle some major garden projects. Here are ten things to do in December:

1. Install a drip irrigation system complete with timer to save water.

2. Create perennial and bulb gardens to reduce planting of annuals, saving water and time spent on maintenance.

3. Develop a wildlife garden in a corner of the yard to attract birds, bees and small critters.

4. Grow plants to give them as holiday gifts.

5. If your landscape has drainage problems, create a drainage swale that might include a retention basin or a simulated creek bed with rocks and boulders.

December: Time to do the heavy work, such as installing a dry creek bed for drainage.

6. Develop a rock garden on a flowing mound to create a feature with ground covers and accent plants.

7. Reduce size of a large lawn area and give the space to water-efficient ground covers.

8. Create interest with ornamental grass accents such as *Muhlenbergia* species.

9. If you have an old garden with woody hedges and overgrown plants, consider giving it a face lift. Remove tired plants and bring new ideas into play with colorful, water-efficient, low-maintenance plants.

10. If an abundance of gravel or other inert ground cover surround your home, replace some areas with living ground covers and shrubs. Place plants at the base of structures to reduce reflected heat on the outside of buildings to help reduce cooling costs inside.

Water-Efficient Irrigation

$\mathcal{H}$OW DO YOU KNOW WHEN YOUR PLANTS NEED WATER? Drying winds, fast- or slow-draining soils, and the inherent water requirements of various plant types differ greatly. For example, established native plants need much less water than tropical and subtropical shrubs and trees, shallow-rooted annuals, perennials and ground covers and lawns. Other factors play important roles. Competition for water from the roots of nearby hedges and trees, age of plant, soil conditions, time of year as well as reflected heat from buildings and walls place extra demands on plants.

Lush tropical plants will require daily watering during the summer and two to three times weekly during the winter. Even low to moderate water users may need irrigation daily or every other day during the summer, depending on water-holding capacity of the soil.

Cacti do well without regular watering. Established cactus gardens can survive with hand watering from a garden hose two to four times a year, depending on rainfall. In fact, some years no measurable rain falls in the Coachella Valley! Generally, monthly or bimonthly watering through the summer is appreciated by even the least thirsty of plants.

All cove and dune areas of the valley have soils that are well drained and retain little water. The best water-holding soils exist along the Whitewater Stormwater Channel from Rancho Mirage to Indio, in the lower cove of La Quinta, in the Indio and Coachella areas and most of the lower valley. In some areas these soils may actually be poorly drained.

Plants and Their Day-to-Day Water Needs

Plants lose most water through their leaves when temperatures are high. Greatest loss occurs between noon and 3 p.m. Roots absorb water both day and night but, on a hot day, transpiration through the leaves may exceed absorption through the roots. If the loss is too great, plants show their distress by wilting.

Above: A drip-irrigation emitter applies water slowly where it is needed most: in the plant's root zone.

Left: An automatic, programmable irrigation system will save you water, money and time, and can provide plants with the proper amounts of moisture for health and growth.

A CIMIS station gathers local weather information and sends it to Sacramento for analysis. This information is then distributed to local irrigators.

If there is enough moisture in the soil, moisture content in the leaves will return to normal at night. Irrigation in early morning or at night gets water into the soil without undue loss through evaporation.

Watering in evening has as added benefit of high water pressure. Greatest demand on water is between 8 a.m. and 6 p.m. to 8 p.m. Sprinklers work at peak efficiency when water demand is at its lowest—later in the evening or early morning. For plants susceptible to mildew such as roses, morning watering is best, allowing leaves to dry before night.

Deep soaking of trees, shrubs, palms and vines, young or old, helps them develop deep root systems. Deeper, more extensive roots have access to reservoirs of moisture in the soil that will supply extra moisture to counter the demand caused during heat or extended dry periods.

When weather turns cool, homeowners often neglect watering Bermudagrass lawns. These lawns should never be allowed to become bone dry, even if they are not overseeded. Irrigate so they will continue cool weather development and recover more promptly in spring.

Following are some practical and important rules to make watering plants less of a chore and help them grow more successfully:

❏ Don't operate sprinklers during windy periods, which are most frequent in the afternoon. Winds blow water away and cause it to evaporate more rapidly.

❏ Create furrows or basins around plants so water will soak into the root zone.

❏ Install automatic watering systems where possible for regulated applications by both bubblers and underground sprinklers.

❏ Adjust automatic clocks to increase or decrease the amount of water applied as seasons change.

❏ Control weeds. They steal valuable moisture and nutrients that should go to your plants.

❏ Use mulches to increase retention of moisture in the soil and to keep roots cooler during hot weather. See Mulching, page 22.

❏ Apply water during the night or early morning in summer for highest water pressure and to avoid loss through evaporation.

❏ Light hand sprinkling from a hose on shrubs, trees and vines does little good. Soak the soil deeply.

❏ The appearance of green scum on the soil surface indicates too much water being applied. This often occurs in late summer or fall with a cooling trend. Reduce water applied, and check for leaks in irrigation system.

Suggestions for watering special kinds of plants can be found in the chapter Special Gardens, Special Plants, pages 137 to 151. These include containers, page 143; roses, page 144; citrus, page 146; and annuals, page 149.

Irrigating Ground Covers

Irrigating lawn with a drip system is not practical and using drip for ground covers can be a challenge. If a flowing, rolling ground cover is acceptable or desirable, the gardener may plant from flats in areas moistened by emitters. If not, gallon-sized plants with a wide-spreading growth pattern should be used, with one emitter per plant. Jet spray or microspray should be spaced for head-to-head coverage for watering consistency and uniform growth.

Avoid microspray heads in windy, exposed locations where watering efficiency can be so low the plant suffers.

Technology: Telling us How Much and When to Water

Computer technology applied to current localized weather conditions is now available to help the home gardener irrigate precisely to replace plant water los.

Developed and operated by the California Department of Water Resources primarily for agricultural irrigation, the California Irrigation Management Information System (CIMIS) is especially helpful to provide lawn irrigation to the home gardener. A home computer is not necessary, although it could make the information more useful.

Evapotranspiration (ET) and Irrigation

A computer in Sacramento regularly polls several automatic weather stations throughout the state, including the Coachella Valley. It records local weather data such as temperature, relative humidity, dew point, wind speed, soil temperature, rainfall and net radiation. The computer stores the accumulated data and calculates hourly a reference figure for the total amount of water a plant needs to maintain itself. This *evapotranspiration* (ET) rate varies by plant type. Precise figures for many landscape plants have not yet been calculated, but the reference ET, or ET°, gives the home gardener a good starting point.

If the daily reference ET is known, little additional information is needed by the average home owner to accurately calculate daily irrigation need. Irrigation system controllers can be programmed to deliver that amount to plants.

Moisture stress—replacing less moisture than ET losses—can cause plants to temporarily stop growing. By irrigating established plants at 80 percent of ET, the home gardener can mow the lawn and prune hedges less frequently without damaging the plants. They simply will grow about 50 percent less. Irrigating at less than 80 percent will cause plants listed in this book as *high water use*

to weaken and slowly decline, becoming more susceptible to disease and pests.

Fruit trees and vegetable gardens should always be irrigated at 100 percent of the ET rate unless they are solely ornamental. Without 100 percent, harvest quality and quantity will be greatly diminished.

CIMIS Computer

After obtaining a password from the Department of Water Resources, anyone with a computer and modem can access the CIMIS computer in Sacramento. The Coachella Valley Water District water management specialist can supply a contact name and telephone number. A link to CIMIS data also is available through the CVWD's web site: www.cvwd.org, which, incidentally, also supplies updates to this book.

No computer? No problem. Coachella Valley Water District and the National Weather Service announce local ET information every day on KIG 78, the Coachella Valley weather radio station (162.4 MHz). Inexpensive radios that receive only the weather station are available in electronics stores. No weather radio? Access the information by telephone through the district's taped weather forecast: (760) 398-7211, or (760) 345-3711.

Irrigation Guide for Trees, Shrubs and Ground Covers in the Coachella Valley

Trees & Shrubs	Jan.	Feb.	Mar.	Apr.	May	June	July	Aug.	Sept.	Oct.	Nov.	Dec.
*High	45	56	53	59	60	59	59	57	63	52	44	42
*Med.	31	35	33	38	39	38	38	37	41	33	28	28
*Low	14	21	16	17	18	181	18	17	18	16	14	14

Gallons per day for established trees and large shrubs (15 to 20 feet high and as wide)

Ground covers	Jan.	Feb.	Mar.	Apr.	May	June	July	Aug.	Sept.	Oct.	Nov.	Dec.
*High	2.4	2.8	2.8	3.1	3.0	3.1	3.1	3.0	3.2	2.8	2.3	2.1
*Med.	1.8	1.9	1.8	2.0	2.0	2.0	2.0	2.1	1	1.8	1.6	1.4
*Low	.7	.9	.9	1.0	.9	.9	.9	.9	1.0	.9	.7	.7

Gallons per day for small shrubs and ground covers

Irrigation Days per Week

	2	3	4	5	6	7	7	6	5	4	3	2

Plants are categorized as high, medium or low water use in the chapter Plants for Desert Success. See pages 43 to 135.

To calculate how long to water with a drip system, multiply the gallonage ratings of your emitters by the gallons per irrigation day by 60 minutes. For example, a 1-gallon emitter on a plant requiring 8 gallons per cycle: multiply 1x8x60 for a required irrigation time of 480 minutes, or 8 hours. Large trees naturally require more and larger emitters. Four 2-gallon emitters would apply the same amount of water in one hour as a single 1-gallon emitter in 8 hours.

Installing a Water-Efficient Irrigation System

Drip and Lawn Irrigation

Drip-irrigation systems are well-suited to most landscapes that contain only shrubs and trees. And a properly programmed automatic sprinkler system is a must for efficient lawn watering. Water buyer, gardener and plants all benefit from irrigation systems.

Drip places water in the root zone on a regular basis to encourage superior growth and healthier plants. Only the root zone is irrigated. No water is wasted on open spaces between plants. This reduces water loss to evaporation by as much as 60 percent and reduces the home gardener's workload because there is less wet ground surface to sprout weeds.

Sandy soils drain so rapidly that water moves little horizontally in the soil. Emitter spacing must be closer in such soils to obtain sufficient coverage of the root zone. If the area isn't windy, microspray heads may be more efficient than drip heads for plants in sandy soils.

Fine-textured soils allow drip emitters to produce larger soak areas, reducing the number of emitters needed. Gallonage requirements per plant, as shown in the chart on page 31, remains the same. But any reduction in number of emitters must be accompanied by a compensating increase in delivery time. For example, if you water every other day, double the daily gallonage shown in the chart.

Often, many different plant types are planted close together in the home garden, and some need more moisture than others. Drip emitters with different flow rates can be used at the same operating pressure to meet individual plant needs. Multiple outlet emitters also can be installed to apply more water to large trees or shrubs.

Debris entering broken irrigation lines is a common problem in the Coachella Valley. The debris is carried by flowing water causes filters, valve ports and sprinkler nozzles to clog and perform poorly. Once a broken line has been repaired, it is important that the line be thoroughly flushed out. This can be accomplished by first removing the closest sprinkler head and flushing the material out of the sprinkler riser. Then remove the end-of-the-line sprinkler head and flush until the water runs clear for at least 30 seconds.

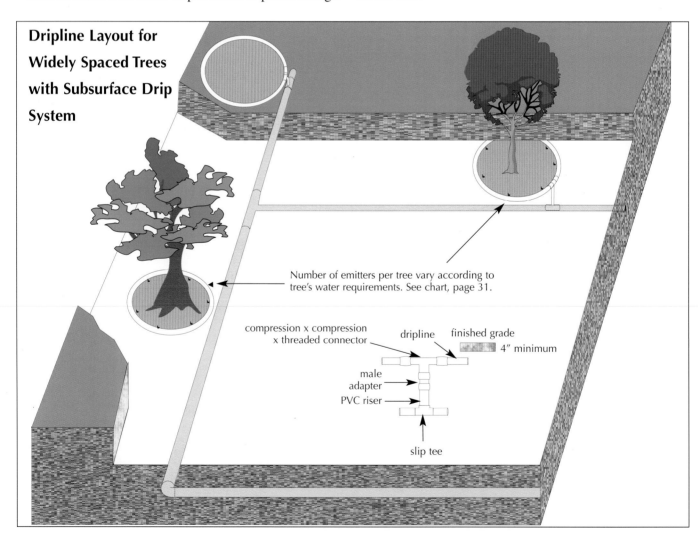

Dripline Layout for Widely Spaced Trees with Subsurface Drip System

Number of emitters per tree vary according to tree's water requirements. See chart, page 31.

compression x compression x threaded connector
dripline
finished grade
4" minimum
male adapter
PVC riser
slip tee

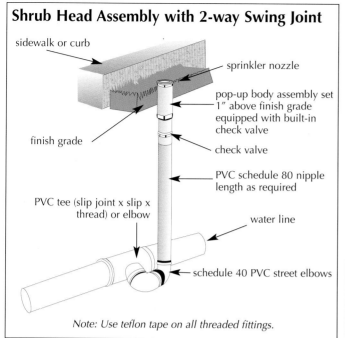

Shrub Head Assembly with 2-way Swing Joint

sidewalk or curb

sprinkler nozzle

pop-up body assembly set 1″ above finish grade equipped with built-in check valve

finish grade

check valve

PVC schedule 80 nipple length as required

PVC tee (slip joint x slip x thread) or elbow

water line

schedule 40 PVC street elbows

Note: Use teflon tape on all threaded fittings.

Lawn Head Assembly with 3-way Swing Joint
For easy adjustment of sprinkler to grade

sidewalk or curb

finish grade

sprinkler nozzle

pop-up body assembly (install flush with finish grade)

check valve

PVC schedule 10 street elbow

PVC schedule 80 nipple length as required

PVC tee (slip joint x slip x thread) or elbow

irrigation water line size as required

PVC schedule 40 street elbow

PVC schedule 80 nipple length as required. In final position, riser shall be at a 15-degree angle.

PVC schedule 10 street elbow

Note: Use teflon tape on all threaded fittings.

Irrigation System Design and Installation

Whether the homeowner decides to design and install his own system, install a professionally designed system, or contract for both design and installation, he will need certain information. This includes water source and meter size or connection size and location; static water pressure; electric power source and location; and dimensions or, if possible, a map drawn to scale, of the area to be irrigated.

Assuming a complete "do-it-yourself" job, the homeowner first should check what irrigation equipment is available locally. Before going to see an irrigation equipment supplier, the homeowner should make a list of required materials. The best way is to prepare a sketch of the system. If the irrigation plan is neatly drawn to scale, the irrigation equipment supplier should be willing to provide a list of supplies, along with a total price.

After obtaining supplies, the homeowner is ready to stake out the irrigation head locations, mainline routing and valve locations. Next, a trench is dug for the PVC mainline and wire. Then the mainline, wire and electric valves are installed. Next, trenching is dug for the irrigation heads and lateral piping, which are installed before the project is completed. The connection of wiring to the electric controller is last.

It is important to develop a landscape layout before an irrigation system is designed. Large trees and shrubs should be planted before installing the system so piping can be routed around them with ample clearance. The drip irrigation system should show exact details and specifications of what and where the pipe and emitters are to be installed—whether the work will be done by the gardener or a contractor.

An irrigation system designed by a professional irrigation consultant or designer is often well worth the cost. In fact, it may save the homeowner more money (in the form of reduced water bills) than the cost of the service.

If a contractor installs the system, all prospective contractors must have the same plan so bidders can develop proposals based on the same materials and layout.

Even though the drip system is designed for a specific landscape, it should be flexible enough to accept modification to meet changing needs of the homeowner and the landscape.

Microirrigation systems must be designed to accommodate plants when they reach mature size. They should be able to complete all irrigation cycles during peak-use months in 12 hours or less.

When planning emitters, determine gallons per hour each plant will require and number of emitters necessary. Systems are easier to size for gallons per hour per plant if trees and large shrubs are on separate valves from small shrubs and ground covers. When possible, cacti and other low-water plants should also be on a separate valve.

Most plants perform best when 50 percent or more of the soil volume within the drip line is moistened by the irrigation system.

Irrigation System Components

Stores that specialize in irrigation supplies can provide expert assistance and carry a wide range of specialty parts. Home-improvement and hardware stores, while not offering the same quality of service or variety of parts, usually sell systems prepackaged for the do-it-yourselfer with detailed written instructions. Avoid purchasing unknown brands. Equipment often cannot be interchanged with that of other manufacturers, so once a system is installed it is important to be able to have a dependable source of parts for replacement and expansion.

Filtration—Emitters must be supplied with filtered water to prevent clogging. The small tubing, which discharges water at 1 to 6 gallons per hour, requires a fine mesh filter that is easy to clean or replace. Mesh size should be in accordance with filtration requirements of the emitters.

Pressure gauge and regulator—Water in desert regions generally contains minerals or salts that can build up over time. The pressure gauge, installed downstream from the filter and pressure regulator, lets the gardener know when it's time to clean the filter.

Noncompensating emitters—These emitters have a set flow rate at a given pressure and are used on level ground. The non-compensating emitter requires less filtration and should be more resistant to clogging.

Compensating emitters—For use where there are elevation extremes of more than 10 feet. They produce a nearly constant flow rate regardless of pressure fluctuation.

Automatic controller—Electronic controllers are especially effective with drip-irrigation systems. They allow the user to match watering frequency and volume, taking into consideration various soil drainage conditions and plant requirements. With automatic controllers, a variety of plants with different water requirements can be served on a single system without sacrificing efficiency.

Automatic valves—Success of drip irrigation depends on accurate water application on a regular schedule. Automatic valves should be able to operate on low pressure and low volume.

Sprinkler Heads

Sprinkler heads with plastic components and with pop down springs are currently preferred to brass or metal.

Pop-up spray—Pop up height of 3 to 4 inches is ideal for a lawn, while 6- to 12-inch popups work best for planter beds.

Check for: debris screens to reduce clogging and seals

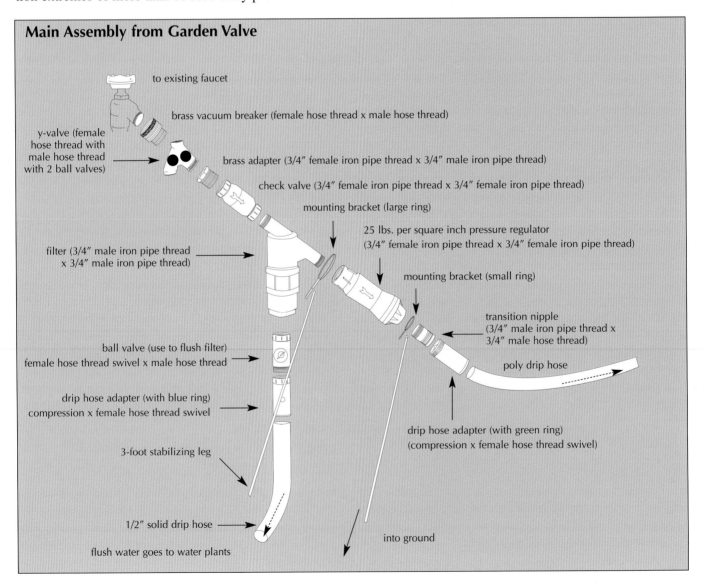

Main Assembly from Garden Valve

to existing faucet

brass vacuum breaker (female hose thread x male hose thread)

y-valve (female hose thread with male hose thread with 2 ball valves)

brass adapter (3/4″ female iron pipe thread x 3/4″ male iron pipe thread)

check valve (3/4″ female iron pipe thread x 3/4″ female iron pipe thread)

mounting bracket (large ring)

25 lbs. per square inch pressure regulator (3/4″ female iron pipe thread x 3/4″ female iron pipe thread)

filter (3/4″ male iron pipe thread x 3/4″ male iron pipe thread)

mounting bracket (small ring)

transition nipple (3/4″ male iron pipe thread x 3/4″ male hose thread)

poly drip hose

ball valve (use to flush filter) female hose thread swivel x male hose thread

drip hose adapter (with blue ring) compression x female hose thread swivel

drip hose adapter (with green ring) (compression x female hose thread swivel)

3-foot stabilizing leg

1/2″ solid drip hose

flush water goes to water plants

into ground

around risers to protect from sand abrasion and limit water blow-by. Heads should be available in several nozzle patterns and radii (color-coded ones preferred) to provide coverage on small irregular areas, as well as low angle nozzles for windy areas. Look also for check valves to prevent low head drainage on slopes, flow devices to control radius and misting and pressure regulation built into the head.

Pop-up rotor—Higher quality heads have metal risers and are resistant to sand abrasion. A minimum 3-inch pop up is required for lawns and 12-inch pop up for planter beds.

Check for: debris screens to reduce clogging, strong pop down spring, riser seals to protect from sand abrasion and minimum amount of wearing parts. Several color-coded nozzle sizes should be available to balance water output between full circle, 180° and 90° arc and low-angle nozzles for windy areas. Check valves should be present to prevent low head drainage on slopes.

Bubblers

Use to water planter beds by flooding or place them near individual plants according to their gallons-per-minute requirements.

Adjustable—Better ones require a tool to adjust..

Check for: wide range of flow adjustments, debris filters, set flow adjustments that hold.

Nonadjustable—More tamper-resistant than adjustable types.

Check for: availability of several flow models, pressure compensation to deliver same flow over wide pressure range and debris screens.

Valves

Above ground with anti-siphon—Brass is preferred if it will be located in full afternoon sun.

Check for: handle for emergency shut-off or flow adjustment, replaceable solenoid assembly, threaded body and ability to work with flows less than 2 gallons per minute if used for microirrigation.

In-line underground—Brass preferred if pressures will exceed 85 pounds per square inch.

Check for: handle for emergency shut off or flow adjustment, replaceable solenoid assembly, valve with pressure rating of 200 pounds per square inch, threaded body, pressure regulating module, ability to handle flows less than 2 gallons per minute for microirrigation.

Controllers

Electronic—Run off house current.

Check for: battery or other backup to retain program during power failure; dual or multi-program capability; minimum of three start times per program per day; 14-day calendar or programmable day intervals; metal case, lockable if it is to be installed outside; water budget feature; programmable by the hour for drip irrigation; master valve terminal and programmable booster pump terminal; programmable for rainy day shutoff; sensor input terminal strip with minimum of three inputs for program override to shut-off system due to high soil moisture, wind, rain or

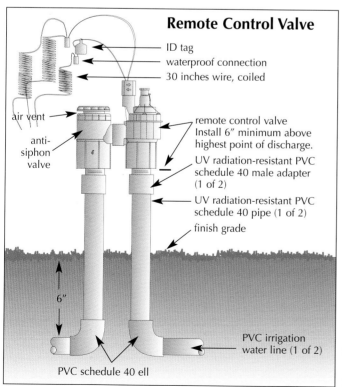

Remote Control Valve

ID tag
waterproof connection
30 inches wire, coiled

air vent
anti-siphon valve

remote control valve
Install 6" minimum above highest point of discharge.

UV radiation-resistant PVC schedule 40 male adapter (1 of 2)

UV radiation-resistant PVC schedule 40 pipe (1 of 2)

finish grade

6"

PVC irrigation water line (1 of 2)

PVC schedule 40 ell

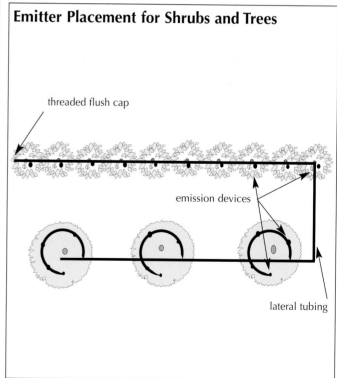

Emitter Placement for Shrubs and Trees

threaded flush cap

emission devices

lateral tubing

other unsatisfactory watering conditions; remote access by modem or radio; programmable to use ET data from CIMIS. (See page 30 to 31.)

Electro-mechanical—Usually single program.

Check for: minimum 3-minute cycle for spray heads; maximum 60-minute cycle for rotor heads and drip; minimum three starts available per day; 14-day calendar. For outside installation, check for gasket-sealed door and lockable, metal case.

Installation Tips

After installing basic equipment, PVC or other pipe is installed to connect main lines to valves. Then tees are cut into the lateral lines at plant locations after trees and shrubs have been planted.

Right after planting, basins should be created for hand watering until the drip heads are installed. Basins can be removed after the drip system is up and running. Prior to installation of drip or micro jet heads, flush all lines to remove soil debris.

The simplest installation of drip for home or small commercial application is to use an existing garden valve with pressure regulator and polyethylene hose or tubing to plants. Water them with the proper number and sizes of emitters according to the plant's inherent water needs.

Emitter placement is important. On slopes, place uphill 12 to 18 inches from the base of the plant so water will flow down toward the plants to provide more adequate root zone coverage.

Microirrigation Systems

For commercial and public properties, irrigation systems should be strongly constructed, resistant to vandals, operate with a minimum of supervision and be hidden. Often, home systems are more fragile, laid out on top the soil and require careful watching to be sure emitters and microsprays continue to function.

Professional-quality landscape microirrigation equipment was developed initially for agricultural use. Coachella Valley farmers have been world leaders in developing and using microirrigation techniques. Homeowners in the Coachella Valley benefit by having easy access to several irrigation speciality stores. Speciality irrigation stores are excellent sources for equipment and advice. There irrigation professionals are available to suggest problem-solving steps and provide expert guidance.

Residential drip systems generally use clean pressurized drinking water delivered by a public purveyor, but adequate filtration and pressure regulation is still necessary. Filtration requirements are determined by emitter and micro spray needs. Pressure regulation is determined by incoming static pressure and amount of pressure the emitters, hose, tubing and piping can accommodate.

A regulator is required to keep microirrigation hose pressure below 30 psi. Surface-laid polyethylene hose (residential use only) should have compression fittings that grip the hose from the outside. They grip tighter with increased pressure and are less likely than insert fittings to

Irrigation Guide for Lawns in the Coachella Valley

	Jan.	Feb.	Mar.	Apr.	May	June	July	Aug.	Sept.	Oct.	Nov.	Dec.
Spray head *according to captured water after 15-minute test*												
*1/4"	6	9	12	16	17	19	20	16	15	11	7	4
*3/8"	4	6	9	11	11	13	13	10	10	7	4	3
*1/2"	3	5	6	9	9	9	9	8	8	5	3	2
Rotor head *according to captured water after 30-minute test*												
*1/8"	21	32	45	61	63	71	74	61	57	40	24	17
*3/16	14	21	38	41	42	54	49	41	39	26	17	11
*1/4"	11	16	23	31	31	36	38	30	29	20	12	8
Irrigation frequency: daily												
	7	7	7	7	7	7	7	7	7	7	7	7

Perform the sprinkler coverage test as described on pages 37 to 38. Operate spray head sprinklers for 15 minutes. Operate rotor head sprinklers for 30 minutes. Measure the water in the containers, all which should be the same size. Refer to the chart above to learn how many minutes to irrigate each day. For example, 1/2 inch of water captured on a spray head system would require 9 minutes per day in April, seven times a week.

Installed and operated correctly, an automatic sprinkler system is the ideal way to irrigate lawns.

come apart during the heat of summer. Insert fittings grip the hose on the inside and can come loose with fluctuating pressure.

Commercial systems typically use buried PVC piping. Here, the emitter outlet is the only visible part. Standard installation will have an emitter at each plant except for trees. These will have three or more emitters, depending on water requirements. Multiple outlet emitters with microtubes to each plant should be avoided in commercial applications because raking and cultivation can disturb or cut the small tubing, causing the plant to die of thirst. If multiple-outlet emitters are used, they must be in an access box and the micro tubes must be deeply buried with the ends exposed and anchored. Length of the microtube should be limited to less than 10 feet.

Subsurface drip systems must have chemically treated emitters that roots won't penetrate or have physical barriers that keep roots out. These systems are used to irrigate trees, shrubs and planter beds. Lawns generally require sprinkler irrigation to germinate seeds and for complete coverage of established turf.

Subsurface drip should be used with caution on plants that are sensitive to salts. This is particularly true in salty soils when irrigation water may also contain salts. This is because salts can accumulate near the soil surface when the irrigation is supplied from below.

The best drip system for a vegetable garden is *irrigation tape* used in commercial agriculture. It is a thin-walled drip hose that has holes placed every few inches to discharge water. Lay out a hose tape for each row of planting. It can be left on the soil surface or buried one or two inches. You can install a ball valve at each row.

Lawn Irrigation Systems

Installed and operated correctly, an automatic lawn sprinkler system can be an important water-conservation tool for the homeowner. To help ensure proper irrigation, follow these few simple procedures.

To find out if water is being applied evenly throughout the lawn area, perform this simple test. First, set empty coffee cans, tuna cans or other straight-sided containers throughout the lawn in a grid pattern between sprinklers. Run spray head sprinklers for 15 minutes; run rotor head sprinklers for 30 minutes. With a ruler, measure and record the depth of collected water in each container. By using containers that are all the same size (with identical surface areas), water volume for separate areas around the lawn can be compared by pouring them into a kitchen measuring cup. If there is a large difference—more than 20 percent—between maximum and minimum, some changes or adjustments in the irrigation system should be done before proceeding.

Most spray head irrigation systems spaced 12 to 15 feet apart should accumulate about 1/2 inch of water in 15 minutes of operation. Most irrigation systems using larger rotor sprinklers spaced 25 to 40 feet apart will accumulate about 1/8-inch of water in 30 minutes.

The lawn irrigation chart on page 36 is for established lawns, watered during the cooler hours of the day, and assumes the use of Bermudagrass throughout the year. If you must have a green lawn during cool months when Bermudagrass is dormant, and you overseed with more water-intensive ryegrass, adjust this schedule upward from October to November to meet the germination needs of the rye. See page 142 for information on overseeding.

The chart assumes normal weather conditions and 70 percent sprinkler uniformity. Sprinkler coverage should be adjusted or the operating time should be increased to compensate for dry spots if uniformity is poor. Irrigation time must be increased when temperatures are above normal or conditions are windy.

Retrofitting an Irrigation System

Usually, in retrofitting an irrigation system to drip, most of the existing PVC piping can be utilized.

Although the home owner should try to use as much of the existing system as practical, any galvanized piping must be replaced or abandoned. Only existing plastic piping in good condition should be used. Because the new gallonage will be reduced, there probably will be a need to consolidate several valve circuits—either electrically or physically. Where several valves are on a manifold, that piping is best replumbed into one valve. The operation of existing valves should be checked at low flow. Existing valves may need to be replaced with smaller valves designed for reduced flows.

Drippers or microjet sprays may be installed on existing lateral piping and irrigation-head risers. However, PVC pipe or above-grade tubing may have to be run to individual plants. Make sure at least 50 percent of the soil volume within the plant's dripline is receiving water. This is especially important for large trees.

If there are no reasons to avoid having above-grade black plastic tubing (vandalism, appearance), it can be run from existing valves and "snaked" where necessary to water all the plants. Bury just below the soil surface.

It is usually best to install a small filter and pressure-reducing device at each valve, but this depends on pressure and elevation changes within the system.

The drip-irrigation controller must be capable of long cycle watering—from 1 to 6 hours. If it is electronic, it probably can be programmed by the hour, minute or even second. Electromechanical controllers usually have 30- to 60-minute maximum start times per station. If there will be a combination of lawn and shrubbery on an existing electromechanical station, it is best to replace it. If only shrubs and trees will be served by the controller, it may be possible to wire several controller stations together.

When converting an existing sprinkler irrigation system to serve the home-owner's microirrigation needs for other landscaping, the variety of plant sizes, water needs and growing conditions can make selecting emitter sizes confusing. Consider each plant's water requirement. Using the irrigation chart on page 31, the needs of each plant can be matched to emitter size and water use.

If some plants are growing beneath trees or in the shade of a structure, water needs will probably be less than for the same plant in an exposed location. Often, however, plants that prefer shade are high users of water and may require more than the trees providing the shade.

Because of the big difference in the comparative water requirements of small shrubs and large trees, they should be placed on separate valve circuits. Mid-sized plants generally can share any valve circuit available.

Irrigation of established plants should be applied at the plant's *drip line*—the widest circumference of branches. It is important, however, to match new drip coverage to the existing root system to prevent shock, especially during the first summer after the switch.

Microspray emitters provide the best water distribution to established plants growing in coarse sandy soil in wind-protected areas. The smallest available microspray emitter, however, delivers about 6 gallons per hour. They are best used on large plants or in planter beds containing many small plants that need the coverage of overhead spraying.

Keep in mind that all plants on the same station will be irrigated for the same amount of time.

Frequency of watering will depend on soil type and weather conditions. Information about these variables can be found on page 30 and pages 9 to 10.

Drip emitters usually come in 0.5, 1 or 2 gallons per hour single-outlet styles. Six gallons per minute and larger emitters are usually multi-outlets with up to 24 gallons per hour total flow. Microspray emitters vary from 6 to 30 gallons per hour with various radii of throw. Bubblers with fixed flow range from 0.25 to 4 gallons per minute. Adjustable flow bubblers range up to 4.5 gallons per minute. Flow regulating screens or disks range from 0.2 to 4 gallons per minute to make fixed flow bubblers.

Windy weather can play havoc with water distribution. If possible, operate when breezes are at a minimum.

Maintaining and Troubleshooting Your Irrigation System

When plants wilt or die, the cause may be traced to an irrigation system problem. Regular maintenance of the system usually can prevent this. When problems occur, troubleshooting techniques can speed repairs. Maintenance and repairs are easier if planning goes into the initial installation. Controller wiring should be arranged so all valves operate in sequence as you walk around the house. Some controllers have a two-minute per station check schedule built in.

Electrical problems can prove to be troublesome. Again, prevention is the best policy. Wire connectors at electric valves must be properly waterproofed or, better yet, use all UL approved connectors made for direct burial. Controllers should be on their own circuit breaker to prevent loss of power if another appliance malfunctions. Heat causes a lot of controller problems. If possible, position them out of direct sun, especially afternoon sun, and away from heat thrown off from air conditioning units. Replace backup batteries in time clocks at the beginning of each summer.

Preventative Maintenance of Lawn Systems
Operate the test cycle manually from the controller after each mowing to check for malfunctioning sprinkler heads.

All heads must pop up to clear the grass and pop down at the end of the cycle. If they do not, sand and debris are clogging them. Clean and flush out of the heads.

Look for heads tilted out of alignment, part-circle heads twisted out of horizontal alignment with sidewalk or curb, clogged nozzles and rotors not turning. Check for *head-to-head* sprinkler coverage. Each sprinkler should throw water to reach the adjoining sprinkler. If not, it could be caused by a major loss of pressure due to a broken head or pipe, which will need immediate repair. A broken sprinkler head can waste at least 500 gallons of water a week and also cause other sprinklers on the system to malfunction.

A "double swing" joint usually prevents major damage. The best time to include the joint is when the system is installed. To make a double swing joint, lateral tees and ells are installed at 90° to vertical and two threaded street ells are installed before installing the sprinkler riser. On existing systems, flexible risers should be installed to prevent damage. Without breakage, ingestion of debris—the next most common problem—also is prevented. If your irrigation system experiences clogging due to debris, the steps to take to remove it are described on page 32.

Homeowners: Be aware of possible injury and liability problems caused by sprinkler heads. Be sure all heads are below grade of adjacent walkways. If necessary, the heads may require pop up bodies to give the necessary coverage.

If lawns slope toward a structure or sprinklers throw water onto a structure, moisture can enter the wall and cause damage. Regrade planted areas to drain away from the building. Replace or redirect errant sprinklers.

Operate the test cycle. It allows you to see if each valve is coming on and shutting off properly, without hesitation.

Preventative Maintenance of Irrigation Systems

Spray heads and bubblers—Check for proper flow and leaks and for plants overgrowing spray heads, preventing proper radius of throw. Prune plants or move the sprinkler to provide proper coverage.

Emitters and microsprays—Check for clogs, outlets are above ground, there are no leaks and emitters aren't stuck in the flushing mode, causing flooding or erosion.

Planter irrigation systems—Operate as often as necessary to check for malfunctioning heads before plants are damaged from lack of water. Perform this check once a week in the summer and once or twice a month during the winter. Check all plants to see that they are receiving proper amounts of water. More than half the soil within the drip line of each plant must be getting water.

Drip system filters—Flush as often as necessary to keep system flowing without pressure loss. Checking pressure downstream with a pressure gauge or a Schrader test valve (similar to a tire valve stem) is a good way to determine a need to flush.

Drip system lines—Flush lines after breaks are repaired. For general maintenance, flush them at least once or twice a year to keep silt and other small particulates from accumulating. An automatic flush valve installed at the end of the line or at the low point will help.

Pressure gauge or Schrader test valve—Used at the end of a microirrigation system to diagnose leak or pressure regulator problems.

Water meter—Check the flow routinely when irrigation system is running. Changes in flow rate will warn of problems. Unusually fast flow is indicative of a leak. An abnormally slow flow indicates clogged filters or emitters. Some systems use electronic flow meters connected to controllers to automatically shut off a system or valve when the flow rate goes outside preset limits. When this happens, an error message is left for the user.

Controller—Check regularly that the correct time and day of week are displayed. If the controller is electronic, check to be sure it is running the personalized program instead of the default. If the default program is running, check the battery backup system.

Irrigation schedule—For heavy water users, make sure to check to determine if at least 80 percent of daily evap-

A single dry spot that suddenly appears in the lawn is probably the result of one sprinkler failing. For example, one rotor head is not turning or there is a clogged nozzle.

otranspiration (ET) requirements are being met. Low-water use plants may require only 40 to 60 percent of daily ET, while lawns in late spring or early summer may need 100 percent ET. See charts, page 31 (landscape plants), and page 36 (lawns).

Timing—Sprinklers should operate during the coolest time of the day in summer and early enough in the day in winter so plants are dry before dark. Drip- and flood-irrigated planter beds may be watered any time.

Runoff—Check for runoff before the end of an irrigation cycle. If water is running off, divide application into two or more cycles during the day separated by an hour of "soak time."

Controller program—Check and adjust every couple of weeks during spring and fall and every month or two during summer. Keep pace with changing weather conditions unless a soil-moisture sensor override system is used.

Diagnosing Irrigation Problems

Many sudden dry spots between heads—Probably the result of low pressure or valves not coming on. Turn on the valves from the controller. This checks the operation of the controller, wire and valve solenoid. If water comes on, look for a broken pipe or riser. Dry spots a few feet from rotor heads with green interlinking rings farther out between heads or, in the case of spray heads, green around the head and dry in between, is typical of low pressure.

A single dry spot that suddenly appears in the lawn is probably the result of one sprinkler failing, i.e., rotor head not turning or a clogged nozzle. It could also be an under sized nozzle in a rotor.

Valve doesn't come on—Check to see if the controller has power. If it does, check other stations to see if they come on. If they do, the problem is isolated to the wire or valve. Attempt to turn on the valve manually by bleeding. If this starts water flowing, power is not getting to the valve or valve solenoid. If there is another valve adjacent to the problem valve, switch (one at a time) the solenoid wire and the power wire. This should isolate the problem to either the wire or the solenoid. If the solenoid doesn't operate, replace it. If power is not getting to the valve, check all wire splices and look for signs of gopher activity, construction or other disturbances that could have caused a broken wire.

Reoccurrence of dry spots in same locations—usually caused from sprinklers placed too far apart or undersized nozzles in surrounding heads. Reoccurring broken heads at the same location can be eliminated by installing swing joints or flex risers. Be sure to thoroughly flush any broken pipe or sprinkler risers after repairing.

Plants often overgrow spray heads, preventing proper "radius of throw," or appplications of water. Using a pop-up sprinkler head as shown helps avoid these problems.

Plants for Desert Success

SELECTING PLANTS FOR VALLEY GARDENS IS A DAUNTING TASK, largely because the choices are so numerous and varied. Our sunny climate, mild winters and long growing season allows such a wide range of plants to grow and thrive.

Gardeners and home owners have among their choices "traditional" landscape plants—those that have been grown in the Valley for decades. Sweeping expanses of lawn bordered by hedges and bracketed by skyline palms, brought to life with colorful beds of annuals in the foreground, are common scenes.

Although appealing to many, these types of landscapes require a tremendous amount of water to establish and maintain. And water is the desert's most precious resource, one that is becoming even more coveted as the population swells throughout the Southwest region, increasing demand.

New plants that are attractive and colorful yet require less water to grow and thrive are recent additions to our plant palette. Years of testing and research by pioneering landscape professionals, nurserymen and growers have made them more readily available. Many are native to our region; others come from arid climates around the world. With a thoughtful eye toward design, these plants are gradually changing the face of the Coachella Valley, while greatly reducing the amount of water it takes to keep our landscapes attractive, healthy and thriving.

You'll find these plants in this chapter. As you look through the following pages, reviewing plants as candidates for your own landscape, consider the need to conserve water in our desert. In the long term, it is wise for all of us to select plants that are lush *and* water-efficient.

Left: Barrel cacti, penstemon (background) and verbena combine for a colorful and appealing low-water planting.

Above: *Baccharis* hybrid 'Starn' Thompson with mesquite overhead create a cool and refreshing scene at the Coachella Valley Water District's Palm Desert office.

In this chapter, the simple colored drawings shown below help explain at a glance the exposure and water requirements for each plant.

 Full Sun

 Partial Sun

 Shade

 High Water

 Moderate Water

 Low Water

Use these only as a general guide. The health, age, location in the garden and soil conditions will affect a plant's culture. Sometimes plants accept a wide range of exposures and water applications. Be a regular observer of your plants so you can take action to correct problems early on.

Acacia species, Acacia

Acacias are native to Australia, Africa, Mexico, Texas, South America and the southwestern United States. Evergreen and deciduous species are available. All have a tolerance to heat and are low to moderate water users once established. Provide acacias with deep, infrequent watering to help establish deep roots.

Acacia aneura, MULGA TREE OR SHRUB

An evergreen and thornless acacia to 20 feet high and 15 to 20 feet wide. Makes a fine windbreak and screen. Yellow catkin flowers are heaviest during late spring into summer. Tree form and small, narrow, silvery gray leaves are leathery, similar to that of an olive tree. Native to Australia. Hardy to 24°F.

Acacia berlandieri, GUAJILLO TREE

Like many acacias, light green leaves are delicate and almost fernlike. Trees grow to 10 to 15 feet high and 12 feet wide. Fragrant, cream-colored puffball flowers bloom in tune with spring weather. Locate in well-drained soil. Smallish thorns are not a serious problem. Gradually prune lower branches to develop small tree form. Native to southern Texas and Mexico. Hardy to 20°F.

Acacia craspedocarpa, LEATHERLEAF ACACIA SHRUB

Grows 10 to 15 feet high with gray-green leaves. A suitable alternative to oleander. Evergreen. Native to Australia. Hardy to 18°F.

Acacia farnesiana, SWEET ACACIA   TREE

(A. smallii, A. minuta). A native of Mexico, with fernlike leaves, thorny branches and vase-shaped form. Deciduous to semi-deciduous, multi-trunk or standard form grows 20 to 25 feet high and as wide. Yellow puffball flowers are profuse in spring and produce a wonderful sweet fragrance. Suckers after heavy pruning. Hardy to 20°F.

Acacia pennatula, SIERRA MADRE ACACIA   TREE

Admired for its tropical fernlike growth that is similar to *Albizia julibrissin,* silk tree. (See page 47.) Develops an evergreen canopy 20 to 30 feet wide to 15 to 20 feet high. Puffball flowers are yellow. Native to Mexico. Hardy to 20°F.

Acacia redolens, PROSTRATE ACACIA   GROUND COVER

'Desert Carpet'™ is an improved selection with a more prostrate growth habit. Generally reaches 1-1/2 to 2 feet high and can spread 8 to 10 feet wide. Some mounding occurs at crown. Remove vertical growth shoots as they occur. Rapid coverage on slopes and for erosion control. Accepts no traffic. Low water use once established. Native to Australia. Hardy to 18°F.

Acacia salicina, WILLOW ACACIA   TREE

An alternative to weeping willow, which is often short-lived in desert regions. Pendulous, graceful, evergreen foliage to 20 to 40 feet high. Creamy white puffball flowers bloom in late summer into winter. Water deeply to avoid blow over. Native to Australia. Hardy to 20°F.

Acacia saligna, BLUE LEAF WATTLE, WEEPING WATTLE   TREE

Rapid, aggressive, vertical growth with a dense canopy to 20 feet high with an

Opposite page: *Acacia aneura,* mulga, is an evergreen and thornless acacia growing to 20 feet high and 15 to 20 feet wide.

Below left: *Acacia saligna,* blue leaf wattle, becomes covered with large, yellow puffball flowers in spring.

Below: Yellow flowers of *Acacia farnesiana,* sweet acacia, are profuse in spring and produce a wonderful fragrance.

equal spread. Evergreen leaves drape gracefully toward the ground. In spring, large yellow flowers adorn stems. Native to Australia. Hardy to 22°F.

Acacia stenophylla, SHOESTRING ACACIA   TREE

Strong, vertical and graceful, stringy, soft gray-green, evergreen leaves up to 4 inches long hang from its branches. Can reach 25 to 30 feet high and spread only 15 to 20 feet wide, ideal for narrow spaces. A clean tree that does not produce much litter—useful around pool and patio areas. Requires minimum pruning. Native to Australia. Hardy to 20°F.

Achillea tomentosa, WOOLLY YARROW   PERENNIAL

Mat-forming perennial with gray-green, fernlike foliage and golden flower spikes 6 to 10 inches high. Flowers bloom in late spring. Use in a border or as a foreground plant. Sun or partial shade. Low water use. Cold hardy.

African daisy—*see Dimorphotheca sinuata*

African sumac—*see Rhus lancea*

Agapanthus orientalis, LILY-OF-THE-NILE   PERENNIAL

Produces large clusters of blue flowers on 2-foot stems surrounded by dark green, straplike, evergreen leaves. Fleshy roots store moisture. Effective in containers as well as in a natural garden design. Locate where plants will receive afternoon shade; they burn in summer sun. Cold tender. 'Albidus',

Acacia stenophylla, shoestring acacia, can reach 25 to 30 feet high and spread only 15 to 20 feet wide, ideal for narrow spaces.

white lily-of-the-Nile, produces large clusters of white flowers. 'Peter Pan', dwarf lily-of-the-Nile, has more narrow leaves. Flowers are blue and bloom in clusters on 12- to 15-inch stems. 'Peter Pan Albus', dwarf white lily of the Nile, has white flower clusters on 12- to 15-inch stems.

Agave americana, CENTURY PLANT   ACCENT

Evergreen, grayish blue-green leaf blades. Grows 6 to 10 feet high with an even greater spread—too large for an accent plant in many gardens. Plants typically flower after they are 10 years old or more. The single bloom stalk can reach 15 to 30 feet high, after which the plant dies. Hardy to 20°F.

Agave vilmoriniana, OCTOPUS AGAVE   ACCENT

Evergreen with long, curving, blue-gray, thornless leaf blades. Graceful, sculptural appearance is softer than *Agave americana.* Grows to 4 feet high, sprawling 5 to 6 feet wide. Blooms after five years or more then dies. Hardy to 25°F.

Ajuga reptans, CARPET BUGLE   GROUND COVER

The creeping stems and dark green leaves of carpet bugle create a thick, mat-like background for its showy blue flower spikes in spring. Grows best in shade or beneath a tree canopy that allows filtered light. Semi-deciduous in winter. Accepts some traffic. Grows 3 to 4 inches high in shade. High to moderate water user, depending on the season. Transplants well from root divisions made at plant crown; plant 6 to 12 inches apart. Mow planting after bloom has passed to renew. Cold hardy. 'Atropurpurea,' bronze ajuga, has bronze leaves and dark purple flowers, which are splendid in contrast with green-foliaged plants. Accepts minimum traffic. Prefers a little more shade than *Ajuga reptans.*

Albizia julibrissin, SILK TREE, MIMOSA TREE   TREE

Deciduous tree to 25 to 35 feet high at maturity. Sometimes short-lived. Creates a wide canopy with graceful, light green, feathery foliage. Produces an abundance of rich pink, silky flowers in summer, sporadically other times of the year. As flowers and pods drop, they create a fair amount of litter. A nice tree to view from above. Low to moderate water use but deep watering is essential. Native to Asia. Hardy to 15°F.

Left: *Albizia julibrissin,* silk tree, creates a wide canopy with graceful, light green, feathery foliage. Produces an abundance of rich pink, silky flowers in summer, sporadically other times of the year.

Below: *Agave vilmoriniana* is graceful and more sculptural in appearance compared to *Agave americana.* Grows to 4 feet high, sprawling 5 to 6 feet wide.

Above: *Aloe vera* is the aloe known and used for its medicinal qualities. Yellow flowers bloom late winter and into spring, appearing on 12-inch spikes above the narrow, gray-green leaves.

Above right: Hummingbirds and butterflies flock to the tubular, orange to red flowers of *Anisacanthus quadrifidus* var. *brevifolius* 'Mountain Flame'™.

Algerian ivy—*see Hedera canariensis*

Aloe arborescens, GIANT ALOE   ACCENT

The strong, spreading, basal growth of this aloe makes it a good accent plant. Tall, vertical stems are tipped with orangish flowers in spring. Attracts hummingbirds. Native to South Africa. Hardy to 30°F.

Aloe vera, ALOE VERA, TRUE ALOE   ACCENT

(*A. barbadensis*). This evergreen succulent grows to 2 feet high, spreading to 3 feet wide. Yellow flowers bloom late winter and into spring, appearing on 12-inch spikes above the narrow, gray-green leaves that do not have spots. This is the aloe used for its medicinal qualities. Attracts hummingbirds. Moderate water, best in partial shade. Hardy to 25°F.

Ammi majus, BISHOP'S FLOWERS   ANNUAL

This plant is similar in appearance to Queen Anne's lace, growing to 3 feet high. White flowers bloom in summer, set off by finely dissected leaves that have toothlike margins. Excellent cut flower. Plant in full sun in almost any soil. Easy to start from seed.

Angel's hair—*see Artemisia schmidtiana* 'Silver Mound'

Anisacanthus species, DESERT HONEYSUCKLE   SHRUB

Two *Anisacanthus* species share the common name of desert honeysuckle. Hummingbirds and butterflies flock to the tubular, orange to red flowers that are loaded with nectar. They are deciduous and excellent for wildlife habitats. Plants grow 3 to 5 feet high and as wide with a natural form. Well-drained soil important. Low water use after plants are established.

Anisacanthus quadrifidus var. *brevifolius* 'Mountain Flame'™ and *A. quadrifidus* var. *wrightii* 'Mexican Flame'™ are grown for their abundant orange

flower clusters. Most flowering occurs midsummer until frost. Cut plants back to 12 inches in winter for renewed growth in spring. Both are hardy to 10°F.

Anisacanthus thurberi produces orange or yellow tubular flowers that bloom in spring and summer. Native to Arizona and New Mexico. Hardy to 20°F.

Anisodontea hypomandarum, S. AFRICAN MALLOW   SHRUB

A recent introduction to the West, South African mallow blooms on and off throughout the year with a great show of rose-pink flowers. Use this 3 to 4-foot plant in a border or as a foreground to taller plants. Place in groupings or in containers for close-up viewing. Good soil drainage is a must, as is partial shade. Moderate water use. Plants respond to occasional light thinning and trimming, developing fuller growth. Hardy to 25°F.

Antigonon leptopus, QUEEN'S WREATH, CORAL VINE   VINE

A rapid-climbing, deciduous vine that produces profuse, bright pink flowers with deeper pink centers. 'Baja Red' produces bright red flowers. Queen's wreath blooms freely in summer, providing quick, attractive cover to 30 to 40 feet long, with clusters of flowers and 4-inch, heart-shaped leaves. Attracts bees. Plant goes dormant and freezes to ground when temperatures drop below 32°F. It regrows from roots when warm temperatures return in spring.

Antirrhinum majus, SNAPDRAGON   ANNUAL

Tall, 1- to 1-1/2-foot "tetra" forms do best when staked early in their life to support stems. Dwarf types 6 to 18 inches high are ideal for massing and in borders. All forms are colorful as cut flowers. Plant midOctober to February in a sunny location. Thin or space 12 to 15 inches apart. Plants bloom well into spring with regular water and monthly fertilizer. Flood or drip irrigate. Applying water overhead and the water on leaves helps promote rust disease.

Antigonon leptopus, queen's wreath, blooms freely in summer, providing a rapid-growing, attractive cover with clusters of flowers and 4-inch, heart-shaped leaves.

Above: *Aquilegia* hybrids, columbine, produce delicate flowers on long stems in salmon, yellow, lavender or white. Plant in masses for best display.

Above right: *Arecastrum romanzoffianum,* queen palm, grows with a straight trunk to 25 to 40 feet with graceful, arching, feathery leaves.

Apache plume—*see Fallugia paradoxa*

Aquilegia hybrids, COLUMBINE PERENNIAL

Herbaceous plants growing 1 to 3 feet high with gray-green leaves. Large delicate flowers on long stems may be salmon, yellow, lavender or white. Plant in masses for best display. Locate where plants will receive afternoon shade in a rich, organic soil. Loved by hummingbirds. Moderate water use. Cut back winter-dormant plants for regrowth the following spring.

Arecastrum romanzoffianum, QUEEN PALM FEATHER PALM

(Syagrus romanzoffianum). Grows with a straight trunk to 25 to 40 feet with graceful, arching, feathery leaves. Responds to regular moisture and fertilizer, but avoid encouraging too rapid growth or it can cause fronds to break. Use in areas protected from strong winds. To reduce mite infestations, rinse foliage monthly. Can be damaged when temperatures drop below 25°F to 30°F or with sustained high temperatures of 110°F to 120°F. A clean plant around pools.

Artemisia schmidtiana, ANGEL'S HAIR PERENNIAL

'Silver Mound' is low growing to 2 feet high with interesting, silvery gray, fernlike evergreen leaves. Excellent for rock garden or borders, especially in contrast with brightly colored flowers. Prefers sunny exposure. Hardy to 20°F.

Asclepias subulata, DESERT MILKWEED PERENNIAL

Grows to 4 feet high with slender, gray-green stems. Flat-topped, pale yellow flowers bloom in clusters from spring into fall. Seed pods to 3 inches long split and send out silvery seed fluffs. Great accent around rock-studded drainage swales or courtyards. Good soil drainage important. Attracts butterflies. Native to the southwest desert region. Hardy to 20°F.

Asclepias tuberosa, BUTTERFLY WEED　　　PERENNIAL

Clusters of bright orange, umbrella-shaped flowers are borne on multiple flowering stems, attracting butterflies. Grows 1 to 3 feet high. Plant in well-drained soil; avoid rich or heavy clay soils. Full sun or partial shade. Cold hardy.

Ash—*see Fraxinus*

Asparagus densiflorus, ASPARAGUS FERN　　　PERENNIAL

'Sprengeri' has small leaves on arching branches that make a rich, fluffy, bright green mound—useful as cut foliage in arrangements. Use as ground cover, border, filler or container plant. This South African native is a tough, versatile plant that accepts exposures ranging from shade to full sun. Hardy to 24°F. 'Myers' is similar but with dense, clean, plumelike stems that are more refined. Accepts semi-shade. Slightly less hardy than 'Sprengeri'.

Asparagus macowanii　　　PERENNIAL

(A. myriocladus, A. retrofractus). Tufts of rich green, threadlike foliage appear like billows of green smoke. Many long, slender stems to 1-1/2 to 2 feet long rise in clumps that form tuberous roots. Plant in shade only. Hardy to 25°F.

Asparagus plumosus, FERN ASPARAGUS　　　GROUND COVER

A vigorous fern with small, dainty, lacelike leaves that are deep green. Good cut foliage for indoor arrangements. Climbing vining habit or ground cover. Plant in shade only. Hardy to 25°F.

Aucuba japonica, JAPANESE AUCUBA　　　SHRUB

Shade-loving and bold, this green-leafed tropical shrub produces a colorful array of bright red berries that remain on the plant for many months. Grows 4 to 5 feet high. Locate in shade only. Native to Japan. 'Variegata', gold dust plant, is a small compact evergreen with large, glossy green leaves speckled with gold. Cold hardy.

Below left: *Asclepias tuberosa*, butterfly weed, produces bright orange, umbrella-shaped flowers on multiple flowering stems. Grows 1 to 3 feet high.

Below: The dense, clean, plumelike stems of *Asparagus densiflorus* 'Myers'.

Above: *Baileya multiradiata,* desert marigold, is a perennial wildflower that blooms almost continuously from spring to fall.

Above right: *Bauhinia blakeana* produces abundant maroon to pink flowers from December to April.

Azalea cultivars, AZALEA   SHRUB

Produces a long season of color during winter. Grow only in shaded areas, and be sure to avoid reflected sun. Must have well-drained, acid-type soil. Supply with regular moisture. Ideal plant in foreground with camellias or other shade plants, in containers, or even useful as a short-term flowering house plant indoors. Hardy 0°F to 20°F, depending on plant type.

Baby blue eyes—*see Nemophila menziesii*

Baby tears—*see Soleirolia soleirolii*

Baccharis X 'Centennial'   GROUND COVER

A low-growing, wide-spreading hybrid of *Baccharis sarothroides* and *B. pilularis.* Grows well under both dry and moist conditions, roots deeply to prevent erosion and presents a good-looking, year-round appearance. Grows 1 to 2 feet high, spreading 3 to 6 feet wide. Plant 2 to 3 feet apart for ground cover. Heat and drought resistant. *Baccharis* hybrid 'Starn' Thompson is a more uniform and compact selection. (See photo, page 43.) Low water use; drip irrigation ideal. Cold hardy to 15°F.

Bachelor button—*see Centaurea cyanus*

Baileya multiradiata, DESERT MARIGOLD   WILDFLOWER

This perennial grows 1 to 1-1/2 feet high, with bright yellow, daisylike flowers that bloom on tall stems. Blooms almost continuously from spring to fall. Woolly gray leaves form a clump to 6 inches high. Cut back in winter to stimulate new growth and flowers in spring. Reseeds readily. A wonderful color plant in a natural garden design. Low water use, but more flowers and better reseeding with moisture during dry periods. Hardy to 20°F.

Baja fairy duster—*see Calliandra californica*

Baja ruellia—*see Ruellia peninsularis*

Bambusa multiplex, GOLDEN GODDESS BAMBOO   SHRUB

(B. glauscens). 'Golden Goddess' is an improved selection, with slender yellowish stalks rising 6 to 8 feet high. Stalks form an open, arching, clump effect.

Clumping type of root structure. Native to the Orient. Hardy to 15°F.

Bambusa oldhamii, GIANT TIMBER BAMBOO SHRUB

Forms erect clumps that are ideal for heavy tall screens or as single accents to 50 feet high. Stems to 3 inches in diameter are most effective when planting is thinned out on a regular basis. Dense foliage. A clumping type bamboo, it is easy to control. (Be aware that *running type* bamboos can be invasive.) Needs regular moisture to look attractive. Native to China. Hardy to 15°F.

Barrel cactus—*see Echinocactus grusonii* **and** *Ferocactus wislizenii*

Bat-faced cuphea—*see Cuphea llavea*

Bauhinia species, ORCHID TREE TREE

Bauhinia blakeana, Hong Kong orchid tree, has heart-shaped leaves 4 to 6 inches long that are narrow and leathery. It grows 15 to 20 feet high and remains more evergreen than *B. variegata.* However, trees can suffer cold damage at 28°F, and severe winds often cause limb damage. Abundant maroon to pink flowers bloom from December to April, and are quite dramatic in size and color. There is some leaf drop during bloom time. Moderate but deep watering at drip line of tree is essential. Plant in well-drained soil. Native to China.

Bauhinia lunarioides, white orchid tree, is a desert native that grows in a shrubby form to 15 feet high. It is deciduous, producing large clusters of small, fragrant, white or purple flowers in spring. Hardy to 10°F.

Bauhinia purpurea, purple orchid tree, is semi-deciduous with gray-green leaves. To 30 feet high with umbrella canopy. Native to India. Hardy to 25°F.

Bauhinia variegata is a subtropical tree, creating a dense, medium green crown up to 30 feet high. Narrow, leathery leaves are 4 to 6 inches long. Profuse magenta to purple, orchidlike flowers cover the branches in late winter. Many mature trees can be seen thriving throughout the Coachella Valley. Becomes semi-deciduous prior to flowering period. Native to India and China. Hardy to 25°F.

Below right and bottom: *Bougainvillea* are popular color plants in the Coachella Valley. Shrub and vining forms produce masses of flowers from their *bracts,* which are modified leaves that surround the actual tiny white flowers. Select a warm microclimate for a planting site since bougainvillea is prone to frost damage.

Below: *Berlandiera lyrata,* chocolate flower, produces a fragrance similar to chocolate. Sprays of flowers in shades of yellow bloom in spring and early summer on 1-1/2-foot plants.

Beaumontia grandiflora, EASTER LILY VINE   VINE

Fast growing, large evergreen with beautiful, large, dark green leaves. Fragrant, showy trumpet-shaped white flowers bloom in spring. Best in partial shade and rich soil. Protect from cold when temperatures drop below 30°F.

Beaver tail cactus—*see Opuntia species*

Bellflower—*see Campanula isophylla 'Stella'*

Bergenia crassifolia, SIBERIAN TEA   PERENNIAL

This evergreen perennial forms clumps to 1-1/2 feet high and 2 feet wide. The large, round leaves have wavy edges. Rose, lilac or purple flower spikes to 8 inches high bloom January and February. Use as edging or ground cover in shade. High water use. Cold hardy.

Berlandiera lyrata, CHOCOLATE FLOWER   PERENNIAL

To 1-1/2 feet high with 2-foot spread. Sprays of flowers in shades of yellow bloom spring to early summer and produce a fragrance similar to chocolate. Flowerheads expand in morning, drooping in afternoon. Leaves are green

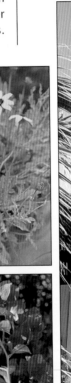

above, whitish underneath, making it a fine companion plant with other gray-leaved plants such as salvias. Native to North America. Hardy to 10°F.

Bird of paradise—*see Caesalpinia gilliesii*

Bishop's flowers—*see Ammi majus*

Black dalea—*see Dalea frutescens*

Black-eyed Susan—*see Rudbeckia hirta*

Bladderpod—*see Cleome isomeris*

Blanket flower—*see Gaillardia grandiflora*

Blazing-star—*see Mentzelia lindleyi*

Blue carpet juniper—*see Juniperus horizontalis 'Wiltonii'*

Blue fescue—*see Festuca ovina var. glauca*

Blue flax—*see Linum perenne subsp. lewisii*

Blue Italian cypress—*see Cupressus sempervirens 'Glauca'*

Blue leaf wattle—*see Acacia saligna*

Blue marguerite—*see Felicia amelloides*

Blue queen sage—*see Salvia X superba 'Blue Queen'*

Blue thimble flower—*see Gilia capitata*

Boston ivy—*see Parthenocissus tricuspidata*

Bottle-brush—*see Callistemon viminalis*

Bottle tree—*see Brachychiton populneus*

Bougainvillea species, BOUGAINVILLEA VINE AND SHRUB

Bougainvillea species are popular "workhorse" plants in the Coachella Valley. Shrub and vining forms produce volumes of color from their *bracts,* which are modified leaves that surround the actual tiny flowers. Select a warm microclimate for a planting site since bougainvillea is relatively frost-tender. After young plants are established, keep *Bougainvillea* on the dry side, which encourages more flowers. Native to South America. Cultivated varieties come in wide range of colors; here are a few favorites.

Bougainvillea spectabilis (B. brasiliensis) is an indescribable sight with purple flower bracts that bloom in clusters. Must have full sun. Hardy to 20°F. 'Barbara Karst' produces cascading masses of large, brilliant red flower bracts that are borne almost continually. Plants bloom at an early age. Full sun. 'California Gold' has rich golden bracts that bloom profusely for several months, in contrast to its deep green leaves on vining branches. 'Jamaica White' has exotic, tropical, lush green foliage. Spectacular masses of frothy, sea foam white bracts cascade from branch tips. Blooms occasionally take on a slight pink tinge with cooler weather. Hardy to 30°F. 'Orange King' is covered with bronzy orange-gold flower bracts in graceful sprays during the warm season. Attractive foliage. 'Texas Dawn' produces myriad, gracefully formed rose bracts suspended from long arching sprays. A sunny location is ideal. Hardy to 30°F. 'Crimson Jewel' and its luxurious, dark green leaves create a harmonious setting for hundreds of brilliant, glowing, red bracts. Plant becomes a vigorous bush form 3 to 5 feet high. 'La Jolla', with red bracts, is more compact. Good choice for containers. 'Temple Fire' is partially deciduous with bronze-red bracts. Hardy to 30°F.

Brahea armata, Mexican blue fan palm, is prized for its silvery blue fronds and small stature. It grows to 20 to 30 feet high at a very slow rate.

Brachychiton populneus, BOTTLE TREE TREE

Well adapted to hot, dry, windy desert conditions. Evergreen, shiny, dark green leaves cover a pyramidal form that grows rapidly 30 to 50 feet, spreading as wide as 30 feet. Install drip or bubbler heads at tree's drip line (see page 152) to encourage deep rooting. Remove dead wood in winter. Keep splayed branches under control. Leaf drop occurs in early spring as new leaves crowd out old. Give extra iron to avoid chlorosis. Native to Australia. Hardy to 18°F.

Brahea armata, MEXICAN BLUE FAN PALM FAN PALM

Grows 20 to 30 feet high at a very slow growth rate. Well-suited to small gardens. Silvery blue fronds are an attractive feature. Summer flowers grow in creamy clusters 6 to 10 feet long. Native to Baja California. Hardy to 18°F.

Brahea edulis, GUADALUPE PALM FAN PALM

Light green fronds. Trees reach 30 feet at maturity. Slow growth rate. Ideal accent in small areas. From Guadalupe Inlands in Baja California. Hardy to 24°F.

Bristol fairy gypsophila—*see Gypsophila paniculata*

Brittle bush—*see Encelia farinosa*

Brunfelsia pauciflora 'Floribunda'
YESTERDAY, TODAY & TOMORROW SHRUB

B. calycina) Spring-blooming evergreen to 10 feet high but can be kept smaller by pruning. Foliage is light green. Flowers open to a deep violet and fade to light violet or white, lasting about three days. Ideal in shade. Hardy to 20°F.

Buddleia marrubifolia, WOOLLY BUTTERFLY BUSH SHRUB

Useful in shrub or perennial beds, plus the vivid yellow and orange, ball-shaped flowers attract butterflies. Grows to 5 feet high and as wide. The toothed, gray, woolly leaves blend well with brittlebush, lavender, salvia and bougainvillea, as well as other gray-foliaged plants. Provide soil with good drainage, and prune to control and renew plants as needed. Low water use. Native to the Chihuahuan Desert of Mexico. Hardy to 15°F.

Bull Grass—*see Muhlenbergia emersleyi*

Bushy senna—*see Senna*

Butia capitata, PINDO PALM   FEATHER PALM

(Cocos australis). Native to Brazil, Uruguay and Argentina. Accepts frost and extreme heat, sun and hardship of every kind. Grows slowly to 10 to 20 feet high. Gray-green, feathery leaves are long and graceful, ideal as an accent plant. Apply iron if foliage pales. Low to moderate water use. Hardy to 15°F.

Butterfly iris—*see Dietes vegeta*

Butterfly weed—*see Asclepias tuberosa*

Buxus microphylla var. japonica, JAPANESE BOXWOOD   SHRUB

Standard boxwood and grow to 10 feet high. 'Nana' is evergreen and compact 2 to 4 feet high with small, round-tipped bright green leaves. Excellent, upright, small shrub for hedges or trained specimens. Can be kept as low hedge in formal landscaping. Accepts sun to partial shade. Hardy to 0°F.

Caesalpinia cacalaco, CASCALOTE   TREE

Develops into an attractive small tree up to 15 feet high and almost as wide. Spikes of clear yellow flowers bloom at the branch tips in late winter to early spring. Luxuriant foliage is armed with thorns about the size of rose thorns. Locate away from pedestrian traffic. Prune after winter-flowering season to control ungainly growth. Plant in well-drained soil in frost-free location. Native to Vera Cruz, Mexico. Hardy to 20°F, but flowers are damaged at 30°F.

Caesalpinia gilliesii, YELLOW BIRD OF PARADISE   SHRUB

Grows 5 to 8 feet high, sometimes more, with an equal spread. Foliage is sparse and feathery, with a growth habit that is ungainly and "top heavy." However, the individual yellow flowers with red stamens can be showy. If possible, use

Below left: *Brachychiton populneus,* bottle tree, has evergreen, shiny, dark green leaves. Grows rapidly to 30 to 50 feet high, spreading as wide as 30 feet.

Below center: The vivid yellow and orange, ball-shaped flowers of *Buddleia marrubifolia,* woolly butterfly bush, attract butterflies. Here its silvery gray foliage contrasts nicely with *Bougainvillea.*

Below: The foliage of *Caesalpinia gilliesii,* yellow bird of paradise, is sparse and feathery, with a growth habit that often becomes "top heavy." However, the individual yellow flowers with red stamens can be very showy.

Above: The refined, dark green foliage of *Calliandra californica*, Baja fairy duster, grows to 6 feet high and 4 to 5 feet wide. Striking red puffball flowers with long stamens bloom spring into fall.

Above center: *Calliandra eriophylla*, fairy duster, presents a graceful, airy mood, with pinkish red flower clusters in the spring, set off by its refined foliage.

Above right: *Calliandra haematocephala*, pink powder puff, is grown for its winter flowers that look like powder puffs.

Right: A must for summer color in the Coachella Valley, *Caesalpinia pulcherrima*, red bird of paradise, flowers profusely from early summer to fall.

as background behind smaller, fuller plants to hide the bare lower stems. Provides color late spring to fall. Grows in almost any soil. Moderate water use. Native to Argentina. Not as many flowers as *C. pulcherrima*, but tolerates temperatures to 20°F.

Caesalpinia pulcherrima, RED BIRD OF PARADISE   SHRUB
Brilliant red and yellow flowers bloom from early summer to fall. Another workhorse plant for the Coachella Valley. Typically grows 5 to 8 feet high, with fine-textured, almost luxuriant leaves, but can get much larger in mild climates. Due to its stature and deciduous nature, use as background plant. Accepts almost any soil but full sun is a must. Low water use. Cut stems back to 18 inches after winter dormancy, prior to surge of new spring growth.

A yellow-flowering selection has recently become available. Its bloom season is slightly later in the warm season, lasting later in the year. Native to the West Indies. Foliage freezes at 28°F to 30°F.

Cajeput tree—*see Melaleuca quinquenervia*

Calendula officinalis, CALENDULA   ANNUAL
Flower colors range from bright yellows to deep orange, with best appearance in late winter and early spring. Growth is vigorous to 18 inches high. Place in

separate beds from other annuals because plants tend to sprawl. Space 15 to 18 inches apart. If water is applied by overhead sprinklers, plants tend to develop mildew. Apply in early morning so moisture on leaves will dry in the sun, and flood irrigate. Accepts any exposure except north. needs good soil drainage.

California blue bells—*see Phacelia campanularia*

California fan palm—*see Washingtonia filifera*

California fuschia—*see Zauschneria californica*

California live oak—*see Quercus agrifolia*

California pepper tree—*see Schinus molle*

California poppy—*see Eschscholzia californica*

Calliandra californica, BAJA FAIRY DUSTER   SHRUB

The refined, dark green foliage of Baja fairy duster is attractive when combined with other native or subtropical plants. It grows to 6 feet high and 4 to 5 feet wide. Red puffball flowers with long stamens bloom spring into fall. Hummingbirds are attracted to the flowers. Prune lightly in late spring to encourage a fuller plant from the ground up. Low to moderate water use. If growth becomes excessive, decrease water. Plant in soil with good drainage. Native to Baja California. Hardy to 20°F to 25°F.

Calliandra eriophylla, FAIRY DUSTER   SHRUB

Produces pinkish red flower clusters in the spring, set off by its refined foliage. Mature height and spread is 3 to 5 feet. Similar to *Calliandra californica,* but its growth habit is more controlled. Graceful and airy, it's at home in a natural garden design. Pruning back branches may help create more fullness. Do not prune into square or round forms; allow plants to grow naturally and they will produce more flowers. A low water-use plant that prefers full sun and well-drained soil. Native to California and the Southwest. Hardy to 20°F.

Calliandra haematocephala, PINK POWDER PUFF   SHRUB

A desirable, hospitable evergreen for an unusual accent planting or trained wall. In winter, a profusion of bright, reddish pink stamens shaped like huge powder puffs contrast with rich green, graceful, compound foliage. Very color-

Flower colors of *Calendula officinalis,* calendula, range from bright yellows to deep orange. The best show of color occurs in late winter and early spring. Plant are vigorous growers to 18 inches high.

Callistemon viminalis, weeping bottlebrush, grows as a small tree, large shrub or screen to 20 to 30 feet high. Evergreen pendulous branches are covered with red, bottlebrush flowers midspring and summer.

ful. Accepts full sun to partial shade. Provide ample water and well-drained soil. Native to Bolivia. Hardy to 30°F.

Callistemon viminalis, WEEPING BOTTLE-BRUSH   SHRUB, TREE

An exceptional small tree that grows 20 to 30 feet high with a 15-foot spread. This freely branching evergreen has pendulous branches covered with magnificent, red, bottlebrush flowers midspring and summer. Attracts butterflies. *Callistemon citrinus* is similar but upright in form. Stake the first two years to help tree develop good form. Excessive water can cause trees to become chlorotic. Full sun. Native to Australia. Hardy to 20°F.

Calylophus hartwegii, CALYLOPHUS   GROUND COVER

A clumping ground cover with masses of large yellow flowers to 2 inches wide. Blooms in spring, summer and fall. Grows 1 to 1-1/2 feet high and spreads to 2 feet wide. Leaves are narrow and bright green. Attractive when tucked in among boulders or massed in clusters. Plant in soil that has good drainage. Water frequently in summer to encourage more flowers. Cut back to 8 inches high in fall after blooming stops to reshape and renew plant for spring growth. Plants are dormant in winter. Native to southeastern Arizona. Hardy to 5°F.

Camellia species, CAMELLIA SHRUB

These charming shrubs flower in late fall and winter. The waxy petaled flowers are available in many colors, from white to red and various forms such as single, double, rose and peony. Leaves are glossy dark green on graceful plants. Growing camellias in containers is ideal in desert climates, allowing use of specialized soil, fertilizer and exposure requirements. Must have shade and protection from reflected sun. Provide a well-drained soil and regular moisture. Use an acid-type fertilizer during growing season. Native to eastern Asia. Foliage is hardy to 20°F, but flowers tolerate less cold.

Campanula isophylla, ITALIAN BELLFLOWER PERENNIAL

Grows with trailing stems to 18 inches, suited as hanging basket or as a ground cover. 'Stella Blue' has violet-blue flowers; 'Stella White' has white flowers that bloom spring to fall. Best in partial shade. Native to Italy. Moderate to high water use. Hardy to 15°F.

Campsis radicans, TRUMPET VINE VINE

This eastern United States native is tolerant of the harsh summer growing conditions in the Coachella Valley. It is vigorous and self-climbing to 20 feet or more high and wide. The dark green leaves are deciduous in winter. Clusters of 3-inch, orange or red flowers bloom summer and fall. Rapid growth rate. Use as a color accent, shade or screening. Grows best in partial shade. Provide moderate water to maintain flowers and dense foliage. Cold hardy.

Canary Island pine—*see Pinus canariensis*

Canna species, CANNA PERENNIAL

Subtropical evergreen color spring to fall. Lush foliage and flowers grow to 3 to 10 feet high. Gingerlike flowers come in many bright colors. Effective as a background when planted in groups. Full sun. High water use. Hardy to 40°F.

Carob—*see Ceratonia siliqua*

Carolina jessamine—*see Gelsemium sempervirens*

Calylophus hartwegii, calylophus, is a flowering ground cover that grows 1 to 1-1/2 feet high and spreads to 2 feet wide. Masses of large yellow flowers up to 2 inches across bloom in spring, summer and fall.

Carnegiea gigantea, saguaro cactus, is a symbol of the desert Southwest. Mature cactus can reach up to 60 feet high, with several arms. Large white flowers bloom in summer.

Carissa grandiflora, NATAL PLUM   SHRUB

(C. macrocarpa). White flowers are followed by red fruit.'Boxwood Beauty' has a compact form, growing to 2 feet high with a semi-upright, compact growth habit. Foliage is an intense deep green, densely arranged on unique, tight, short branches. Makes a good dwarf hedge but spines can be a hazard. Protect from frost by locating in a warm microclimate such as the south side of a building under a wide overhang. 'Fancy' has lush green foliage, outstanding fruiting qualities and boldly branching upright growth to 6 feet. Tasty, bright orange-red fruit. Large, fragrant, white flowers. 'Green Carpet' has dense growth to 1-1/2 feet high. Its spreading habit makes it exceptionally good as a ground cover. Foliage is lush and resembles a carpet of green. Locate in full sun. 'Tuttlei' has a more upright form to 2 to 3 feet high. It has a spreading, tight-branching growth habit enhanced with rich green foliage.

Full sun. All natal plums are low-water use plants once established. Native to South Africa. Hardy to 26°F to 28°F.

Carnation—*see Dianthus species*

Carnegiea gigantea, SAGUARO CACTUS   ACCENT

This columnar cactus is a well-known symbol of the Southwest. Extremely slow growing to 50 to 60 feet high, it towers over the desert landscape. Large white flowers appear wreathlike atop arms in summer, followed by edible red fruit. Low water use; avoid winter irrigation. Requires good soil drainage. Young plants can freeze at 30°F; mature specimens are hardy to 10°F to 20°F.

Carpet bugle—*see Ajuga reptans*

Cascalote—*see Caesalpinia cacalaco*

**Cassia species— ***see Senna*

Catchfly—*see Silene armeria*

Catclaw—*see Macfadyena unguis-cati*

Catharanthus roseus, VINCA   ANNUAL

(Vinca rosea). Outstanding flowering annual that blooms with a vengeance from spring into summer, and often into fall. Many flower colors are available including white, red, pink and magenta. Most varieties grow 12 to 15 inches high but smaller forms are available. Plant in late spring, spacing 9 to 12 inches apart. Feed with diluted liquid fertilizer monthly to keep foliage rich green and to maintain blooming plants. Excellent in containers. Low to moderate water use. Tolerates heat and sun. Provide good soil drainage and rotate plantings to new beds every year or two to help prevent fungus disease.

Centaurea cineraria, DUSTY MILLER   PERENNIAL

Compact perennial to 2 feet high. Velvety white leaves have broad, roundish lobes. Solitary flower heads are purple or yellow. Plant in full sun. Good soil drainage important. Be aware there are several different plants known by the common name dusty miller.

Centaurea cyanus, BACHELOR'S BUTTON   ANNUAL

This annual grows to 2 feet high with blue flowers. The foliage is gray-green with blue or pink flowers at the end of the stems. Accepts full sun or partial shade. Reseeds easily. Grows in almost any soil. Native to Europe.

Century plant—*see Agave americana*

Cephalophyllum aestonii, ICE PLANT GROUND COVER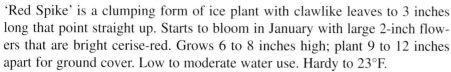

'Red Spike' is a clumping form of ice plant with clawlike leaves to 3 inches long that point straight up. Starts to bloom in January with large 2-inch flowers that are bright cerise-red. Grows 6 to 8 inches high; plant 9 to 12 inches apart for ground cover. Low to moderate water use. Hardy to 23°F.

Cerastium tomentosum, SNOW-IN-SUMMER GROUND COVER

This low-growing perennial with soft, whitish gray foliage grows to just 4 to 6 inches high. Small white flowers to 3/4-inch across bloom late spring into summer. For good contrast use it next to a green cover such as *Baccharis* X 'Centennial'. Plant 1-1/2 to 2 feet apart. Trim spent flowers and tired stems at least once each year after flowering. Sun-loving and drought tolerant, it thrives with little care. Low to moderate water use. Cold hardy.

Ceratonia siliqua, CAROB, ST. JOHN'S BREAD TREE

A large, wide-spreading evergreen tree to 20 to 40 feet high, its round-headed form is densely branched. Slow to establish. Compound leaves are shiny deep green and cast dense shade. Female plants develop long brown seed pods that can be messy. To avoid, grow male plants. Low water use. Water deeply and infrequently to encourage deep rooting. Hardy to 22°F to 25°F.

Cercidium species, PALO VERDE

These desert trees provide a definite personality to the landscape, characterized by their blue-green to green bark and natural, multiple trunks. Most are wide spreading to 25 to 35 feet with a similar height, which varies according to the species, depth of moisture and soil type. Masses of fragrant yellow flowers bloom April and early May. They are some of the best trees to create a desert

Cercidium species, palo verde, evokes a sense of the desert. Unique green bark, profuse yellow flowers in spring and low-water requirement make them coveted trees in the Coachella Valley landscape.

Above: *Cercidium microphyllum,* little leaf palo verde, has bark, stems and leaves that are yellow-green. Form is more dwarf than *Cercidium floridum*—to just 20 feet high.

Above right: *Cercidium floridum,* blue palo verde, is one of the most colorful desert trees. Typically grows as a multitrunk form to 35 feet high and 30 feet wide, producing filtered shade. Golden yellow flowers appear March and April.

atmosphere in home gardens, and excellent for wildlife habitats. All tolerate extremes of heat and full sun, and prefer well-drained soils such as sand, loam, gravel or decomposed granite. Except for *Cercidium praecox,* which suffers damage at 25°F, most palo verdes are cold hardy to the low 20°s F.

Cercidium floridum, BLUE PALO VERDE   TREE
Blue palo verde is one of the most colorful desert trees. The strong, multitrunk form has a spreading canopy to 35 feet high and 30 feet wide, producing filtered shade. Luxuriant golden yellow flowers appear in profusion March and April. Bark on young trees is bluish green; with age, bark on main trunk darkens. Encourage natural, angular form and avoid heavy pruning, which interrupts growth patterns. Low water use, increasing to moderate in summer. Native to the Sonoran Desert in Arizona, California, Baja California and northern Mexico. Hardy to 24°F.

Cercidium microphyllum, LITTLE LEAF PALO VERDE   TREE
Bark, stems and leaves are yellow-green. At 20 feet high, more dwarflike and stiffer appearance than *Cercidium floridum.* Semideciduous—leaflets drop in cold or drought. Pale yellow flowers appear April through May. Slow growing but rate can be accelerated with additional moisture. Twiggy growth and low canopy provide shelter for wildlife. Ideal as a background or for screening. Selectively thin branches if you want to show off trunk structure. Excellent as a small patio tree with character. Native to Arizona and Baja California at 500 to 4,000 feet Full sun. Low water use. Hardy to 15°F.

Cercidium hybrid 'DESERT MUSEUM'   TREE
This superior *Cercidium* is a result of hybridizing work involving *C. floridum, C. microphyllum* and *Parkinsonia aculeata,* Mexican palo verde, done at the Arizona-Sonora Desert Museum in Tucson. Growth pattern of ascending branches provides sturdy structure and strong vertical form. Mature height is 25 feet to 30 feet with 20-foot spread. Flowers are rich yellow and bloom during spring. Plant in deep soil. Hardy to 15°F.

Cercidium praecox, PALO BREA, SONORAN PALO VERDE   TREE

Grows slowly into a 15- to 30-foot tree. Vivid yellow flower clusters bloom in April and May. Palo brea has a more upright structure and thornier branches that other *Cercidium* species, with distinctive, sculptural, angular branches. Bark on trunks and branches remains green. Low to moderate water but deep watering improves appearance. Hardy to 25°F.

Cestrum parqui, WILLOW-LEAFED JASMINE   SHRUB

Dense and upright shrub to 6 to 10 feet high with light green leaves. Insignificant in appearance, greenish white flowers emit a heavy sweet fragrance at night. Plant in partial shade. Native to Chile. Hardy to 28°F.

Chamelaucium uncinatum, GERALDTON WAX FLOWER   SHRUB

Medium-sized, upright shrub to 10 to 15 feet high. Multibranched with fine, needlelike green leaves. The foliage serves as a background for the magnificent display of rosy lavender flowers that bloom along branches in spring. Cut back after bloom to stimulate more dense growth. Excellent as a cut flower. Full sun. Needs good soil drainage. Native to Australia. Hardy to 22°F to 25°F.

Chamaerops humilis, MEDITERRANEAN FAN PALM   FAN PALM

A slow-growing, multitrunked fan palm. Grows faster and larger with regular fertilizer and water. Dwarfish in habit, a fine palm for a specimen. Attains height of 10 to 12 feet at maturity. Leaves are small and abundant, the *petioles* (see page 153) armed with sharp spines. Some plants sucker freely and form a dense clump, becoming a handsome tub plant or a featured plant for pool land-scaping. Accepts full sun to partial shade. Moderate water use. Hardy to 18°F.

Chaparral sage—*see Salvia clevelandii*

Chaste tree—*see Vitex agnus-castus*

Cheiranthus cheri, WALLFLOWER   ANNUAL

Bushy annual grown for its sweet fragrant flowers in shades of yellow and red. Grows to 2 feet high. Plant in full sun and in soil with good drainage. Under

Above left: *Cercidium praecox*, palo brea, has a different appearance that other *Cercidium* species. It is more upright with an angular structure and thornier branches.

Above: *Chamaerops humilis*, Mediterranean fan palm, is a slow-growing, multitrunked fan palm. It remains dwarfish in habit, reaching 10 to 12 feet at maturity.

the right conditions it is cold hardy and drought tolerant. Easy to grow from seed. Wallflower is rarely considered a wildflower in the U.S. but is added to wildflower mixes because it does well in meadows, adding its bright color.

Chilopsis linearis, DESERT WILLOW   TREE

This native to the Chihuahuan and Sonoran Deserts has three definite seasons: deciduous during the winter months, lush, willowlike growth and orchidlike flowers in the spring, and then a transition into summer and fall when the numerous, slender seed capsules create a ragged look. (These can be removed with some patient pruning.) The multiple trunks of this light, airy, 25- to 30-foot tree provide structure for graceful light-green leaves and white, pink, lavender and purple flower clusters. Many selections are available that have great variations in flower color. Shop during spring and early summer when plants are in flower to get a look at flower color selection. 'Lucretia Hamilton' is a superior cultivar. Deciduous to just 15 to 18 feet high, with dark purple flowers in spring, summer and fall.

Do any heavy pruning during the deciduous period—November into February. Prune to control growth, create new flowering wood and to display handsome trunks. Best in soil with good drainage. Low to moderate water, but irrigate deeply. Full sun, accepts extreme heat and cold. Hardy to 5°F to 10°F.

Chinese houses—*see Collinsia heterophylla*

Chinese pistachio—*see Pistacia chinensis*

Chitalpa tashkentenis, CHITALPA   TREE

A selected form from Russia that is a cross of two genera: *Chilopsis linearis* and *Catalpa bignonioides*. Chitalpa combines the best characteristics of both plants. It is more evergreen and has large, vivid flower clusters. Availability at nurseries may be limited. Mature size of 20 to 30 feet is ideal for small gardens. Hardy to 25°F.

Chocolate flower—*see Berlandiera lyrata*

Below and below right: Chilopsis linearis, desert willow, grows with multiple trunks, producing an airy, 25- to 30-foot tree. A range of flower colors are available, including white, pink, lavender and purple.

Chorisia speciosa, SILK FLOSS TREE, KAPOK   TREE

Native to Brazil, this tree produces prodigious amounts of rose to wine-colored flowers in fall to late winter. Also called the drunkard's tree due to large sharp spines on trunks of young trees. Seeds are covered with white cottony kapok, once used to stuff life vests. Adapted to grow along the coast, inland valleys and in low-elevation desert areas such as the Coachella Valley. The pyramidal growth can reach to 30 to 50 feet high and spread 25 to 40 feet, so not a good choice for a small garden. Deciduous prior to bloom period. Avoid windy locations. Moderate but deep water required. Hardy to 27°F.

Chrysactinia mexicana, DAMIANITA   SHRUB

Similar in appearance to *Ericameria laricifolia,* turpentine bush, with compact, needlelike growth. Damianita bears solid yellow, daisylike flowers from April to September. Evergreen plants grow to 2 feet high with an equal spread. After a long flowering season, lightly prune spent flowers to improve appearance. Good soil drainage is important. Hardy to 0°F.

Chrysanthemum frutescens, MARGUERITE   PERENNIAL, ANNUAL

Marguerite is a perennial but typically grown as an annual in the Coachella Valley. It reaches 2 to 3 feet high and as wide, taking on an almost shrublike appearance. Available in white, yellow or pink flowering forms, each offset by bright green divided leaves. Use blue pansies or violas in foreground for a color treat. Tender to heavy frost but usually recovers. Plant from October through February for spring flowers until April 1. Space at least 3 to 4 feet apart and locate in full sun in the ground or in large containers. Thin the vigorous leaves once in early spring and remove dead blooms to encourage new flowers. Plants rarely continue flowering beyond June 15. Moisture needs increase to high as plants mature, due to their extensive root development.

Above: Shasta daisy is a perennial chrysanthemum.

Below left: *Chorisia speciosa,* silk floss tree, can reach 30 to 50 feet high and spread 25 to 40 feet.

Below: The trunk of silk floss tree is studded with large thorns, so plant with caution around pedestrian traffic areas.

Chrysanthemum X superbum, SHASTA DAISY   PERENNIAL

(C. maximum). White ray flowers surround yellow disks. The stem is straight or slightly branched and the basal leaves are deeply toothed. Plant from contain-

ers in spring or fall. Attractive in borders and as cut flowers. Divide plants every two years to develop more vigorous growth. Plant in sunny location. Cold hardy.

Chrysanthemum X morifolium, CHRYSANTHEMUM   ANNUAL

This is the garden-variety chrysanthemum, which is grown as an annual. Also known as florist's chrysanthemum. Plants are available in a range of flower colors, Reaching 1 to 1-1/2 feet high. Best in full sun. Moderate water use.

Chrysothamnus nauseosus, GOLDEN RABBIT BUSH   SHRUB

This deciduous shrub with silvery blue, narrow leaves grows to 3 to 5 feet high. It produces a profuse display of pungently scented, brilliant yellow flowers in fall. Plant with *Salvia greggii* or *S. leucantha* for a dramatic color combination when few other plants are in bloom. Prune after blooming ceases. Low water use in a natural garden design. Hardy to cold.

Chuperosa—*see Justicia californica*

Clarkia amoena, FAREWELL-TO-SPRING   ANNUAL WILDFLOWER

This annual wildflower grows to 2 feet high with slender stems that support cup-shaped flowers in shades of pink, lavender or red. Several flowers often bloom on a single flowering stalk. Easy to grow from seed, but does not do well in hot humid climates when temperatures climb above 80°F. Plant in fall or early spring in a sunny location.

Clematis X 'Ramona', CLEMATIS   VINE

Large lavender-blue flowers make a striking picture during summer. Vigorous grower. Deciduous. Locate in partial shade only. Prune to ground in fall. Moderate to high water use. Cold hardy.

Cleome isomeris, BLADDERPOD   SHRUB

(Isomeris arborea). A native of western Mojave Desert. The 4- to 6-foot shrub has light green foliage and bright yellow, snapdragonlike flowers borne in clus-

Below: *Chrysactinia mexicana*, damianita, is similar in appearance to *Ericameria laricifolia*. Damianita bears daisylike flowers from April to September. Plants grow to 2 feet high with an equal spread.

Below right: *Cleome isomeris*, bladderpod, becomes a 3- to 4-foot shrub, with bright yellow, snapdragonlike flowers. After flowers complete bloom, inflated green capsules develop with the seeds inside.

ters at the tips of branches. Flowers are a great source of nectar for bees and hummingbirds. After flowers complete bloom, inflated green capsules develop with seeds inside. Plants blend well with *Encelia farinosa, Aniscanthus* species and *Salvia greggii.* Easy to grow from seed sown directly in place. Well-drained soil important. Supply low to moderate moisture during summer dormancy. Hardy to 25°F.

Clivia miniata, KAFFIR LILY   PERENNIAL
Orange flowers bloom in clusters on stout stems to 2 feet high in early spring. Leaves of Belgian hybrids are wider, dark green. Great container specimen. Plant in shade. Moderate water use. Cold tender.

Clytostoma callistegioides, LAVENDER TRUMPET VINE   VINE
Evergreen vine for sun or shade. Pale lavender to violet trumpetlike flowers 3 inches long bloom in spring and summer. Glossy green leaves. Prune in late winter to control and to renew plants. Native to Argentina. Hardy to 20°F.

Cocculus laurifolius, LAUREL-LEAF COCCULUS   SHRUB
Glistening leathery leaves on graceful arching branches make this handsome, upright, medium-size shrub desirable. Develops slowly. Good cut foliage for arrangements. Accepts some sun but better with eastern exposure (afternoon shade) or in partial shade beneath canopy trees. Hardy to 26°F.

Collinsia heterophylla, CHINESE HOUSES   ANNUAL
The name Chinese houses comes from the arrangement of flowers, which look like miniature pagodas. Violet or white flowers bloom spring to early summer. Will grow to 2 feet high in full sun or shade and tolerates most soil conditions. Native to California.

Columbine—*see Aquilegia hybrids*

Convolvulus cneorum, SILVER BUSH MORNING GLORY   SHRUB
Dwarf, compact, evergreen shrub 2 to 3 feet high, with soft silvery foliage. Masses of white to pink flowers bloom late spring and summer. Plants located

Above: *Cordia boissieri,* Texas olive, grows 10 to 12 feet high and spreads to 10 feet wide. Leaves are blue-green and leathery, backing clusters of white flowers to 2-1/2 inches wide.

Above right: *Cordia parvifolia,* littleleaf cordia, is similar to *Cordia boissieri* but plants grow to just 4 to 6 feet high with a similar spread. Leaves are smaller and white flowers are 1 to 1-1/2 inches across.

in full sun have fuller, more dense growth. In partial shade form is more open. Plant in well-drained soil. Native to southern Europe. Hardy to 25°F.

Convolvulus mauritanicus,
GROUND MORNING GLORY   GROUND COVER

Fast-growing, trailing evergreen perennial 1 to 1-1/2 feet high, spreading 2 feet wide. Small, round, gray-green leaves are covered with 1-inch-wide, lavender-blue flowers all summer. Plant in full sun only. Requires good soil drainage. Trim plants back in winter to renew. Hardy to 15°F.

Coolibah tree—*see Eucalyptus microthea*

Coral bells—*see Heuchera sanguinea*

Coral vine—*see Antigonon leptopus*

Cordia boissieri, TEXAS OLIVE   SHRUB OR SMALL TREE
This superior plant has blue-green, leathery leaves and clusters of white flowers to 2-1/2 inches wide. Grows 10 to 12 feet high and spreads to 10 feet wide. Generally a warm-season bloomer, however, flowering extends into winter in the Coachella Valley. Accepts partial shade. Prefers well-drained soil. Remove dead interior branches and lower branches for a small tree effect. Native to Mexico and the Rio Grande Valley in Texas. Hardy to 20°F to 24°F.

Cordia parvifolia, littleleaf cordia, is similar to *C. boissieri* but smaller in stature with smaller leaves and small white flowers 1 to 1-1/2 inches across. Plants grow 4 to 6 feet high with a similar spread. Form is more open and airy.

Cork oak—*see Quercus suber*

Coreopsis lanceolata, LANCE-LEAF COREOPSIS   PERENNIAL
Plants grow to 2 feet high with yellow daisylike flowers on long stems that bloom spring into early summer. 'Early Sunrise' grows to 1-1/2 feet high with double golden yellow flowers. Coreopsis are great border plants or cut flowers. Plant in full sun in regular garden soil. Moderate water use. Hardy to 10°F.

Corokia cotoneaster, KOROKIA   SHRUB, VINE

This New Zealand native is well adapted to the Southwest. It is an 8- to 10-foot shrub that can also become a handsome vine on a wall. Some enjoy it as a natural bonsai in a container. Its unique growth habit includes a branch structure zigzagged with nearly black twigs covered with whitish leaves 3/4 inch long, producing a silvery look. Star-shaped yellow flowers bloom midspring; orange to red egg-shaped berries follow by midsummer. Requires good soil drainage. Your nursery can order plants if they're not available. Hardy to 20°F.

Cortaderia selloana, PAMPAS GRASS   ORNAMENTAL GRASS

The recent introduction of *Cortaderia selloana* var. *pumila,* dwarf pampas grass, is a blessing to those who like pampas grass but want a more compact and manageable plant. This variety grows to 4 to 6 feet high—much more suited to today's smaller garden. Moderate water use. Cut back to 18 inches every year or two in fall to regenerate fresh growth. Cold hardy.

Cosmos bipinnatus, COSMOS   ANNUAL

Open and airy color plant, with soft fernlike leaves and daisylike flowers in pink, red or white. Plant form is informal to 3 to 5 feet high so locate in the back of a natural border. Easy to grow from seed. Plant in moderately rich soil in full sun location in fall or early spring. High water use. Native to Mexico.

Crape myrtle—*see Lagerstroemia indica*

Creeping fig—*see Ficus pumila*

Creosote bush—*see Larrea tridentata*

Crown of thorns—*see Euphorbia milii*

Cuphea llavea, BAT-FACED CUPHEA   SHRUB

Small shrub to 2 feet high and 3 feet wide with crisp, dark green foliage. Blooms spring, summer and fall. Unusual red flowers with purple centers remind one of a bat's face. Provide ample water during warm months, particularly if plants are located in full sun. Best with afternoon shade in the Coachella Valley. A longer-lived alternative to annuals in flowerbeds. Hardy to 20°F.

Upper left: *Cortaderia selloana pumila,* dwarf pampas grass, grows to 4 to 6 feet high. It is better suited than the species for today's smaller gardens.

Top: *Coreopsis lanceolata,* lance-leaf coreopsis, grows to 2 feet high. Yellow daisy-like flowers on long stems bloom spring into summer.

Above: *Cuphea llavea,* bat-faced cuphea, is a perennial with unusual red flowers with purple centers that look similar to a bat's face.

Above: *Cupressus arizonica*, Arizona cypress, is one of the best medium-sized evergreens as a windbreak or tall screen for low-water, low-maintenance situations. Grows to 30 to 40 feet high and 30 feet wide with a pyramidal form.

Above right: *Dasylirion wheeleri,* desert spoon, is an outstanding accent plant, growing 3 to 5 feet high. Typically, after many years, flower spikes to 12 feet high appear in late fall, but the age when plants begin to bloom is unpredictable.

Cupressus arizonica, ARIZONA CYPRESS TREE

Arizona cypress is one of the best medium-sized evergreens as a windbreak or tall screen for low-water, low-maintenance situations. Grows to 30 to 40 feet high and 30 feet wide with a pyramidal form. Gray-green, scalelike foliage varies from plant to plant. 'Gareei' is a grafted selection, which means plants will consistently have rich, silvery, blue-green foliage. Grows 30 to 40 feet high. Branches have a distinct whipcord texture. Thrives in low-rainfall areas when established. Cold hardy. Resistant to cypress canker. Hardy to 0°F to 5°F. Note: *Cupressus arizonica* is often referred to as rough-barked Arizona cypress and *C. glabra* as smooth-barked Arizona cypress.

Cupressus sempervirens, ITALIAN CYPRESS TREE

Cutting-grown rather than propagated by seed to insure particular outstanding qualities. Narrow and dense columnar form to 20 to 60 feet high. A tall, vertical accent in expansive formal landscapes. 'Glauca' has attractive, bluish green, juniperlike foliage. Control red spider in summer. 'Stricta' is similar in form and size with dark green foliage. All are hardy to 10°F.

Cycas revoluta, SAGO PALM FEATHER PALM

A dwarf and compact palmlike plant , with many, long, shining, dark green leaves. The leaves appear as if they've been waxed, growing as a crown on top of the short trunk. Thick, heavy stem in small plants resembles a pineapple. Makes a splendid specimen container plant or include in a grouping of similar-sized palms. Reaches choice height of 6 to 10 feet, but grows very slowly. Locate where plants receive partial filtered shade; protect first year from direct sun with shade cloth. Native to Japan. Hardy to 15°F.

Dalea frutescens, BLACK DALEA SHRUB

One of the many valuable *Dalea* species. Compact and airy to 3 feet high and 4 feet wide. Expect partial leaf drop in extreme cold or during drought. Rose-purple flowers put on a show in fall and winter when most plants have ceased blooming. 'Sierra Negra' is an improved selection. Lightly prune, maintaining natural form, in spring. Locate in well-drained soil. Native to Chihuahuan Desert. Hardy to 0°F.

Dalea greggii, TRAILING INDIGO BUSH   GROUND COVER

This Chihuahuan Desert native is admired by gardeners seeking a low-water use ground cover. Plants grow to 1 to 1-1/2 feet high with foliage that remains a handsome gray to gray-green all year long. Dainty purple flowers bloom in spring. A single plant can spread to 10 to 15 feet in diameter! Little pruning required unless plants are used in small spaces such as along curbs or walks. Once established, water need is low. With moderate water, growth is more vigorous. Ideal for erosion control. Install drip head or bubbler 18 to 24 inches from plant crown and, if on a slope, position on the uphill side. Hardy to 15°F.

Dalea pulchra, INDIGO BUSH, BUSH DALEA   SHRUB

This shrub has contrasting, intertwining gray foliage with violet-blue flowers in late winter into spring. Grows 3 to 5 feet high and to 4 feet wide. Adds great interest when combined with other native desert plants. Best in full sun and in well-drained soil. Low water use. Hardy to 5°F.

Dame's rocket—*see Hesperis matronalis*

Dasylirion species, DESERT SPOON   ACCENT

Dasylirion wheeleri grows 3 to 5 feet high, eventually developing a trunk with a mature size of 6 to 8 feet high, spreading to 5 feet. Usually after many years, flower spikes to 12 feet high appear in late fall, but the age which plants actually begin to bloom is unpredictable. Narrow, gray-green leaves are sharply toothed along the edges. Full sun, with low water use. Native to southwest U.S. Hardy to 10°F.

D. acrotriche, green desert spoon, is a close relative with an almost identical appearance, but leaves are bright green rather than gray-green. For a more subtropical mood, select this plant. *D. wheeleri* is better suited for a desert-theme landscape. Slightly less hardy—to 20°F.

Date palm—*see Phoenix dactylifera*

Daylily—*see Hemerocallis hybrids*

Dalea species come in wide range of sizes and forms. Below: flowers of Dalea pulchra; below left, Dalea frutescens 'Sierra Negra', a shrub form, and below, Dalea greggii, a wide-spreading ground cover.

Delphinium species, LARKSPUR ANNUAL

A perennial that is treated as annual in the Coachella Valley. Set out year-old plants from containers in October for best results. Blend one cup of bone meal into planting hole backfill soil before planting. Position plant crown slightly above ground level so it will remain dry. Locate plants away from heavy winds and add 4-foot stakes early on to support tall flower stems. Feed monthly with liquid fertilizer high in nitrogen. Because of tall stature of plants (some grow to 6 feet high) place in background, along walls or among tall shrubs. Prefers rich, loam soil in east exposure or in filtered shade.

Desert honeysuckle—*see Aniscanthus species*

Desert ironwood—*see Olneya tesota*

Desert milkweed—*see Asclepias subulata*

Desert spoon—*see Dasylirion wheeleri*

Desert willow—*see Chilopsis linearis*

Dianthus species, CARNATION ANNUAL

Treat as an annual in the Coachella Valley. Plant October to January for late winter to spring flowers. Colors range from white, pink, red, purple and shades between. Flowers have a delightful, spicy fragrance; bring them indoors to enjoy in bouquets. Space plants 1 to 1-1/2 feet apart in enriched, well-drained soil. Stake early to support tall flower stems. Pinch young plants to develop strength and to create more flowers. Remove spent flowers regularly for more blooms. Accepts full sun to partial shade. Moderate moisture.

Dicliptera resupinata, DICLIPTERA PERENNIAL

Low-growing perennial to 2 feet high and as wide. Rose-purple flowers provide a long season of color from May through October. Use in small garden areas such as patio or courtyard. Trim back after cold weather just prior to spring to

Below: Flowers of *Dianthus* species, carnation, range from white, pink, red, purple and shades between. Many gardeners cut flowers and bring them indoors to enjoy their delightful, spicy fragrance.

Below right: *Dimorphotheca sinuata,* African daisy, is an easy-to-grow annual wildflower. Flower colors range from yellow, salmon, rose, white and orange. Sow seed in fall for flowers in early spring.

renew growth. Dark green heart-shaped leaves are 1 inch long. Well-drained soil is deal. Native to the Southwest. Hardy to 20°F.

Dietes bicolor, PEACOCK FLOWER   PERENNIAL

(Moraea bicolor). An evergreen perennial that grows from rhizomes. Plants grow to 2-1/2 feet high with stiff, upright leaves. Lemon yellow flowers with maroon spots bloom for several months during the warm season. Accepts full sun. Moderate water use, but more flowers with more moisture. Hardy to 25°F.

Dietes vegeta, BUTTERFLY IRIS   PERENNIAL

(Moraea vegeta, M. iridoides). Evergreen perennial from rhizomes to 2 feet high with stiff upright leaves. Small, white, irislike flowers bloom spring to fall. Accepts full sun to partial shade. Similar culture as *Dietes bicolor.*

Dimorphotheca sinuata, AFRICAN DAISY   WILDFLOWER

This easy-to-grow annual puts on a spectacular early spring show. Use in masses in borders or landscape perimeter. Sprightly flower colors range from yellow, salmon, rose, white and orange. Grows readily from seed with rapid germination. Plant September 15 through February for bloom March through May. Thin seedlings to 12 to 15 inches apart. Grows to 1 foot high or more with an equal spread. Provide regular moisture after seeding and to establish plants. Once seedlings reach a few inches high, reduce water to encourage more flowers. Accepts almost any soil with good drainage. Reseeds to come back year after year. Native to South Africa.

Dodonaea viscosa, HOP BUSH, HOPSEED BUSH   SHRUB

Ruggedly handsome substitute for oleanders if you need a vigorous plant 10 to 12 feet high and almost as wide. Capable as low windbreak or screening; space 4 to 5 feet apart. The dense green foliage stands up to wind, heat and cold.

The casual growth habit of *Dodonaea viscosa,* hop bush, is ideal for a natural garden design. For a screen or low windbreak as shown above, space plants 4 to 5 feet apart. The dense bright green foliage stands up to wind, heat and cold.

Above: *Echinacea purpurea*, purple coneflower, is known for its purple cone-shaped flowers and is also a popular herbal remedy. Flowers are favorites in a natural garden.

Above right: The dense, fine-textured, dark green leaves of *Ericameria laricifolia*, turpentine bush, become blanketed with bright yellow, daisylike flowers in fall. Develops into a shrub 2 to 3 feet high and as wide. Excellent in combination with purple-flowering plants, such as *Dalea* species, as shown.

'Purpurea', purple hop bush, has bronzy purple leaves and is less hardy—to 20°F. Accepts most soils but prefers well-drained soil with deep irrigation. Can be lightly shaped or allow to grow naturally. An Arizona native. Hardy to 10°F.

Drunkard's tree—*see Chorisia speciosa*

Dusty miller—*see Centaurea cineraria*

Dwarf cup flower—*see Nierembergia hippomanica*

Dwarf rosemary—*see Rosmarinus 'Lockwood de Forest'*

Dwarf running myrtle—*see Vinca minor*

Easterlily vine—*see Beaumontia grandiflora*

Echinacea purpurea, PURPLE CONEFLOWER   PERENNIAL
Purple cone-shaped flowers are long lasting and a favorite in a natural garden. Grows 2 to 4 feet high and 2-1/2 feet wide. Accepts many soil conditions but does need full sun. Grows easily from seed and competes well with grasses. Native to prairies in midwestern U.S. Moderate water use. Cold hardy.

Echinocactus grusonii, GOLDEN BARREL CACTUS ACCENT

One of the best cactus for landscaping due to its symmetrical, globular shape and brilliant, golden spines that seem to light up in the sun. Grows slowly to 2 feet high or more, but remains a manageable size in most gardens for many years. Flowers appear in spring on the crown. Plant in sandy, well-drained soil. Water infrequently, perhaps once a month, slightly more often during summer. Native to Chihuahuan Desert. Hardy to 15°F; young plants slightly less hardy.

Elephant's food—*see Portulacaria afra*

Encelia farinosa, BRITTLEBUSH, INCIENSO SHRUB

Brittlebush is an abundant shrub in desert areas throughout the Southwest. It also plays a versatile role in home gardens, particularly in natural designs with other native plants. Evergreen gray to light green leaves are soft and velvety to the touch, covering the 2- to 3-foot plants. Bright, yellow, daisylike flowers are borne on tall stems well above the foliage in spring. After flowering has passed, cut plant back by one-third and water thoroughly for a repeat bloom. Basic needs include well-drained soil and full sun. Does not need fertilizer. Low-water use. Hardy to 25°F.

English ivy—*see Hedera helix*

English lavender—*see Lavandula angustifolia*

Ericameria laricifolia, TURPENTINE BUSH SHRUB

In the fall, turpentine bush's dense, fine-textured, dark green leaves becomes blanketed by bright yellow, daisylike flowers. The refined growth can develop into a shrub 2 to 3 feet high and as wide. Best used in masses or clusters in out-of-the-way places, on slopes or in combination with other low-water use plants. Give the foliage a rub between your hands and you will smell the turpentine scent. Well-drained soil, full sun or partial shade and low water are basic cultural requirements. Native to west Texas, New Mexico, Arizona and Mexico. Hardy to 0°F.

Above left: *Echinocactus grusonii,* golden barrel cactus, is a superior accent plant. It is admired for its low-water use, slow growth and brilliant, golden spines that light up in the afternoon sun. Flowers appear in spring on the crown.

Above: *Encelia farinosa,* brittlebush, is grown for its gray to light green leaves and bright, yellow, daisylike flowers in spring. It's a versatile, easy-to-grow shrub, especially for natural garden designs.

Above: *Eucalyptus polyanthemos*, silver dollar gum, grows 20 to 50 feet high. Grayish green leaves are almost round (thus its common name) when trees are young. Eventually, leaves become more narrow, with light red margins and veins.

Above right: *Eucalyptus spathulata,* swamp malee, has a different appearance than most eucalyptus. Graceful, ribbonlike leaves are 2 to 3 inches long. Smooth, reddish to tan, peeling bark adds a sculptural effect. Grows 15 to 30 feet high and is excellent as a screen or windbreak.

Eriobotrya japonica, LOQUAT, JAPANESE PLUM   TREE, SHRUB

A small to medium (10 to 15 feet), evergreen tree or shrub with decorative, dark green leaves. The pear-shaped, orange-yellow fruit are edible. Produces a subtropical effect with strong, open, branching habit. Best in partial shade. Moderate water requirement. Hardy to 10°F.

Eschscholzia californica, CALIFORNIA POPPY   WILDFLOWER

California poppy is the trademark wildflower of the West, and the state flower of California. Orange to yellow, cup-shaped flowers bloom on 12- to 18-inch stems from spring into early summer. Plants reseed readily, or you may collect the dry seed pods before seed is dispersed and sow where you want plants to grow. Easy to grow from seed in most soils and in a range of climates. Does not like soil that is continuously moist or overly rich. In mild climates sow in fall for spring flowers. Plant in full sun to partial shade. Drought tolerant.

Eucalyptus species, EUCALYPTUS

Dozens of eucalyptus have been grown and selected for commercial use and in home landscapes in the West. Initially, they served as windbreaks to protect orchards and homesites, and they continue this utilitarian role today.

Selecting eucalyptus for a home landscape requires some thought and planning, because many species grow up to 60 feet or higher—much too large for most residences. Generally, smaller species such as *Eucalyptus spathulata* are more successful and better suited to the size and scale of most home lots. Be particularly careful if power lines are part of your landscape. This is true with any trees for that matter. Encourage deep roots with deep (and wide) watering with drip irrigation.

Eucalyptus cinerea, SILVER-DOLLAR TREE   TREE

Small to medium tree to 20 to 50 feet high. Fast growing in youth. Attractive, gray-green, rounded leaves grow as opposites on the stem. Juvenile leaves are excellent for cut foliage. Tolerates wind. Low water use. Hardy to 14°F to 17°F.

Eucalyptus microtheca, COOLIBAH TREE   TREE

Evergreen and graceful tree to 20 to 40 feet high. Tolerates heat, wind and drought. Occasional leaf and twig litter may be a nuisance. Canopy provides substantial shade. Suitable for use as a windbreak. Hardy to 25°F.

Eucalyptus polyanthemos, SILVER-DOLLAR GUM   TREE

Medium size to 25 to 50 feet, sometimes more. Low branching. Grayish green leaves are almost round when trees are young, eventually (after several years) trees produce more narrow leaves with light red margins and veins. White flowers bloom in September. Hardy 18°F to 22°F.

Eucalyptus sideroxylon, PINK, RED IRONBARK   TREE

Medium to tall, 20 to 60 feet high, with rough, brownish red bark and long, dark green leaves. Pink flowers are borne in large clusters. Low to moderate water use. Hardy to 20°F to 25°F.

Eucalyptus spathulata, SWAMP MALEE   TREE

Evergreen, compact and handsome, with multiple trunks. Smooth, reddish to tan, peeling bark adds a sculptural effect. Grows 15 to 30 feet high with graceful, ribbonlike leaves 2 to 3 inches long. Makes an excellent screen or windbreak. Tolerates salty, poor soil. Low water use. Hardy to 15°F to 20°F.

Euonymus japonicus, EUONYMUS   SHRUB

Fast-growing, upright shrub to 8 to 12 feet high with large, shiny, deep green leaves. Needs regular moisture to maintain healthy, overall lush and vigorous appearance. Compact branching habit accepts shearing well.

Above: Eschscholzia californica, California poppy, is one of the best wildflowers for Coachella Valley gardens. Easy to grow and a prolific bloomer from spring into early summer.

Above left: *Eucalyptus cinerea,* silver dollar tree, makes a distinctive small tree for almost any size garden. Fast growing in youth, its attractive, gray-green, rounded leaves grow as opposites on its stems. Juvenile leaves are excellent for cut foliage in bouquets and arrangements.

Above: *Feijoa sellowiana,* pineapple guava, has attractive, gray-green leaves that serve as the background for waxy white flowers with red stamens. Flower petals are edible and can be used in salads.

Above right: *Euphorbia rigida,* gopher plant, is a striking spring-flowering perennial with blue-gray, textured, spreading branches that grow to 2 feet high, spreading up to 4 feet wide.

'Aureo-variegata', gold spot euonymus, is more compact, to 4 to 6 feet high. It has leaves blotched with yellow and well-defined, dark green margins. Best in partial shade. 'Microphyllus Improved', boxleaf euonymus, is a dwarf selection to 2 to 4 feet high. It is erect with small, closely arranged, dark green leaves. Compact with a formal appearance that does not require pruning. Locate in full sun or partial shade. Native to Japan. All are cold hardy.

Euphorbia milii, CROWN OF THORNS   ACCENT

Perennial that doubles as an accent. This relative of poinsettia is shrublike with thorny stems. Clusters of red flowers bloom most of the year. Accepts heat. Drought tolerant, but better appearance with regular summer irrigation. Cold tender.

Euphorbia rigida, GOPHER PLANT   PERENNIAL

(E. biglandulosa). Unique spring-flowering perennial with blue-gray textured vertical and spreading branches that grow 2 feet high by 4 feet wide. Color of flowers on tips of branches is brilliant chrome yellow. Most effective in sunny location. Mass in small areas in well-drained soil or plant in containers. After flowers complete bloom cycle, cut back extended branches to encourage new growth. Native to the Mediterranean. Hardy to 0°F.

Euphorbia tirucalli, PENCIL BUSH   ACCENT

Leafless plant grown for its unusual, pencil-thick branches with see-through patterns. Sap is irritating to people and animals. Tender to cold. Grow in containers so plants can be moved to frost-free location during cold weather.

Euryops pectinatus 'Viridis', GREEN GOLD   PERENNIAL

Workhorse evergreen perennial that is often used a small shrub, 'Viridis' is an improved selection. Grows 3 to 4 feet high with fine-textured, deep green leaves. Yellow daisylike flowers to 2 inches across bloom fall into early winter. Good container plant. Tolerates a wide range of climates, from the desert to the coast. Accepts drought conditions. Hardy to mid 20s°F.

Evening primrose—*see Oenothera species*

Fairy primrose—*see Primula malacoides*

Fallugia paradoxa, APACHE PLUME SHRUB

Admired for its graceful, airy, upright stems and branches and spring flowers. White flowers are 1 inch across, and look similar to single rose blossoms. Seed heads that are silky pink plumes adorn plants from May to December. Adds long-term interest in borders, to 3 to 6 feet high, but is deciduous in cold winters. Locate in partial shade to full sun; accepts reflected heat. Well-drained soil essential. Low water use. Native to Utah to Texas south to Mexico. Cold hardy.

Farewell to spring—*see Clarkia amoena*

Fatshedera lizei, BOTANICAL WONDER VINE, SHRUB

A hybrid between two plant genera: *Fatsia* and *Hedera*. Semi-climbing vine or shrub with large, glossy green leaves. Evergreen, tropical appearance. Provide with shade to partial shade exposure. Will not tolerate windy locations. Develops more compact growth with numerous light prunings during the year. Hardy to 15°F to 25°F, except new growth, which is cold-tender.

Fatsia japonica, JAPANESE ARALIA SHRUB

Attractive, tropical-appearing evergreen, grown for its large, deeply cut, glossy, dark green, leathery leaves. Small white flowers bloom fall and winter, followed by shiny black fruit. Rapid growth to 4 feet. Plant in shade only. Native to Japan. Hardy to 25°F.

Feather tree—*see Lysiloma species*

Feijoa sellowiana, PINEAPPLE GUAVA SHRUB

Fast growing, evergreen shrub, growing 10 to 18 feet high. Gray-green leaves are attractive, as are the waxy white flowers with red stamens. Flower petals are edible and can be used in salads. Flowers bloom May through June and are followed by tasty fruit. Fruit quality and quantity is better in cooler climates. Locate in full sun to partial shade. Native to South America. Hardy to 20°F.

Above: *Euryops pectinatus* 'Viridis', green gold, is a dependable evergreen perennial that is often used a small shrub. Grows 3 to 4 feet high with fine-textured, deep green leaves. Yellow daisylike flowers to 2 inches across blanket plants fall into early winter.

Above left: *Fallugia paradoxa*, Apache plume, is a airy shrub reaching 3 to 6 feet high. Silky pink seed heads (as shown) are an attraction on plants from May to December.

Above: *Ferocactus wislizenii,* fish-hook barrel cactus, makes a fine accent plant. Orangish flowers bloom spring and summer, followed by decorative fruit.

Right: *Felicia amelloides,* blue marguerite, is one of the best blue-flowering perennials for warm-summer areas. Bright blue, daisylike flowers with yellow centers bloom for several months during the warm season.

Felicia amelloides, BLUE MARGUERITE　　　PERENNIAL

Evergreen in warm climates to 2 feet high or more. Bright blue, daisylike flowers with yellow centers bloom for several months during the warm season. Use in containers, borders or color accent. Accepts full sun in most climates; better with afternoon shade in Coachella Valley. Native to South Africa. Moderate water use. Hardy to 20°F.

Fern pine—*see Podocarpus gracilior*

Ferocactus wislizenii, FISH-HOOK BARREL CACTUS　　　ACCENT

Green, spined, rounded barrel cactus 2 to 10 feet high. Spring and summer flowers are orange. Overwatering may cause plants to rot and die. Helpful to plant in sandy, well-drained soil. Hardy to 0°F.

Festuca ovina var. glauca, BLUE FESCUE　ORNAMENTAL GRASS

A blue-gray, highly ornamental grass, growing in roundish tufts 6 to 10 inches high. The blue-gray foliage creates an interesting pattern in borders or as a foreground planting to taller perennials and shrubs. Plant 18 inches apart. Seed heads rise above clumps in the fall, creating a shaggy effect. Cut back to 3 to 4 inches high in winter for renewed growth the following spring. Will not tolerate wet, poorly drained soil. Full sun. Low to moderate moisture. Cold hardy.

Ficus benjamina, WEEPING FIG　　　　　　TREE

Superb subtropical plant, growing rapidly to 10 to 20 feet high. Bright green leaves on graceful, weeping branches make an attractive small indoor tree, one of its common uses. Also excellent for espaliers, containers, specimen, hedge, screen or patio tree where hardy. Native to India. Tender to frost and susceptible to wind damage. Cold tender: hardy to 32°F.

Ficus pumila, CREEPING FIG, ROCK FIG   VINE

Evergreen, self-clinging vine. Creates an interesting tracery pattern on walls, growing to 30 feet or more high. Juvenile leaves are small and oval; mature leaves are large and lobed, similar to fig leaves. Cutting plants back after they have reached the mature stage will cause them to revert to juvenile form. Full sun to partial shade exposure. Tough plant once it is established, but can be slow to get started. Low water use. Hardy to 10°F to 20°F.

Figs, fruit-bearing—*see page 146*

Five spot—*see Nemophila maculata*

Flanders field poppy—*see Papaver rhoeas*

Forget-me-not—*see Myosotis sylvatica*

Fouquieria splendens, OCOTILLO   ACCENT

This native cactus look-alike is actually a shrub. Ocotillo is one of the most distinctive plants of the desert Southwest. A few to many unbranched thorny canes, 10 to 15 feet long, arch up out and away from the plant's base, creating a vase-shape. Small bright green leaves cover the canes during periods of rain and humidity, dropping during dry conditions as plants become dormant. Spikes of flame orange flowers bloom at branch tips during spring. Excellent accent plant, especially as silhouette and when backlit by the sun. Prefers nutrient-poor, rocky soil. Avoid overwatering; accepts drought. Hardy to 10°F.

Fraxinus uhdei 'Majestic Beauty', EVERGREEN ASH   TREE

Exceptionally large, compound, glossy dark green leaves add splendor to this medium-sized, round-headed tree. More evergreen and more uniform growth than other ashes. Vigorous growth, reaching 50 to 60 feet high with 50-foot spread. Strong branching habit. Moderate water use. Deep irrigation helps reduce surface rooting. Hardy to 22°F.

Fraxinus velutina 'Modesto', MODESTO ASH   TREE

Medium-sized, deciduous tree to 20 to 30 feet high. Sturdy branches form a rounded crown. Lustrous green leaves turn gold in the fall. A vigorous shade tree. Low to moderate water use. Hardy to 10°F to 15°F.

Gaillardia X grandiflora, BLANKET FLOWER   PERENNIAL

This plant is a hybrid of G. *aristata* and G. *puchella.* It is a long-blooming perennial, flowering continuously from spring to frost. Many varieties are available. Striking red and yellow flowers are set off by glossy green leaves. Plants range in size from less than 1 foot to 4 feet high, depending on the selection. They are easy to grow. Sow seed in spring or fall in full sun in well-drained soil. Stake flowers of taller varieties. Low water use. Hardy to 15°F.

Gaillardia pulchella, INDIAN BLANKET   ANNUAL

Often used in western region wildflower seed mixes for its easy, aggressive growth. Plants grow to 1-1/2 to 2 feet high. Long slender stems are topped with 2-inch red, yellow and gold flowers. Easy to start from seed. Plant in full sun and in soil with good drainage. Blooms from midsummer to frost.

Fouquieria splendens, ocotillo, is a well-known vertical accent plant in the Coachella Valley. Accepts the toughest conditions and low-water situations.

Gardenia jasminoides, GARDENIA SHRUB

This is the well-known evergreen with large, creamy white, extremely fragrant flowers and glossy green leaves. Flowers bloom April to October. Apply acid fertilizer monthly from March to September for best results. Good soil drainage is required; include ground bark in soil mix. Prefers partial shade. 'Mystery', bushy and compact to 5 feet high. 'Veitchi', everblooming gardenia, is a free-flowering evergreen. Compact and upright to 2 to 3 feet high. Produces bright green foliage and fragrant, white flowers. Hardy 15°F to 20°F.

Gazania hybrids, GAZANIA GROUND COVER

Permanent bedding or border plant. Clumping growth becomes a low-growing mat of gray-green foliage. Daisylike flowers to 2 inches in diameter come in a wide range of bright colors. Accepts dry conditions but moderate water encourages optimum growth and flowers. Grows 6 to 10 inches high. Plant 12 inches apart. Accepts no traffic. Hardy to 24°F.

'Copper King' is grown for its immense, bronze-red flowers that bloom in profusion that many consider the most striking of all gazanias. Tolerates lower temperatures than other selections. 'Fiesta' has reddish copper flowers and glossy, dark green foliage. 'Chansonette Mixture' grows to 10 inches high with a compact habit. Wide range of flower colors available, including yellow, orange and red. Reseeds readily. Plant in full sun. Low to moderate water use.

Gazania rigens leucolaena, TRAILING GAZANIA GR. COVER

(G. leucolaena). Clean, silvery green foliage spreads rapidly, forming an attractive cover. Grows 6 to 10 inches high. Daisylike gazania flowers in many colors are borne in profusion practically every month of the year. Useful on banks for erosion control. Acceptable growth in relatively poor soil. Plant in full sun, spacing 1-1/2 to 2 feet apart. Requires partial shade in reflected heat locations. No traffic. Avoid overwatering. Tolerates drought. Hardy to 26°F.

Geijera parviflora, AUSTRALIAN WILLOW   TREE

Evergreen, graceful, fine-textured tree to 25 to 30 feet high. Growth is uniform but slow. Drought tolerant. Good soil drainage is essential. Best with moderate water; ample water actually inhibits growth. Hardy to 25°F.

Gelsemium sempervirens, CAROLINA JESSAMINE   VINE

An evergreen, twining vine with rich green leaves. Climbs to about 20 feet, but does require support. Profusion of trumpet-shaped, bright yellow, fragrant flowers bloom in late winter to early spring. Accepts full sun to partial shade. Note that all plant parts are poisonous. Hardy to 15°F.

Geraldton wax flower—*see Chamelaucium uncinatum*

Geranium species, GERANIUM   ANNUAL

Geraniums are treated as annuals in low-elevation desert regions and are ideal container color plants. Plant in spring after danger of frost has passed in full sun or partial shade. A well-drained soil is important. Enjoy the spring flowers then move into shade as the warm season comes on in late April and May. Space plants in flowerbeds at least 18 inches apart. Remove dead flowers and leaves on a regular basis to help prevent diseases. Feed with dilute solution of liquid fertilizer. Low to moderate moisture requirement; avoid soggy wet soils.

Gerbera jamesonii, GERBERA, TRANSVAAL DAISY   PERENNIAL

An evergreen perennial color plant in warm climates such as in the Coachella Valley. Daisylike flowers come in a wide range of colors. Gerbera makes a superb cut flower on 12-inch stems. Best with afternoon shade in desert climates. Moderate water requirement. Hardy to 15°F.

Germander—*see Teucrium*

Giant timber bamboo—*see Bambusa oldhamii*

Gilia capitata, BLUE THIMBLE FLOWER   ANNUAL

Plants grow to 2 feet high with tall, slender stems. Blue pin-cushion flowers bloom from summer to fall. Leaves to 4 inches long are finely dissected, adding a light airy feeling to plants. Accepts full sun to shade. Drought tolerant once established. Easy to grow from seed. Native to western North America.

Below left: Geraniums are treated as annuals in low-elevation desert regions. Space plants in flowerbeds at least 18 inches apart.

Below: *Gelsemium sempervirens*, Carolina jessamine, climbs to about 20 feet, with support. Trumpet-shaped, bright yellow, fragrant (but poisonous) flowers bloom in late winter to early spring.

Above: *Hedera canariensis,* Algerian ivy, grows 12 to 15 inches high with large, bright, glossy green leaves to 6 inches long. Leaves are widely spaced along stems. Plant 15 to 18 inches apart for a continuous ground cover.

Above right: *Grevillea robusta,* silk oak, needs room to reach its mature height of 40 to 50 feet. Thick, fernlike, dark green leaves serve as background to clusters of showy, bright, orange-yellow flowers in spring.

Gold dust plant—*see Aucuba japonica*

Golden bamboo—*see Phyllostachys aurea*

Golden goddess bamboo—*see Bambusa multiplex 'Golden Goddess'*

Golden lupine—*see Lupinus densiflorus var. aureus*

Golden rabbit bush—*see Chrysothamnus nauseosus*

Golden shrub daisy—*see Euryops pectinatus*

Goldfields—*see Lasthenia glabrata*

Goldman's senna—*see Senna polyantha*

Grape—*see Vitis vinifera*

Green gold—*see Euryops pectinatus 'Viridis'*

Grevillea robusta, SILK OAK TREE

Large, narrow, columnar evergreen tree to 40 to 50 feet high, spreading to 30 feet wide. Fernlike dark green leaves serve as background to clusters of showy, bright, orange-yellow flowers in spring. Stake to develop form of newly planted trees. Brittle branches are prone to breaking in strong, gusty winds. Invasive and voracious roots can cause problems with nearby plants. Encourage deep rooting with deep watering. Makes a fine tall hedge, growing and filling in rapidly. Messy leaf drop. Moderate water requirement. Native to Australia. Young trees accept temperatures down to 24°F, mature trees are hardy to 16°F.

Grewia occidentalis, LAVENDER STAR-FLOWER   SHRUB

Fast-growing, evergreen shrub to 6 feet high, spreading 4 to 5 feet wide. Lavender, star-shaped flowers bloom throughout the year. Accepts training as an espalier. Full sun exposure. Native to Africa. Hardy to 26°F to 28°F.

Guadalupe palm—*see Brahea edulis*

Guajillo—*see Acacia berlandieri*

Gutierrezia sarothrae, SICKLE BROOM   SHRUB

Grows 1-1/2 to 2 feet high with fascinating, symmetrical, threadlike leaves that support masses of small yellow flowers in late summer. Growth is neat and tidy. Use in the native garden among boulders or as a foreground in the natural border. Prefers full sun and well-drained soil. Low water use. If not available in containers at the nursery it can be started from seed in the fall. Native to high-elevation desert regions in the West. Cold hardy.

Gypsophila paniculata, BABY'S BREATH   PERENNIAL

'Bristol Fairy' is an improved selection, growing to 3 feet high. Large panicles (loose clusters) of double white flowers bloom profusely through summer. Heat and drought tolerant. Full sun. Moderate water use. Cold hardy.

Hall's Japanese honeysuckle—*see Lonicera japonica 'Halliana'*

Heavenly bamboo—*see Nandina domestica*

Hedera canariensis, ALGERIAN IVY   VINE

Algerian ivy grows 12 to 15 inches high with large, bright, glossy green leaves to 6 inches long. Leaves are widely spaced along stems. Grow as a self-climbing vine or continuous ground cover. Once established, plants grows rapidly. High water use. Requires partial shade exposure. Will not accept traffic. Hardy to 24°F.

Hedera helix, ENGLISH IVY   VINE

English ivy is better suited as a ground cover in small shaded areas or borders than its Algerian cousin. Once established, plants cover rapidly, growing 12 inches high with dark green leaves 2 to 4 inches wide. Plant 1-1/2 to 2 feet apart for solid cover. No traffic. Requires ample moisture in a shaded location. Cold hardy. 'Hahnii', Hahn's ivy, is ideal where ground patterns are desired. Provides a softer effect than the species and can be confined more readily. Grows 8 to 12 inches high. No traffic. Plant in shade only. High water use. Hardy to 25°F.

Hemerocallis hybrids, DAYLILY   PERENNIAL

Both evergreen and deciduous hybrids are available. Each form a clump of slender arching leaves. Flowers in clusters bloom at the ends of tall stems mid-spring to early fall. They resemble lilies and come in many colors, including yellow, orange and red and many pastel shades as well. Many cultivars are available, so shop around. Flowers last only one day, but are replaced by new flowers the following day. They add splashes of color anywhere in the garden—borders, among rocks and boulders, grouped in masses or even as a small-area ground cover. Accepts almost any soil. Cut back brown stems and deadhead flowers after bloom season. Moderate water use.

Hemerocallis hybrids, daylily, grow as clumps of slender arching leaves. Lilylike flowers in clusters bloom at the ends of tall stems midspring to early fall. Many flower colors are available.

Heuchera sanguinea, coral bells, creates a feeling of the woods, and requires partial shade in hot-summer areas. Flowers bloom in clusters in coral, reddish pink, white or crimson on top of 1- to 2-foot stems.

Hesperaloe parviflora, RED YUCCA   ACCENT

Evergreen yuccalike plant to 3 to 4 feet high and as wide. Plants are long-term color providers with flowers from late spring into late summer. Vivid reddish coral, bell-shaped flowers on tall spikes are loved by hummingbirds. A variety with pale yellow flowers is also available. Low water use. Hardy to 15°F.

Hesperaloe funifera, giant hesperaloe, is similar but larger to 6 feet high and as wide or wider, with swordlike leaves that are more upright. Flowering stalks to 8 feet high are topped with greenish white blooms late spring to summer.

Hesperis matronalis, DAME'S ROCKET   PERENNIAL

Produces purple and white flowers similar to those of phlox, borne in loose heads at the end of the stems. Plants grow 2 to 3 feet high. Locate in full sun or partial shade in moist, well-drained soil. Easy to grow from seed.

Heuchera sanguinea, CORAL BELLS   PERENNIAL

Plant is low growing with roundish leaves to 6 to 12 inches high. Flower clusters in coral, reddish pink, white or crimson bloom on top of 1- to 2-foot stems. Locate in partial shade in hot-summer areas in fertile, well-drained soil. Moderate water use. Cold hardy.

Hibiscus species, HIBISCUS   SHRUB

These subtropical flowering shrubs grow 6 to 10 feet high. They bloom continuously during the warm season. Foliage varies but most have attractive, glossy, deep green leaves. Flowers come in a wide range of colors; many are multicolored with contrasting throats. Provide afternoon shade and wind protection. Prune June to September. Hardy 28°F to 40°F, depending on variety.

'Agnes Gault' has large, single, bright rose-pink flowers that are heavily veined with a pink and cranberry throat. Fast-growing, vigorous plant. 'Butterfly', vibrant, bright yellow, single flowers are produced in profusion on upright plants. 'Crown of Bohemia', very full double flowers are magnificent golden yellow with deep orange-red throats. 'High Voltage' has large white flowers with contrasting magenta throats. 'Ross Estey', extremely large single flowers with orange edges shading to glowing rose center. These ruffled and tufted flowers last about three days on plants. Foliage is heavy and large with a glossy, hand-polished appearance. 'San Diego Red' produces vivid, bright red single flowers in profuse numbers most of the year. Glossy dark green foliage on vigorous, upright shrub. 'White Wings' produces a heavy crop of attractive single flowers. White petals have a ruby eye in the center accented with a faint red vein in each petal.

Holly—*see Ilex cornuta*

Holly oak—*see Quercus ilex*

Hopseed bush—*see Dodonaea viscosa*

Iceland poppy—*see Papaver nudicaule*

Ilex cornuta, CHINESE HOLLY   SHRUB

One of the most versatile hollies, best in a shady location. Plant in an east or west exposure. Grows to become a dense, bushy, 6- to 8-foot evergreen shrub or tree. Scarlet berries are an attraction in fall. 'Burfordii', burford holly, is a prolific bearer of large, bright red berries. Leaves are deep glossy green and are almost spineless. Berries are sterile. Vigorous, upright, compact-branching plants. Best with some shade. 'Rotunda', dwarf Chinese holly, is a superior, compact holly to 2 to 3 feet high, grown for its dense-branching habit. Ideal for shade or partial shade location. Produces no berries but makes up for it with its outstanding appearance.

Ilex vomitoria 'Stokes Dwarf', DWARF YAUPON   SHRUB

Tiny, rich, dark green leaves are closely held on a dwarf plant to 2 to 3 feet high. Full sun to partial shade. Excellent border or low hedge. Native to southeastern United States. Hardy to 20°F.

Above: *Hesperaloe parviflora,* red yucca, is a valuable and versatile accent and color plant. It provides long-term color late spring into late summer, with minimal care.

Below: Hibiscus are ideal flowering plants for a subtropical effect. Many are cold-tender so locate in a sheltered location to protect against frost. Shown are 'Agnes Gault', left, and 'High Voltage', below.

Above: *Jacaranda mimosifolia,* jacaranda, becomes a large, round-headed, semi-evergreen to 50 feet high. Large clusters of attractive, lavender-blue flowers put on a show in May and June.

Above right: *Juniperus chinensis* 'Torulosa', also known as 'Kaizuka', Hollywood juniper, has a distinctive, wind-blown appearance. Form is upright to 15 feet high.

Imperata cylindrica, JAPANESE BLOOD GRASS   ORN. GRASS

'Rubra' is an improved selection that is semi-deciduous to 18 inches high with a spreading habit. Beautiful red leaves in spring and fall. Best color in sunny exposure. Moderate water use. Hardy to 20°F.

Incienso—*see Encelia farinosa*

Indian blanket—*see Gaillardia pulchella*

Indigo bush—*see Dalea pulchra*

Iris moraea—*see Dietes vegeta*

Ironwood—*see Olneya tesota*

Italian stone pine—*see Pinus pinea*

Jacaranda mimosifolia, JACARANDA   TREE

(J. acutifolia). Large, round-headed, semi-evergreen tree grows to 30 to 50 feet, with lacy, fernlike, green leaves. Large clusters of attractive, lavender-blue flowers bloom profusely May and June. As flowers drop, they produce a fair amount of litter, so avoid locating trees near swimming pools or patios. Needs soil with good drainage. Water deeply to reduce development of surface roots but do not overwater. Suckers if pruned too drastically. Native to Argentina. Hardy to 20°F.

Japanese black pine—*see Pinus thunbergii*

Japanese blood grass—*see Imperata cylindrica 'Rubra'*

Japanese boxwood—*see Buxus microphylla var. japonica*

Japanese plum—*see Eriobotrya japonica*

Japanese aralia—*see Fatsia japonica*

Japanese privet—*see Ligustrum japonicum*

Jasminum magnificum, ANGEL WING JASMINE   VINE OR SHRUB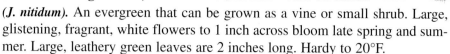

(J. nitidum). An evergreen that can be grown as a vine or small shrub. Large, glistening, fragrant, white flowers to 1 inch across bloom late spring and summer. Large, leathery green leaves are 2 inches long. Hardy to 20°F.

Jerusalem sage—*see Phlomis fruticosa*

Jerusalem thorn—*see Parkinsonia aculeata*

Joshua tree—*see Yucca brevifolia*

Juniperus chinensis, JUNIPER   SHRUB, GROUND COVER

'Armstrongii', Armstrong juniper, is a showy, semi-erect conifer to 4 to 5 feet high. Symmetrical with a close-knit growth habit. More compact than 'Pfitzerana', following. Attractive light green, lacy-textured foliage.
'Hetzii Columnaris', a columnar juniper, is an attractive bright green juniper, growing as a dense, 12- to 15-foot column. Sharp-pointed, needlelike leaves accept trimming well. 'Pfitzerana', Pfitzer juniper, is a handsome, gray-green color. Sharp-needled leaves cover arching branches as plant develops into a showy, spreading shrub 6 to 10 feet high and as wide. Plant form makes a natural security barrier that is difficult to penetrate. 'San Jose' is one of the best prostrate junipers. Sage green and compact to 2 feet high. A husky form with many branches. Locate in partial shade. Excellent specimen for tub or bonsai. 'Torulosa', also known as 'Kaizuka', Hollywood juniper, has rich green foliage. Form is upright to 10 to 20 feet high. Erect branches take on a picturesque wind-blown appearance. Best in partial shade. Handsome shrub for use along fences or for special specimen as an accent.

Juniperus horizontalis, PROSTRATE JUNIPER   GROUND COVER

'Bar Harbor' is a fine prostrate juniper to 1 foot high. Its matted branches hug the ground as they spread. In summer, foliage is a soft blue, gradually taking on a silvery plum hue in winter. Best in partial shade. No traffic. 'Wiltonii', blue carpet juniper, is one of the finest low, trailing junipers growing 6 to 12 inches high, excellent for ground cover or bank planting. Makes a well-mannered carpet of intense, silver-blue leaves, but accepts no traffic.

Juniperus sabina, SAVIN JUNIPER   SHRUB, GROUND COVER

'Arcadia' has rich green, lacy-textured foliage with a semi-spreading growth habit to 2 to 3 feet high. 'Scandia' is low and spreading with feathery green foliage, excellent where a dense, low-growing plant is desired. 'Tamariscifolia', tamarix juniper, is a favorite low, spreading juniper to 3 feet high. Forms heavily covered mounds with attractive blue-green foliage. Useful as ground cover or foreground plant.

Juniperus scopulorum, ROCKY MTN. JUNIPER   SHRUB

'Blue Heaven' makes a neat, pyramidal form 12 to 20 feet high. Compact with distinctive blue foliage. 'Gray Gleam' is a symmetrical, upright, columnar juniper to 20 feet high with attractive gray-blue foliage. Outstanding compact growth. 'Pathfinder' is showy with a dense, pyramidal form 12 to 20 feet high. Blue-gray leaves are attractive in combination with green-foliaged plants.

Three species of *Justicia*, from left to right: *Justicia brandegeana*, shrimp plant, with its masses of pinkish copper, shrimp-shaped flowers. *Justicia californica*, chuperosa, has showy, red, tubular flowers that are most profuse in the spring. It becomes a sprawling, informal shrub to 4 feet high. *Justicia spicigera*, Mexican honeysuckle, produces an almost subtropical effect, with bright orange, tubular flowers and lush, pale green leaves. Ideal in filtered shade.

Justicia brandegeana, SHRIMP PLANT   SHRUB

(Beloperone guttata). Masses of pinkish copper, shrimp-shaped flowers stand out against deep green, luxuriant leaves. Plants grow 2 to 3 feet high, blooming during the warm season. Best in partial shade. Moderate water. Hardy to 28°F.

Justicia californica, CHUPEROSA   SHRUB

Showy, red, tubular flowers are most profuse in the spring, with a smattering in summer and fall. Sprawling, informal growth to 4 feet high, spreading to 6 feet wide. Ideal for a natural garden design. Prefers full sun. Cut plants back severely every two or three years to renew growth. Native to the Sonoran Desert. Hardy to 25°F.

Justicia spicigera, MEXICAN HONEYSUCKLE   SHRUB

Bright orange tubular flowers combine with soft, fuzzy, pale green leaves, creating a luxuriant effect. Hummingbirds flock to plants in bloom, from mid to late spring. Growth is rounded to upright at 3 to 4 feet high. Generally no insect or disease problems. Tolerates some sun, but most lush growth occurs with filtered shade, such as beneath high-canopied trees. Severe damage at low 20s°F.

Kaffir lily—*see Clivia miniata*

Koelreuteria bipinnata, GOLDEN RAIN TREE   TREE

Grown in part for its small, yellow, summer flowers that become inflated papery pods in fall. These resemble miniature Chinese lanterns, thus its common name. As the season progresses, these pods change from a creamy white to orange-red and brown. Makes a nice small shade tree with a mature size of 20 to 35 feet high with an equal spread. Trees develop sturdy trunks that are often irregular, but light pruning of young trees can direct growth. Plant in well-drained soil. Deciduous, so do any major pruning in winter. Hardy to 28°F.

Lady Banks' rose—*see Rosa banksiae*

Lady palm—*see Rhapis excelsa*

Lagerstroemia indica, CRAPE MYRTLE   SHRUB OR SMALL TREE

Vigorous deciduous plant that offers year-round interest. Can be trained to become a quality, 20- to 25-foot tree admired for its striking clusters of flowers

that bloom summer into fall. Foliage turns bright shades of orange, yellow or red in fall. After leaves drop, the smooth, sculptural bark adds close-up interest. Avoid planting in lawn areas, which can cause plants to develop mildew problems, as will excessive humidity. Many cultivars and flower colors available, including white, pink, red and purple. Native to China. Hardy to 20°F.

Lantana camara, LANTANA   SHRUB OR GROUND COVER
Exceptional, compact evergreen shrub or ground cover. Produces masses of color through most of the year, blending with native or introduced dry-climate plants. Rich green leaves cover the thickly branched plants.

Many outstanding selections are available: 'Christine', striking cerise-pink flowers; 'Dwarf White', velvety white flowers; 'Dwarf Yellow', bright yellow flowers; 'Radiation', rich, orange-red flowers; 'Cream Carpet', pert, rich green leaves on spreading branches serve as a background for the carpet of cream-colored flowers; 'Spreading Sunset', bright green leaves on vigorous spreading branches with vivid, orange-red flowers; 'Spreading Sunshine', abundant, bright yellow flowers create a blanket of color on low, spreading compact plants; 'Tangerine', produces blooms that have a true, solid tangerine color. Native to tropical America. Hardy to 26°F.

Lantana montevidensis, TRAILING LANTANA   GROUND COVER
Trailing, prostrate, rapid-growing and free-blooming ground cover to 1-1/2 to 2 feet high. Plants are blanketed with lavender flowers during the fall, winter and spring. If damaged by frost, comes back fast in the spring following a heavy pruning in late winter. Ideal bank cover, especially on sunny slopes, good for erosion control. Accepts no traffic. 'Gold Mound', a hybrid introduction from Texas A&M University, has rich gold flowers and does not produce seeds. Space plants 1-1/2 to 2 feet apart. Hardy to 28°F.

Larchleaf goldenweed—*see Ericameria laricifolia*

Larkspur—*see Delphinium species*

Larrea divaricata subsp. tridentata, CREOSOTE BUSH   SHRUB
Can be seen in abundance throughout low- and high-elevation regions of the desert Southwest. One of the most versatile shrubs for a natural garden design,

Above: *Lagerstroemia indica,* crape myrtle, is a vigorous deciduous tree or large shrub. Admired for its striking clusters of flowers that bloom summer into fall.

Above center: *Larrea divaricata* subsp. *tridentata,* creosote bush, accepts the toughest conditions of intense heat, sun, wind, cold and drought. The dark green, glossy, evergreen leaves are covered with tiny yellow flowers in spring.

Above left: *Lantana camara,* lantana is an exceptional, compact, evergreen shrub or ground cover. Produces masses of flowers through most of the year, blending with native or introduced dry-climate plants.

Above: *Lavandula angustifolia,* English lavender, is an evergreen, flowering herb 3 to 4 feet high with an equal spread. Both flowers and foliage are fragrant.

Below: *Layia platyglossa,* tidy tips, is an annual wildflower. The showy flowers are 1- to 1-1/2 inches wide and bloom on plants to 1 foot high.

accepting the toughest conditions of intense heat, sun, wind, cold and drought. Thrives on low water. The dark green, glossy, evergreen foliage can be most useful as a hedge or screen or individual specimen. Truly maintenance-free. Bees are attracted to small yellow flowers that cover the 5- to 12-foot plants in spring. To develops its deep tap roots, provide new plantings with deep irrigation. If you have inherited creosote bush on your property, additional deep irrigation will make plants more luxuriant. Hardy to 0°F to 5°F.

Lasthenia glabrata, GOLDFIELDS   WILDFLOWER

An annual that grows 6 to 24 inches high with slender stems topped with yellow flowers from spring into summer. Excellent for fast temporary cover and color. Often included in western wildflower mixes; competes well with grasses. Use for soil revegetation and stabilization. Reseeds itself to come back the next year. Accepts full sun to partial shade. Native to northern California.

Lathyrus odoratus, SWEET PEA   ANNUAL

Start with plants in early fall rather than seed for quicker results. If you do start with seeds, soak them in water for several hours before planting. Plant in full sun or morning sun (east exposure) location protected from strong winds. Prepare soil by making a 1-foot deep trench, working in composted manure into lower portion of trench. Dwarf types excel in flower borders or in planters. Protect from birds by covering plants with netting. Install supports for vining types early on, when plants are small. Sweet peas are available in a wide range of colors. Moderate water use. Cut flowers to enjoy them in bouquets indoors, which also causes them to produce more flowers.

Lavandula species, LAVENDER   PERENNIAL

Evergreen flowering perennial herb 3 to 4 feet high with an equal spread. Plants are mound shaped with blue-green foliage. *L. angustifolia* 'Jean Davis' produces white flowers with a pink tinge on compact, plants to 1-1/2 feet high. 'Munstead' is a compact grower to 1- to 1-1/2 feet high. Lavender-blue flower spikes bloom in late spring and summer. Both flowers and foliage are fragrant. *L. stoechas,* Spanish lavender, is the most heat-tolerant lavender. All low to moderate water use. Native to the Mediterranean region. Hardy to 15F.

Lavender star flower—*see Grewia occidentalis*

Lavender trumpet vine—*see Clytostoma callistegioides*

Layia platyglossa, TIDY TIPS   WILDFLOWER

Tidy tips produces yellow daisylike flowers tipped with white. They are 1 to 2 inches across and showy, blooming on plants that grow to 1 foot high. Grows best in well-drained soil in full sun or partial shade. Tolerates heavy soil as long as it does not remain constantly wet. An annual that is easy to grow from seed. In the Coachella Valley sow in fall for late winter color; in colder regions sow in spring after the last frost has passed. Native to California.

Leucophyllum species, TEXAS RANGER

This large group of flowering shrubs have become star performers in the Southwest. More than a dozen species and selections are available and adapted to a large region, from Texas to California. Plants have evergreen silvery, gray to green foliage, dense, well-rounded growth and come in a range of sizes. Low water use, acceptance of full sun and long flowering seasons are more than enough attributes to use them in abundance in most any garden situation. Each species has a unique value that makes it worthy of consideration in plant

groupings. Most are generally cold hardy to 15°F to 20°F and are generally free of insects or diseases. Good soil drainage is important; avoid overwatering. Allowed to grow naturally, plants take on a more informal appearance. Controlling growth by trimming creates a more dense, hedgelike look, but often at the expense of flowers. Avoid pruning in globes or squares. Prune lightly after the fall flowering season has finished. Maintain the plant's form for a more natural but controlled effect.

Leucophyllum candidum, VIOLET SILVERLEAF   SHRUB

'Silver Cloud' has striking, dark violet flowers, excellent in contrast to its silvery white foliage. It is larger than 'Thunder Cloud' but produces fewer flowers. 'Thunder Cloud' is similar to 'Silver Cloud', growing to 3 feet high with indigo flowers. Most profuse bloom for both is during late summer.

Leucophyllum frutescens, TEXAS RANGER, CENIZIO   SHRUB

Grows 6 to 8 feet high and as wide with slightly rangy, open growth habit. Rose-purple flowers bloom most profusely in midsummer. 'Compacta' develops into a dwarf shrub 3 to 4 feet high. 'Green Cloud' has light green foliage; 'White Cloud' produces gray foliage and white flowers.

Leucophyllum laevigatum, CHIHUAHUAN RAIN SAGE   SHRUB

Grows to 4 feet high and as wide or wider with light violet flowers that bloom during summer, especially with humidity. Small, wavy, pale green leaves cover the branches, which turn up at the ends.

Leucophyllum langmaniae, CINNAMON SAGE   SHRUB

'Rio Bravo' has a dense growth habit to 4 to 5 feet high, similar to *L. laevigatum* but with fuller, denser growth. Lavender-blue flowers.

Leucophyllum pruinosum   SHRUB

'Sierra Bouquet' is an improved selection, with silvery gray, deep purple flowers that are the most fragrant of the Texas rangers. Grows to 6 feet high with an equal spread.

Leucophyllum species and hybrids, from left to right: *Leucophyllum frutescens,* Texas ranger, grows to 8 feet high and as wide with somewhat rangy, open growth habit. Rose-purple flowers bloom most profusely in midsummer.
'White Cloud' (center) produces silvery gray foliage and white flowers.
'Green Cloud' (right) has rose-purple flowers set off by light green foliage.

Above: *Leucophyllum langmaniae* 'Rio Bravo' has a dense growth habit to 4 to 5 feet high. Lavender-blue flowers bloom summer and fall.

Above right: *Lobularia maritima*, sweet alyssum, is an easy-care annual that is an all-around excellent companion to bright-colored annuals or perennials. White, rose and purple selections are available.

Leucophyllum X 'Rain Cloud', TEXAS RANGER   SHRUB

'Rain Cloud' is a cross between *L. frutescens* and *L. minus.* Foliage is similar to *L. frutescens* but flowers are blue. Hardy to 5°F to 10°F.

Leucophyllum zygophyllum, BLUE RANGER   SHRUB

'Cimmaron' is an improved selection that becomes a compact shrub 3 to 4 feet high and as wide. Leaves are distinctive in that they cup up. Light blue flowers are attractive against soft gray-green leaves. Hardy to 5°F to 10°F.

Licorice marigold—*see Tagetes lucida*

Ligustrum japonicum, JAPANESE PRIVET   SHRUB

(L. texanum). Fast growing, large, evergreen shrub or tree to 8 to 12 feet high. Dark green, lustrous leaves on heavily branched, upright habit. Clusters of white flowers bloom in spring. Excellent hedge or screen. Hardy to 10°F.

Lily of the Nile—*see Agapanthus orientalis*

Limonium perezii, SEA LAVENDER   PERENNIAL

Plumes of purple flowers bloom on 2-to 3-foot stalks during summer. Medium green leaves 10 to 12 inches long are excellent as underplanting. Requires filtered morning sun or locate beneath canopy trees. Plant in soil with good drainage. Moderate water use. Hardy to 28°F.

Linaria maroccana, TOADFLAX   WILDFLOWER

An annual wildflower growing 1 to 2 feet high. Snapdragonlike flowers bloom in mixed colors. Grows easily from seed; sow in fall in full sun. For best show of color, sow seed in large quantities. Accepts moderate water once plants are up and growing. Reseeds itself to come back the following spring.

Linum grandiflorum 'Rubrum', SCARLET FLAX   WILDFLOWER

This drought-tolerant annual wildflower grows rapidly 1 to 1-1/2 feet high, pro-

ducing brilliant, scarlet flowers at ends of tall stems. Plant in well-drained soil in fall; it will not tolerate soggy soil during the cool season. Accepts full sun to partial shade. Blooms from spring into midsummer. Reseeds readily.

Linum perenne subsp. lewisii, BLUE FLAX   WILDFLOWER
This annual wildflower produces a breathtaking bouquet of dazzling, sky-blue flowers that have a satiny sheen. They open every morning and fade in the afternoon heat. Plants grow to 2 feet high with a light, airy vase shape that allows them to blend well with other wildflowers. It prefers light soil and full sun. Native to California.

Liriope muscari 'Silvery Sunproof'   ORNAMENTAL GRASS
This ornamental grass grows to 1-1/2 feet high. Grasslike leaves that are green with white to golden stripes rise from thick clumps. Erect, lilac blooms in summer highlight this evergreen. Locate in shade only. Native to Japan, China and Vietnam. Hardy to 10°F.

Lobelia erinus, LOBELIA   ANNUAL
Popular and dependable border plant or cover for bulbs, grown for late winter and spring bloom. Flowers are usually light blue to violet with contrasting throats in white or yellow. Also graceful in hanging pots on the patio or in containers. Grows 6 to 8 inches high; plant 12 to 15 inches apart. Provide with rich, improved soil and regular moisture. Can reseed with good growing conditions.

Lobularia maritima, SWEET ALYSSUM   ANNUAL
An easy-care annual that is an excellent companion to bright-colored annuals or perennials. White, rose and purple selections are available. Plant in fall or spring. Grows 6 to 8 inches high. Reliable for fast cover and color. Use as a border or temporary erosion control on slopes, or in containers where it drapes over the sides. Easy to grow from seed or set out plants from packs fall to early spring. Locate in sun to partial shade. Low to moderate water use. Cold hardy.

Above left: *Linum grandiflorum* 'Rubrum', scarlet flax, is an easy-to-grow annual wildflower, producing brilliant, scarlet flowers in spring.

Above: *Limonium perezii*, sea lavender, is excellent as an underplanting. Ideal locations are filtered morning sun or beneath high-canopy trees. Plumes of purple flowers bloom on 2-to 3-foot stalks during summer.

Above and above right:
Lysiloma watsonii var.
thornberi, feather tree,
makes an effective large
shrub or small tree.
Divided, fernlike foliage
provides a lush, tropical
effect. Creamy white,
puffball flowers
cover plants in spring.

Loquat—*see Eriobotrya japonica*

Lonicera japonica 'Halliana', HALL'S HONEYSUCKLE   VINE

Vigorous, twining, evergreen vine or occasionally grown as a rampant ground cover. Fast cover on fences and trellises. Renew growth by cutting plants back severely in late winter every year or two. Highly fragrant flowers are pure white then quickly age to golden yellow. They are most profuse in spring, sporadic in summer. Medium green foliage. Accepts full sun to partial shade. Moderate water use. Cold hardy.

Lord's candle, Our—*see Yucca whipplei*

Lupinus densiflorus var. aureus, GOLDEN LUPINE WILDFLOWER

The golden lupine is an annual native to California, well-adapted throughout the West. Showy, spiked, pealike, golden flowers stand high above the leaves, blooming early spring to early summer. Plants grow to 2 feet high. Sow seed in full sun in fall for flowers the following spring. Prefers well-drained soil.

Lupinus texensis, TEXAS BLUEBONNET   WILDFLOWER

This annual lupine is the trademark flower of Texas, and announces spring with sweeping masses of blue plumed flowers along roadsides and in meadows. A native of Texas that also does well in the western states. Plants grow 1 to 2 feet high. Germination can be sporadic but may be increased by purchasing *scarified* seed. Plant in full sun in fall in well-prepared soil.

Lysiloma watsonii var. thornberi, FEATHER TREE TREE, SHRUB

(*Lysiloma microphylla* **var.** *thornberi*). Finely divided, fernlike foliage provides a lush, tropical effect. Creates dappled shade that can accommodate underplanting of perennials and small shrubs—highly effective in a mini-oasis setting. By the time plants are 6 to 10 years old, the multitrunk growth can reach 15 to 20 feet. Also can be grown as a shrub form. After a spring show of creamy white, puffball flowers, seed pods are numerous enough to create litter in early summer, but are easy to remove. Avoid pruning large branches in summer. Thrives with low to moderate water applications. Plant in full sun in soil with good drainage. Overwatering during summer can create chlorotic conditions. At 25°F becomes deciduous and drops leaves. At 20°F, damage often occurs.

Macfadyena unguis-cati, CATCLAW, YELLOW TRUMPET VINE
Evergreen to partially deciduous vine has slender shoots that cling to any surface and can even pull down stucco on buildings. Dense glossy foliage shows off bright yellow flowers that cover the plant in spring, although flowering is profuse, the season is short lived. Rapid, vigorous growth—can spread 30 to 40 feet vertically or horizontally. Set out 1-gallon-size plants; they seem to establish better than plants from larger-sized containers. Accepts heat and drought, and full sun to partial shade exposures. Low water use. Hardy to 10°F.

Malephora luteola, ROCKY POINT ICE PLANT GROUND COVER
One of the hardiest trailing ice plants, it is used extensively for roadside planting. Medium-sized, gray-green leaves are 1 to 2 inches long. Blooms throughout the year with 1-inch yellow flowers. Hardy to 20°F.

Malephora crocea is similar, blooming in spring and fall with coppery red flowers. Grows 6 to 8 inches high; plant 12 to 18 inches apart for a ground cover. Accepts no traffic. Cold hardy.

Marigold—*see Tagetes erecta*

Marguerite—*see Chrysanthemum frutescens*

Mascagnia macroptera, YELLOW ORCHID VINE VINE
Evergreen twining vine native to central Baja California, central Sonora and south throughout most of Mexico. Clusters of showy, yellow, orchid-shaped flowers appear in spring (if plants did not freeze the previous winter), and in fall. Plants are moderately drought tolerant once established. However, they grow more quickly if given a thorough watering once a week during the growing season. Remove frost-damaged leaves and stems in late winter or early spring. Hardy to mid-20s°F.

Below left: *Lupinus texensis*, Texas bluebonnet, is an annual wildflower. Sweeping masses of blue-plumed flowers are common throughout Texas. Sow seed in fall for flowers the following spring.

Below: *Macfadyena unguis-cati*, catclaw vine, has slender shoots that cling to any surface. Dense, glossy green leaves show off bright yellow flowers that blanket the plant in spring. Flowering is profuse but the season is short lived.

Mascagnia lilacina, purple orchid vine, is a related species. Use on a trellis, chain-link fence or any upright support. Once established, it can reach 20 to 30 feet in one season. Plant in full sun to partial shade. Hardy to 25°F.

Matthiola incana, STOCK — ANNUAL

A dependable workhorse annual for color. Grows 1-1/2 to 2 feet high with an equal spread. Makes a fine background for lower-growing annuals. Space new plantings about 1 foot apart. Most flowering occurs late winter to early spring. Bring cut flowers indoors to enjoy their rich fragrance. Improve soil with amendments to encourage deep rooting; soil must also be well-drained. Plant in early fall in full sun to partial shade location. Moderate water use.

Mealy cup sage—*see Salvia farinacea*

Mediterranean fan palm—*see Chamaerops humilis*

Melaleuca quinquenervia, CAJEPUT TREE, TEA TREE — TREE

Slender, evergreen tree to 20 to 35 feet high, with spongy, light colored, heavily layered and textured bark. Rich green foliage is graceful, thickly covering branches. Some thinning of branches is necessary as tree ages, but avoid heavy topping. Stands up to strong winds. Slender spikes of creamy white flowers adorn branches in summer. Water deeply to encourage deep rooting. Low to moderate water use. Native to Australia. Hardy to 28°F.

Below right: *Muhlenbergia emersleyi* 'Regal Mist' is admired for its graceful, fluffy, purple to pink plumes. They put on a show of color in late summer and fall. Locate plants where the sun will backlight the flowerheads.

Below: One of the attractions of *Melaleuca quinquenervia,* cajeput tree, is its bark: spongy, light colored, heavily layered and textured.

Mentzelia lindleyi, BLAZING-STAR   WILDFLOWER

The star-shaped yellow blossoms of blazing-star have petals that are each near-ly oval, meeting at a reddish orange center. Long yellow stamens contrast nice-ly against the orange centers. Plants grow 1 to 4 feet high and up to 2 feet wide, taking on the form of a small shrub. Tolerates range of soils, including heavy to light, rich to sterile. Requires full sun. Useful addition to wildflower mixes. Sow seed in late fall or early spring for flowers spring into early summer.

Merremia aurea, MERREMIA   VINE

This vine can grow to 25 feet or more with support. Bright yellow, 2-inch, morning glory-type flowers bloom summer and fall, accompanied by dense, bright green leaves divided into five leaflets. Requires full sun for good growth and flowers. Regular water during growing season is also necessary for flower production. Best when planted near a wall, fence or other structure on which to climb. Fast growth allows its use as wind or sun screen. Control rampant growth with pruning. Remove frost-killed vegetation in spring. Native of southern half of Baja California. Freezes back at 32°F but recovers quickly.

Mesquite—*see Prosopis species*

Mexican blue fan palm—*see Brahea armata*

Mexican bush sage—*see Salvia leucantha*

Mexican evening primrose—*see Oenothera berlandieri*

Mexican honeysuckle—*see Justicia spicigera*

Mimosa tree—*see Albizia julibrissin*

Mock orange—*see Pittosporum tobira*

Modesto ash—*see Fraxinus velutina var. glabra*

Moss blue, Moss red, Moss pink, Moss white—*see Phlox subulata*

Mother of thyme—*see Thymus praecox*

Mountain marigold—*see Tagetes lemmonii*

Muhlenbergia capillaris, PINK MUHLY   ORNAMENTAL GRASS

'Regal Mist' is the best known selection of this species, admired for its grace-ful, fluffy, purple to pink plumes. They put on a show of color in late summer and fall. Locate plants where the sun will backlight the flower heads—they'll look as if they are aglow. Pink muhly is evergreen and dwarfish, 3 to 4 feet high and as wide, making it a favorite among golf course designers. Cold hardy.

Muhlenbergia emersleyi , BULL GRASS   ORNAMENTAL GRASS

Introduced from Texas, 'El Toro' is an improved selection, featuring graceful, evergreen leaves that clump to 4 feet or more. Reddish flower plumes reach 4 to 5 feet high in the fall; as they age they turn a cream color. Ideal in clusters among boulders. Prefers afternoon shade in the Coachella Valley. Cut back to 6 inches high in late winter for renewed growth the next spring. Moderate water. Cold hardy.

Muhlenbergia lindheimeri, LINDHEIMER MUHLEY   ORN. GRASS

Low-growing to 1-1/2 to 2 feet high and 3 to 4 feet wide. An improved culti-var is 'Autumn Glow'. Dense, fluffy plumes evoke a dwarfish version of pam-pas grass. Hardy to 10°F.

Above: *Myoporum parvifolium*, myoporum, is one of the best ground covers for the Coachella Valley: tough, hardy and fast-growing with a low-water requirement. Grows 3 to 4 inches high with a spread to 6 to 9 feet wide.

Above right: *Muhlenbergia rigens*, deer grass, develops into a graceful, mounding, grassy accent to 2 to 3 feet high, spreading 4 to 5 feet wide.

Muhlenbergia rigens, DEER GRASS   ORNAMENTAL GRASS

Develops into a graceful, mounding tuft to 2 to 3 feet high, spreading to 4 to 5 feet wide. Hardy to 10°F.

Deer grass, like all *Muhlenbergia* species, accepts heat, cold and low water, and requires little maintenance. Most muhlys require only a once-a-year pruning of grassy foliage and seed stems to 12 inches above ground. This is best done in early spring, allowing plants to renew themselves along with the surge of spring growth.

Murraya paniculata, ORANGE JESSAMINE   SHRUB, TREE

Luxuriant, bright, glossy green leaves and waxy, pure white flowers bloom April to July. They fill the air with an intense orange blossom fragrance. Makes an attractive evergreen hedge or screen to 6 to 12 feet high. May become tree-like to 20 to 25 feet with time if not pruned. Best appearance with some shade but tolerates sun with ample water. Native to southeast Asia. Hardy to 27°F.

Myoporum parvifolium, MYOPORUM   GROUND COVER

One of the best ground covers for the Coachella Valley: tough, hardy and fast-growing with a low-water requirement. Grows 3 to 4 inches high with a spread to 6 to 9 feet wide. Bright green 1-inch leaves with white flowers in summer provide a cooling effect. Branches root as they spread. (Irrigation system note: requires low-volume, low-angle spray to keep soil moist for rooting.) In the Coachella Valley locate in morning sun (eastern exposure). Needs well-drained soil. Excellent as cover on slopes and banks but does not tolerate traffic. Native to Australia. Hardy to 24°F.

Myosotis sylvatica, FORGET-ME-NOT   ANNUAL

This annual produces numerous, small, blue or sometimes pink flowers. It grows 6 to 15 inches high. Prefers regular moisture and slightly acid to neutral soil. Accepts full sun to light shade. Easy to grow from seed.

Myrtle—*see Myrtus communis*

Myrtle—*see Vinca minor*

Myrtus communis, TRUE MYRTLE SHRUB

Grown for its aromatic, dark green, glossy leaves, this shrub has white flowers in the spring and summer. Ideal hedging plant and natural foundation plant to 10 feet high. 'Compacta', dwarf myrtle, has a more compact growth habit. Leaves are smaller and dark green. Grows to 3 to 4 feet high—ideal for low hedging or foreground planting. Accepts shaping well. Low water use. Native to the Mediterranean. Hardy to 10°F.

Nandina domestica, HEAVENLY BAMBOO SHRUB

Evergreen compact shrub to 5 to 8 feet high. This is a most versatile plant for small areas. Appearance is bamboolike, with many vertical stems that display distinctive, lacy green leaves. Foliage may turn brilliant shades of red and orange in fall, depending on extent of exposure to sun and cold. Red berries in winter are also an attraction. Great decorative value in containers. Best with eastern or northern exposure; don't plant on west side. As plants age, remove old stems to renew growth, otherwise little maintenance. Dwarf selections are available. Native to India and east Asia. Hardy to 10°F.

Natal plum—*see Carissa grandiflora*

Nemophila maculata, FIVE SPOT ANNUAL

Flowers are the same as baby blue eyes, following, but are white with vivid purple spots at the tip of each petal. Reaches just 6 inches high, spreading 12 inches or more wide. Grows in a variety of soils, including heavy clay or sand. Attractive when planted in drifts in a meadow or border. Native to California.

Nemophila menziesii, BABY BLUE EYES ANNUAL

Plants grow 6 to 10 inches high with delicate, sky blue flowers marked with white spots. Best with moderate water in shaded areas. Avoid planting in hot or humid conditions. Start from seed either in spring or fall. This wildflower is a prolific bloomer that will reseed itself. Native to California.

Nerium oleander, OLEANDER SHRUB

Oleander has long been a valuable plant in the Coachella Valley, useful as windbreaks and screens. But oleander leaf scorch, a bacterial disease, is

Above: *Myrtus communis,* true myrtle, is grown for its aromatic, glossy leaves and white flowers in spring and summer. It makes an ideal hedging and foundation plant to 6 to 8 feet high. 'Variegata', shown above, has striking variegated leaves.

Above center: The annual *Myosotis sylvatica,* forget-me-not, produces numerous, small, blue or sometimes pink flowers. It grows 6 to 15 inches high.

Above left: *Nandina domestica,* heavenly bamboo, is a most versatile shrub for small areas. Appearance is bamboolike with many vertical stems that display distinctive, lacy green leaves. Grows 5 to 8 feet high; dwarf selections are available that remain much smaller.

Below right: *Nolina microcarpa, beargrass,* is grown for its narrow, grasslike leaves that form a mounding accent to 3 to 6 feet high.

Below: *Oenothera berlandieri,* Mexican evening primrose, makes a colorful ground cover over small areas. 1-1/2-inch, rose-pink blossoms bloom late spring into summer.

Bottom: *Oenothera caespitosa,* white evening primrose, has large, gray-green leaves and masses of large, 4-inch white flowers.

destroying mature plantings throughout California and the Southwest. Currently, older plants, 20 to 30 years old, are most affected. There is no known cure. At this time it is recommended that other plants be selected. Alternatives for oleander windbreaks are listed on page 14.

If you have healthy, existing plantings, continue to maintain them as usual. Prune during warm weather. This exposes interior of plant to sunlight, stimulating new flowering wood. Do not prune into globes or squares. Avoid shearing, which reduces flowering wood. Note that all plant parts are poisonous so do not burn wood or smoke can cause irritation.

Nierembergia hippomanica, DWARF CUP FLOWER PERENNIAL
This low-growing, flowering perennial reaches 8 to 10 inches high. Flowers are 1 inch long, bell-shaped, in rich blue to violet or white. Plant in fall or winter for flowers in summer. Best with afternoon shade or in partial shade. Space plants 8 to 12 inches apart in well-prepared soil. Remove spent blooms (deadheading), which encourages more flowers. Moderate water use. Hardy to 30°F.

Nolina microcarpa, BEAR GRASS ACCENT
Narrow, grasslike leaves to 3 feet long form a mound to 3 to 6 feet high, 5 to 8 feet wide. Leaves have margins with microscopic teeth. Flower stems rise 4 to 5 feet above dense rosette clumps, striking in form but not in color. In garden setting, remove dead basal leaves. Plants thrive in gravelly, sandy, well-draining soil. Low water use. Hardy to cold.

Ocotillo—*see Fouquieria splendens*

Octopus agave—*see Agave vilmoriniana*

Oenothera berlandieri,
MEXICAN EVENING PRIMROSE GROUND COVER
Makes a colorful ground cover for small areas. Grows to 12 inches high with 1-1/2-inch, rose-pink blossoms that bloom late spring into summer. Spreads by underground runners that can invade nearby plantings. Low maintenance. Moderate water use. Full sun. Native to the Chihuahuan Desert. Cold hardy.

Oenothera caespitosa, WHITE EVENING PRIMROSE   PERENNIAL

Evergreen perennial with large, gray-green leaves and masses of large, 4-inch white flowers. Blooms on and off through the year but most prolific in spring. Plants form rounded clumps 1 to 1-1/2 feet high, spreading 3 feet wide. May die out in summer if overwatered. Reseeds readily. Low to moderate water use in well-drained soils. No traffic. Native to western U.S. Cold-hardy, tolerating temperatures to 5°F.

Olea europaea, OLIVE   TREE

A quality, evergreen tree with an informal, picturesque growth habit. Grows to 20 to 30 feet high and as wide, as a standard form, or with multiple trunks. With time, trunks become gnarled, adding to the tree's character. Distinctive, narrow, gray-green leaves reach up to 3 inches long. Olive fruit can be a problem, littering and staining pavement. 'Swan Hill' is a fruitless selection.

 Low water use but additional moisture produces a more handsome tree. Heavy pruning, especially late spring through summer, can allow sun to damage trunks. Olives accept almost any soil, endure heat, cold and wind. Native to the Mediterranean. Hardy to 15°F.

Olneya tesota, DESERT IRONWOOD   TREE

Just as olive trees create a focal point in the landscape, desert ironwood has similar gray-green foliage and trunk character. Lavender, pealike flowers give trees an otherworldly glow April and May and attract bees in abundance. Slow growing to 25 to 30 feet. Requires some patience, yet the reward is worth the wait. Thorns on branches can be a safety hazard near walkways as well as when pruning trees. Requires well-drained soil. Foliage is hardy to about 26°F.

Above: *Olea europaea,* olive, is a well-known evergreen with an informal, picturesque growth habit. A long-lived, quality tree that grows to 20 to 30 feet high and as wide.

Above left: *Olneya tesota,* desert ironwood, is similar to an olive tree in foliage and character. Lavender, pealike flowers cover branches in April and May.

Below: *Optuntia* species come in a wide range of forms and vibrant flower colors.

Bottom: *Orthocarpus purpurascens,* owl's clover, is a hardy annual wildflower. Grows to 8 inches high with rose-pink to purple, plume-like flowers that resemble clover. Here it combines with California poppy.

Below right: *Opuntia basilaris,* beaver tail cactus, branches out with fleshy flattened pads to 1 foot high, spreading 4 feet wide.

Opuntia species, PRICKLY PEAR   ACCENT

A cactus with green pads and often yellow spines, growing 3 to 20 feet high, depending on species. Green and yellow flowers bloom in spring. Hardy to 20°F.

Opuntia basilaris, beaver tail cactus, branches out with fleshy flattened pads to 1 foot high, spreading 4 feet wide. Flowers bloom in spring in yellow to red. Remove pads at joints to control size and shape of plants. Transplant these pads to extend plantings. Hardy to 10°F.

Orange jessamine—*see Murraya paniculata*

Orchid tree—*see Bauhinia species*

Orchid vine—*see Mascagnia macroptera*

Olive—*see Olea europaea*

Orthocarpus purpurascens, OWL'S CLOVER   WILDFLOWER

Reliable annual wildflower for fast cover and color from early spring into summer. Suited to a natural border or in a wildflower mix. Grows to 8 inches high with rose-pink to purple, plumelike flowers that resemble clover. Sow seed in early fall in full sun to partial shade location. Reseeds well and is drought tolerant. Native to the Southwest.

Palo brea—*see Cercidium praecox*

Palo verde—*see Cercidium species* and *Parkinsonia,* **opposite page**

Pampas grass—*see Cortaderia selloana*

Pansy—*see Viola X wittrockiana*

Papaver nudicaule, ICELAND POPPY   PERENNIAL

This is a perennial grown as an annual in the Coachella Valley. Flowers in a range of bright colors bloom on vigorous plants 1- to 1-1/2 feet high. Effective

combined with ranunculus and daffodils. Space 12 inches apart. Cut flowers to enjoy indoors, which also extends flowering season. Locate in a sunny location protected from wind. Moderate moisture requirement once plants are up and growing. Plant October through December for spring color.

Papaver rhoeas, FLANDERS FIELD POPPY ANNUAL

Large, bright red, showy flowers on plants 2 to 4 feet high. Provide light, well-drained soil, moderate water in a full sun to partial shade location. It likes open areas and competes well with grasses. Sow seed in fall or early spring.

Paperflower—*see Psilostrophe tagetina*

Parkinsonia aculeata, MEXICAN PALO VERDE TREE

Semi-deciduous tree for difficult, hot, sunny and dry situations. Fast-growing to 30 feet high, sometimes more, with an equal spread. Overall appearance is airy, with bright green branches and fernlike foliage. Masses of small, bright yellow flowers cover the tree in early summer. A tough tree, accepting wind, heat and drought, although not usually long-lived. Reseeds abundantly. Drought tolerant but more attractive with deep, infrequent irrigations during the warm season. Native to southwest U.S., Mexico and South America. Hardy to 25°F.

A hybrid tree resulting from a cross of *Parkinsonia aculeata, Cercidium floridum* and *C. microphyllum* is also available. See *Cercidium.*

Parthenocissus tricuspidata, BOSTON IVY VINE

A deciduous, vigorous, clinging vine that will attach itself to masonry walls and stonework. Bright green, compound leaves turn to bright, vivid reds and oranges in fall. Locate where plants will receive some shade, preferably in the afternoon. Cold hardy.

Below left: *Parkinsonia aculeata,* Mexican palo verde, is a tough tree for difficult, hot, sunny and dry situations. Fast-growing to 30 feet high with an equal spread. Overall appearance is airy, with bright green branches and fernlike foliage. Reseeds readily.

Below: *Papaver nudicaule,* Iceland poppy, is a perennial grown as an annual in the Coachella Valley. Flowers in a range of bright colors bloom on vigorous plants 1-1/2 to 3 feet high. Effective combined with ranunculus and daffodils.

Above: *Passiflora alato-caerulea,* passion flower vine, is a fast-growing, tropical, evergreen vine with bright green leaves to 30 feet high. Produces masses of large, spectacular flowers in summer.

Above right: *Perovskia atriplicifolia,* Russian sage, is an underused shrubby perennial to 4 feet high and as wide. Small, toothed, gray-green leaves and diminutive spikes of lavender flowers bloom in the summer.

Passiflora alato-caerulea, PASSION FLOWER VINE   VINE

(P. pfordtii). Rapid-growing, tropical, evergreen vine to 30 feet high with tri-lobed, bright green leaves. Masses of large, spectacular flowers bloom in summer. They are 4 inches in diameter, white, with pinkish tints and a purple-blue crown in the center. Moderate to high water use. Hardy to 28°F.

Peacock flower—*see Dietes bicolor*

Pencil bush—*see Euphorbia tirucalli*

Pennisetum setaceum, FOUNTAIN GRASS   ORNAMENTAL GRASS

Select only cultivated varieties of *Pennisetum.* Avoid *Pennisetum setaceum,* fountain grass (white flower plumes). It reseeds and becomes an obnoxious weed. 'Cupreum' makes a low-maintenance accent. Grows 3-1/2 to 4 feet high and as wide. Copper-colored flower spikes add another 1 to 1-1/2 feet. 'Rubrum' is similar with rose-pink flowers. Plants go dormant in winter. Cut back after frost in early spring to 6 inches high. Fresh, new, healthy growth will come on with warmer temperatures. Low to moderate water use. Hardy to 20°F.

Penstemon baccharifolius, ROCK PENSTEMON   SHRUB

Growth is different than most penstemons in that it is more shrublike to 2 feet high. 'Del Rio' is an improved selection, with cherry-colored flowers blooming spring through fall. Loved by hummingbirds. Plants prefer full sun. Provide good soil drainage to prevent root diseases. Native to Texas. Hardy to 5°F.

Penstemon eatonii, FIRECRACKER PENSTEMON   SHRUB

Flowers appear in February, making this plant among the first to bloom each spring. Full sun encourages strong, 3- to 4-foot vertical stems above basal growth to 2 feet across. Avoid shade, which can cause plants to sprawl. Best in well-drained soils. Hardy to 18°F.

Penstemon palmeri, PALMER'S PENSTEMON   PERENNIAL

Tall-growing perennial to 3 feet high with fragrant, white and pink flowers in early summer. Blooms the first season after planting from seed. Sow seed in

fall for spring germination and summer flowers. Requires full sun. Drought tolerant after plants are established. Hardy to 15°F.

Penstemon parryi, PARRY'S PENSTEMON   PERENNIAL
Widely adapted to desert regions. Responds to moderate water and fertilizer. Tall, strongly vertical, 3- to 5-foot stems show off flowers in shades of pink. Attractive in rock gardens, beneath mesquites and acacias or as a foreground among desert shrubs. Accepts full sun, but better with filtered or afternoon shade in low desert. Plant in soil with good drainage After flowers reseed, cut back to top of leaf rosette. Hardy to 18°F.

Periwinkle—*see Vinca major*

Perovskia atriplicifolia, RUSSIAN SAGE   SHRUB
Little-known and underused shrubby perennial to 3 to 4 feet high and as wide. Blends well with *Rosmarinus*, *Salvia*, *Encelia* and *Ericamerica* species. Small, toothed, gray-green leaves are covered with spikes of diminutive lavender flowers in the summer. Plants are not typically bothered by plant diseases or insects. Locate in full sun. Well-drained soil and moderate applications of water help ensure vigorous and healthy growth. Space at least 4 feet apart so they have ample room to reach mature height and spread. Native to eastern Iran and northwest India. Cold hardy.

Above: *Penstemon eatonii*, firecracker penstemon, flowers in February, making this plant among the first to bloom each spring.

Above right: *Penstemon parryi*, Parry's penstemon, is one of the most popular penstemons in the West. Vertical, 3- to 5-foot stems show off flowers in shades of magenta and pink.

Above left: *Pennisetum setaceum* 'Cupreum' grows to 4 feet high with an equal spread. Copper-colored flower spikes add another 1 to 1-1/2 feet in height.

Petunia hybrids, PETUNIA   ANNUAL

Petunias come in a wide range of forms and flower colors. There are compact, low-growing and spreading plant forms. Flowers can be single, double or ruffled. In fact, petunias are the most colorful of all annuals in desert gardens, making the brightest show. Use on banks, in containers or in borders as part of mixed plantings. Plant from packs or pots in October before cool weather settles in. Space 15 to 18 inches apart. Prefers sunny exposure but takes partial shade. Best with regular water and pellet-type fertilizer mixed into soil at planting time. Flowering tapers as extreme heat comes on in late spring. Remove plants by June 15—they'll be weary-looking anyway—to make room for warm-season marigolds, verbena or vinca. Check soil moisture often. Overwatering or poor drainage can cause weak growth and disease problems.

Phacelia campanularia, CALIFORNIA BLUEBELL   WILDFLOWER

Prolific-blooming annual wildflower with rich blue, bell-shaped flowers early spring to early summer. Plants grow 6 to 18 inches high with lush-looking, dark green, fragrant, heart-shaped leaves. Accepts many soil types but performs best in rocky soils with good drainage. Easy to grow from seed. Sow in fall after danger of frost has passed. Reseeds itself. Hardy and drought tolerant.

Philodendron selloum, SPLIT-LEAF PHILODENDRON   SHRUB

A bold foliage plant for that lush, tropical mini-oasis planting. Glossy green deeply lobed leaves. Shade or partial shade, full sun burns plants. Grows well in containers. Native to Brazil. Hardy to 29°F.

Below: Petunias come in a wide range of forms and flower colors, and are considered to be the most colorful of all annuals in desert gardens. Excellent in containers, as shown here.

Below right: *Phoenix dactylifera,* date palm, is abundant in Coachella Valley date groves. Mostly grown for its edible fruit but often used for ornamental purposes. Mature palms can reach up to 80 feet high with time, so best suited to large, expansive projects.

Phlomis fruticosa, JERUSALEM SAGE   PERENNIAL

Evergreen perennial-subshrub to 2 to 3 feet high and as wide. In spring, clear yellow flowers develop atop stems from whorls of gray, feltlike aromatic leaves. Great plant on slopes or combine with other dry-climate plants. Deadhead old flowers for rebloom. Provide good soil drainage and moderate but deep watering. Accepts full sun but prefers afternoon shade. Native to the Mediterranean region. Hardy to 25°F.

Phlox drummondii, ANNUAL PHLOX   ANNUAL

Low, 6- to 12-inch annual that is best massed or as part of a color border. Soft flower colors are common, including shades of salmon, pink, yellow and white. Plant fall into winter, spacing plants 12 inches apart. Prefers full sun to partial shade. Plants and flowers hold up well to late spring and early summer heat. Moderate moisture use. Reseeds well. Cut back straggly growth in early May to stimulate new wave of flowers. Native to Texas.

Phlox subulata, MOSS PINK, CREEPING PHLOX   GROUND COVER

Evergreen to 6 inches high, forming dense mat with tiny, stiff, needlelike leaves. Great for rock gardens or borders. Accepts full sun. 'Blue' produces profuse blue flowers in spring.'Pink' is evergreen to 6 inches, forming a dense mat. 'Red Wing' and 'White Delight' are ground covers to 6 inches high. Each is a prolific bloomer, forming a dense mat. Moderate water use. Cold hardy.

Phoenix dactylifera, DATE PALM   FEATHER PALM

This is the most widely known group of palms cultivated in many parts of the world and abundant in Coachella Valley date groves. Mostly grown for its edible fruit but often used for ornamental purposes. Mature palms can reach up to 80 feet high with time, so they are best adapted to large, expansive projects. Native to the Middle East. Hardy 20°F to 25°F.

Photinia X fraseri, PHOTINIA   SHRUB

Evergreen shrub or screen to 6 to 10 feet high. An attraction is new leaves that are a glistening coppery red on bright red stems. They eventually turn a medium green. Clusters of white blossoms put on a spring show. Partial shade ideal in desert regions. Moderate water use. More mildew resistant than other photinias. Native to eastern Asia. Hardy to 5°F.

Above: *Phacelia campanularia,* California bluebell, is an annual wildflower with rich blue, bell-shaped flowers in early spring to early summer. Plants grow 6 to 12 inches high with lush, dark green, fragrant, heart-shaped leaves.

Above left: *Photinia X fraseri,* photinia, is an evergreen shrub or screen to 6 to 10 feet high. When new leaves first appear, they are a glistening coppery red on bright red stems. They eventually turn a medium green.

Above: *Pinus eldarica*, Afghan pine, grows rapidly to 40 feet high. Accepts heat, strong winds, cold and a variety of soils. Can become an attractive, dense windscreen or featured landscape tree.

Above right: *Pinus halepensis*, aleppo pine, is adapted throughout the Southwest, growing 40 to 60 feet high and 35 to 40 feet wide. Growth is rapid, and trees eventually develop a wide, irregular crown.

Phyllostachys aurea, GOLDEN BAMBOO   SHRUB

Best known of the smaller-growing bamboos, growing 6 to 10 feet high. Stalks appear to have a golden effect at a distance, although leaves are yellow-green. Spreads by *running-type* roots that can invade nearby plantings. Control by installing root guards or grow in a container. Native to China. Hardy to 0°F.

Pindo palm—*see Butia capitata*

Pineapple guava—*see Feijoa sellowiana*

Pines—*see Pinus species*

Pink clover blossom—*see Polygonum capitatum*

Pink ironbark—*see Eucalyptus sideroxylon*

Pink powder puff—*see Calliandra haematocephala*

Pink trumpet vine—*see Podranea ricasoliana*

Pinus species, Pines

Several pines can be grown successfully in the Coachella Valley. Some species can become quite large, so exercise caution when selecting them for residential-scale landscapes. Pines evoke a feeling of the mountains and create a cooling mood, but it can be a challenge to blend them with other arid land plants.

Pinus canariensis, CANARY ISLAND PINE   TREE

Strong, vertical, pyramidal growth to 40 to 60 feet high or more. Develops into a picturesque tree with horizontal branches and dark green needles. Well adapted to low-elevation desert regions. Native to the Canary Islands. Hardy to 20°F.

Pinus eldarica, AFGHAN PINE, MONDALE PINE   TREE

Rapid pyramidal growth to 30 to 40 feet high and to 25 feet wide. Takes heat, severe wind, cold and a variety of soils. In well drained soil, roots penetrate soil for deep rooting and more prolific growth. An attractive dense windscreen or featured landscape tree. Tolerates windy conditions. Native to Afghanistan. Hardy to 0°F.

Pithecellobium flexicaule, Texas ebony, can be a useful security barrier. Its picturesque form and controlled growth under adverse conditions make this a desirable tree for home landscapes, particularly those where space is at a premium.

Pinus halepensis, ALEPPO PINE TREE

This pine is adapted throughout the Southwest, growing 40 to 60 feet high and 35 to 40 feet wide. Growth is rapid, and trees eventually develop a wide, irregular crown. Water deep and at the drip line and beyond so moisture reaches entire root mass. Maintain uniform water supply. Plant in soils with good drainage and avoid caliche soils, if possible. Hardy to 15°F to 20°F.

Pinus pinea, ITALIAN STONE PINE TREE

Broadly conical when young, then becomes spreading and flat-topped and umbrellalike with age. Grows 25 to 40 feet high at a slow to moderate rate. Picturesque trunk and branch structure develop with time. Needles are bright green. Accepts tough conditions of drought and heat. Hardy to 20°F.

Pinus thunbergiana, JAPANESE BLACK PINE TREE

(Pinus thunbergii). Irregular but interesting branching habit on open, pyramidal, 20- to 30-foot tree. Blackish gray bark contrasts with sharp, dark green needles. Decorative in any planting. Can be trained to take on semi-bonsai form. Develops eye-catching, windswept form in windy locations. Cold hardy.

Pistacia chinensis, CHINESE PISTACHIO TREE

Rapid-growing, medium-sized tree to 30 to 40 feet high. Deciduous. Bright green, compound leaves turn intense crimson color in fall months. Accepts a wide variety of adverse conditions. Moderate water use. Hardy to 15°F.

Pithecellobium flexicaule, TEXAS EBONY TREE

The dense, dark green leaves and spiny twigs of Texas ebony can develop into a great security barrier in the landscape. Even without a utilitarian use in mind, its picturesque form makes this a desirable tree for the small garden. Avoid planting near walkways or other pedestrian traffic areas due to its small, sharp thorns. Fragrant cream-colored flowers add color in late spring. Mature height is 20 to 30 feet with a spread of 15 to 20 feet. Low to moderate water. Grows in almost any well-drained soil. Water deeply. Prefers full sun and tolerates heat and cold extremes. Native to Texas and New Mexico. Hardy to 10°F.

Pittosporum phillyraeoides, willow pittosporum, makes a striking vertical accent, growing to 20 feet high and just 10 to 15 feet wide. Handsome form, with light, gray-green, ribbony leaves to 4 inches long. Small yellow flowers add fragrance and color in late winter to early spring.

Pittosporum phillyraeoides, WILLOW PITTOSPORUM   TREE

Handsome, evergreen tree, with light, gray-green, ribbony leaves to 4 inches long. Small, fragrant, yellow flowers bloom late winter to early spring. Makes a fine vertical accent growing to 20 feet high and just 10 to 15 feet wide. Low water use. Native to Australia. Hardy to 15°F.

Pittosporum tobira, MOCK ORANGE   SHRUB

Evergreen shrub 6 to 10 feet high, with glossy green foliage. Fragrant white flower clusters bloom in spring. Becomes a vigorous, sturdy, heavily branching foundation shrub. Prefers partial shade location with filtered sunlight. 'Wheeler's Dwarf' is much more compact to 2 feet high. Dense growth makes it a good choice as a foreground shrub. 'Variegata', variegated mock orange, is a combination of light green and white variegated foliage. Low, compact-branching growth to 4 to 8 feet high. Like the species, it produces fragrant flowers in spring. Locate where plants will receive afternoon shade or partial shade, such as beneath a canopy tree. Hardy to 5°F.

Plum—see Prunus

Plumbago auriculata, CAPE PLUMBAGO SHRUB

(P. capensis). Semi-climbing shrub 6 to 10 feet high (with supports). Produces clusters of 3/4-inch, azure-blue flowers for a long period during summer. Semi-evergreen, light green leaves cover long, vinelike branches. Overall form is mounding. Full sun. Moderate water use. Cut back in late winter every two or three years to renew growth. Native to South Africa. Hardy to 25°F.

Plumbago scandens, WHITE DESERT PLUMBAGO SHRUB

Grows to 3 feet high and as wide, becoming a rambling, vining, ground cover-shrub. Glossy green, evergreen leaves turn red to purple with cold weather. Produces small, white tubular flowers in spring. Better appearance when grown in afternoon shade. 'Summer Snow' is an improved selection. Native to southern Arizona and Mexico. Will accept 25°F, probably freezing back at 20°F.

Podocarpus gracilior, FERN PINE SHRUB

Loose, informal, large shrub, grows 15 to 20 feet high. Provides a tracery pattern of soft, fernlike, 1- to 2-inch, green leaves. Easily shaped and an ideal subject for espalier training. Provide afternoon shade. In fact, tolerates considerable shade, so it's useful against atrium or patio walls. Hardy to 25°F.

Podocarpus macrophyllus, YEW PODOCARPUS SHRUB OR TREE

Differs from *P. gracilior* in that leaves are larger—to 4 inches—more firm and deeper green. Shape is more slender and columnar to 15 to 20 feet high and 10 feet wide (much less with a little pruning). Commonly used as container plant. Ideal for patio or small garden, especially for a formal effect. Best in an exposure with some shade. Hardy to 25°F.

Podranea ricasoliana, PINK TRUMPET VINE VINE

Vigorous vining plant with stems up to 20 feet long. Rich green leaves are divided into 9 to 11 leaflets. Clusters of pink flowers to 2 inches long bloom summer and fall. New plants need regular irrigation to become established then require infrequent watering. Fast growth with moderate water. Minimal pruning required. Stems damaged by frost recover rapidly in spring. Use in full sun to partial shade as a self climber on trellis or chainlink fence. Ideal plant for mini-oasis. Native to southern Africa. Hardy to 25°F.

Above: 'Variegata' is a variegated cultivar of *Pittosporum tobira*. It is similar in form but its foliage is a combination of light green and white.

Above left: *Pittosporum tobira* 'Wheeler's Dwarf' is a compact shrub to 2 feet high. Dense growth makes it a good choice as a foreground plant to larger shrubs or trees.

Above and top: *Prosopis glandulosa glandulosa*, honey mesquite, is a rapid-growing, Texas native to 30 feet high and to 35 feet wide. Thorny and deciduous. Its leaves (as shown here) resemble those of *Schinus molle*, California pepper.

Above right: Native mesquites are excellent for home landscape use. New growth is bright green, announcing that spring has come to the desert.

Polygonum aubertii, SILVER LACE VINE VINE

Twining vine to 20 feet high with masses of slender stems and light green leaves. Long fleecy clusters of fragrant, greenish white flowers bloom June to September. Cut back heavy deciduous growth in winter to control and renew plants. Moderate water use. Native to Tibet. Cold hardy.

Polygonum capitatum, PINK CLOVER BLOSSOM GROUND COVER

Attractive bronze-green foliage on trailing plant to 8 inches high. Masses of pink flowers bloom throughout most of the year. Growth is vigorous if given adequate water during warm weather. Covers the ground at a rapid rate, rooting along as runners spread. Plant 12 inches apart for ground cover. Accepts no traffic. Grow in partial shade or out of afternoon sun. Hardy to 28°F.

Pomegranate—*see Punica granatum*

Portulacaria afra, ELEPHANT'S FOOD ACCENT

A succulent native to South Africa that is well adapted to the Coachella Valley. It's an excellent container plant with an interesting, flowing growth habit that also is at home among boulders and native plants. Often confused with jade plant, *Crassula argentea*, which it resembles. Elephant's food grows more rapidly, has more open growth, with limber and tapering branches. Stems are a brownish color covered with 1/2-inch, glossy green, succulent leaves. Best with afternoon shade, but too much shade can cause plants to become a bit straggly. Can be damaged with exposure to high heat. Hardy to 28°F.

Potentilla tabernaemontani GROUND COVER

(Potentilla verna). There is increasing interest in this plant because of its attractive, strawberrylike leaves and flowers. Plants spread rapidly to form a dense, matlike cover to 3 to 6 inches high. Leaves are an attractive dark green. Bright yellow flowers bloom over a long period spring into summer. Accepts full sun as well as some shade. Mow plantings for a more tailored look. Tolerates light foot traffic. Plant 12 inches apart for a ground cover. Moderate to high water requirement. Native to Europe. Cold hardy.

Prickly pear cactus—*see Opuntia species*

Primula malacoides, FAIRY PRIMROSE ANNUAL

Adds splashes of color in shaded or partially shaded locations. Delicate-textured leaves are pale green, oval, to 3 inches long. They grow in rosettes close to ground. Vertical flower stems 8 to 10 inches high bloom in spring in shades of white, pink, red and mauve. Plant October to February, spacing plants 6 to 8 inches apart. Moderate to high water use. Native to China.

Prosopis species, MESQUITE

Mesquites offer quite a lot to Coachella Valley gardeners. Their size, form, color and texture are in tune with the desert. In fact, native mesquites are excellent for home use. Their fast rate of growth, cooling, sheltering shade and low maintenance make mesquites natural choices. In recent years, the number of selections available to home gardeners has increased. Each has special merit.

Prosopis alba, ARGENTINE MESQUITE TREE

Thorny, upright, rapid-growing, lush, dark green, fernlike foliage is semi-deciduous, dropping leaves for a short time in winter. 'Colorado' is consistently thornless and drought tolerant. It performs well in turf with deep watering and is hardy to 10°F. Reaches 30 to 35 feet high and as wide, with a distinctive, umbrella-shaped crown. Growth can be rapid during summer months. Thin drooping branches as well as inside the crown to reduce top heavy growth, which can lead to wind damage. Encourage deep rooting at perimeter of the tree's drip line. Hardy to 18°F.

Prosopis chilensis, CHILEAN MESQUITE TREE

Similar growth habit as Argentine mesquite but without thorns. Admired for its ability to provide fast shade and screening. Both species grow with great vigor in youth, growing up to 6 feet or more in one season. Young trees need staking and adequate ties to help support heavy top growth. Water deeply and wide (see *Prosopis alba*), to encourage deep rooting. Thin no more than 20 percent of interior growth at any one time to prevent sunburn damage. Hardy to 18°F.

Prosopis glandulosa glandulosa, HONEY MESQUITE TREE

Rapid growing to 30 feet high and to 35 feet wide. Thorny and deciduous. Bright green leaves resemble *Schinus molle*, California pepper. Low water use

Prosopis chilensis, Chilean mesquite, is a common tree in the Coachella Valley. It is admired and planted for its ability to provide fast shade and screening. It grows with great vigor in youth, putting on up to 6 feet or more in one season.

Above and above right: *Prosopis velutina*, velvet mesquite, grows to 30 feet high. Foliage is gray-green, and deciduous. Stems develop thorns. Flowers form as long catkins, as shown.

Right: *Punica granatum*, pomegranate, is a deciduous small tree or shrub. Fruiting varieties are also available; see page 146.

after trees are established. Native to the Chihuahuan Desert. Hardy to 15°F.

Prosopis velutina, VELVET MESQUITE   TREE
This North American native mesquite grows to 30 feet high. Foliage is gray-green, deciduous, and stems develop thorns. However, thorns become less abundant with maturity. With age, trunks take on a gnarled and shaggy appearance, resulting in trees of great character. Young trees are slow growing and character is more like shrubs than trees. Cold hardy.

Prostrate germander—*see Teucrium chamaedrys*

Prunus caroliniana 'Bright 'n Tight', CHERRY LAUREL   SHRUB
Specially selected strain of Carolina laurel cherry with showy, compact growth 8 to 20 feet high. Has glossy, deep green, evergreen leaves on upright form. Don't plant in saline or alkaline soils. Best with afternoon shade in Coachella Valley. Hardy to 20°F.

Prunus cerasifera 'Krauter Vesuvius', PURPLE PLUM   TREE

Open, rounded, tree 15 to 25 feet high, with attractive, dark purple, almost black foliage. Pink flowers bloom in spring. Deciduous. May bear fruit in summer. Species native to the Mediterranean. Moderate water use. Cold hardy.

Psilostrophe tagetina, TEXAS PAPERFLOWER   SHRUB

An extravagant, shrubby perennial that covers itself with bright yellow flowers from spring through summer and late fall. Mounding growth to 1-1/2 feet high with a 3-foot spread. Use in natural gardens, among boulders with well-drained soil and in wildflower plantings. After the blossoms dry and turn papery, they maintain their yellow color—excellent in dried arrangements. Locate in full sun to partial shade. Plants can be started from seed. Once established, provide widely spaced irrigations. Shearing faded flowers can cause a new wave of blooms. Native to Texas. Cold hardy.

Psilostrophe cooperi, paperflower, is a related species that is actually more common than the above. Yellow flowers about 1 inch in diameter cover plants for long periods spring through fall. Native to southwest desert region.

Punica granatum, POMEGRANATE   SHRUB OR TREE

Deciduous small tree or shrub adapted to the Coachella Valley. 'Chico', dwarf carnation-flowered pomegranate, grows to only 1-1/2 feet to 2 feet high. 'Legrelle' grows 6 feet to 8 feet high and has double creamy flowers with coral-red stripes. 'Nana', dwarf pomegranate, is more evergreen with dense growth to 3 feet high. A dependable performer with orange-red, single flowers and small, dry, red fruit. 'Wonderful' grows 10 to 12 feet high and bears red, 4 inch flowers. A great hedge and security barrier plant. Prune when dormant in winter. High water use in summer if flowers and fruit are desired, otherwise moderate water. (See page 146.) Does well in alkaline soils. Hardy to 20°F.

Purple coneflower—*see Echinacea purpurea*

Purple fountain grass—*see Pennisetum setaceum 'Rubrum'*

Purple plum—*see Prunus cerasifera 'Krauter Vesuvius'*

Above: *Pyracantha fortuneana* is a vigorous, upright shrub 8 to 12 feet high. Produces large, dark green leaves and thorns. Outstanding landscape interest throughout the year due to its clusters of white spring flowers and large, long-lasting, red winter berries.

Above left: *Psilostrophe cooperi*, paperflower, produces yellow flowers about 1 inch in diameter cover plants for long periods spring through fall. After the blossoms dry they turn papery, adding interest.

Above: *Quercus ilex*, holly oak, makes an excellent, medium-sized evergreen tree to 20 to 30 feet high with small, finely toothed, dark green, hollylike leaves.

Above right: *Quercus suber*, cork oak, is an evergreen tree with a broad, rounded crown. An interesting feature is the thick, deeply furrowed, corky bark, which is harvested as cork for commercial use.

Pyracantha fortuneana 'Graberi', PYRACANTHA   SHRUB

A vigorous, thorny, upright shrub to 8 to 12 feet high. Produces large, dark green leaves. Outstanding landscape interest throughout the year due to its clusters of white spring flowers and large, long-lasting red berries in winter. Accepts espalier training. Native to China. Cold hardy.

Pyracantha X 'Santa Cruz Prostrata'   GROUND COVER

Unique prostrate growth habit to 2 to 4 feet high allows this pyracantha to be used for ground cover, bank planting or as a low shrub. Covers itself with masses of white flowers in spring and red berries in fall. Evergreen, with attractive, glossy, deep green foliage. Moderate water use. Cold hardy.

Queen palm—*see Arecastrum romanzoffianum*

Queen's wreath—*see Antigonon leptopus*

Quercus agrifolia, CALIFORNIA LIVE OAK   TREE

Large, round-headed, evergreen tree 30 to 50 feet high. Rough, dark brown bark on broadly spreading, picturesque branches. Dark green, spiny leaves. Best adapted to Palm Springs areas near foothills or canyons. Hardy to 10°F.

Quercus ilex, HOLLY OAK   TREE

Excellent, medium-sized evergreen tree to 20 to 30 feet high with small, finely toothed, dark green, hollylike leaves. A showy specimen with dense foliage. Low to moderate water use. Hardy to 10°F.

Quercus suber, CORK OAK TREE

Evergreen tree with broad, rounded crown that produces deep shade. Slow growth to 25 to 40 feet high with a short trunk. Leaves are lustrous, dark green above, grayish beneath. Thick, deeply furrowed, corky bark adds close-up interest. It is harvested as cork for commercial use. Low water use. Native to the Mediterranean area. Hardy to 5°F.

Quercus virginiana, SOUTHERN LIVE OAK TREE

Quality evergreen tree that grows 50 to 60 feet high with an equal spread. 'Heritage' is an improved selection, proven to be adapted to desert heat and wind. Grows rapidly, producing impressive branches and trunk. Best performance in well-drained soil. Thrives on moderate to high but deep irrigation. Native to southeastern U.S. Hardy to 10°F.

Rain cloud sage—*see Leucophyllum species*

Red yucca—*see Hesperaloe parviflora*

Red bird of paradise—*see Caesapinia pulcherrima*

Raphiolepis indica, INDIAN HAWTHORN SHRUB

(Rhaphiolepis indica). Evergreen shrub 3 to 4 feet high and 5 to 6 feet wide with a dense, rounded form. From January to April, the dark green leaves are blanketed by magnificent clusters of flowers. Many cultivars are available: 'Clara', white; 'Jack Evans', bright pink; 'Springtime', deep pink; 'Ballerina', rosy pink. Well-drained soil is important. Accepts partial shade. Avoid overhead watering in sunny locations. Native to southern China. Hardy to 15°F.

Rhapis excelsa, SLENDER LADY PALM FAN PALM

An exceptionally decorative and rare palm, lady palm forms dense clumps of many individual stems 6 to 8 feet high. Good specimen plant in tubs or planters indoors. Best growth in bright, indirect light and nutrient-rich soil; it responds to applications of fertilizer. Moderate water use. Hardy to 20°F.

Below left: *Quercus virginiana*, southern live oak, is a large-scale, quality evergreen tree that grows 50 to 60 feet high with an equal spread.

Below: *Raphiolepis* species, raphiolepis, are dense, rounded evergreen shrubs 3 to 4 feet high. Numerous clusters of flowers blanket the dark green leaves from January to April.

Rhus lancea, AFRICAN SUMAC   TREE

A dense, wide-spreading, evergreen tree with a slight weeping or drooping growth habit. Mature trees 20 to 25 feet high may spread to 40 feet or more. A workable tree for a small garden but can be messy. Reddish stems and shiny, medium green leaves are borne in three slender leaflets. Female plants produce tan to reddish berries in clusters. Avoid heavy pruning at a single session. Native to South Africa. Hardy to 10°F.

Rhus lanceolata, PRAIRIE FLAMELEAF SUMAC   TREE, SHRUB

A deciduous tree native to west Texas. Grows 12 to 15 feet high and 10 feet wide. Foliage turns to red and orange in fall. Thrives in dry rocky soils but provide with deep irrigation in summer. Hardy to 0°F to 5°F.

Rhus ovata, SUGAR SUMAC   SHRUB

A dense, slow-growing evergreen that can be used as a large screen or hedge, growing 10 to 18 feet high and 12 feet wide. Curling leathery leaves provide a sturdy background to the 1-inch clusters of red buds that open into white or pink flowers. These are followed by orange to red berries. This plant seldom needs pruning. Prefers deep, well-drained soil. Hardy to 5°F.

Below right: *Rudbeckia hirta,* gloriosa daisy, is grown for its large, showy, yellow-orange flowers that bloom through summer and into fall. Flowers are excellent for cutting. Plants grow to 3 feet or more high so place them in back of the border.

Below: *Ruellia brittoniana* 'Katie' is a dwarf, herbaceous form of ruellia. It grows to just 10 to 12 inches high, spreading by underground runners. Blue, bell-shaped flowers to 2 inches across bloom summer into fall, set off by 4- to 6-inch medium green leaves.

Roses, garden—*see page 144*

Rosa banksiae, LADY BANKS' ROSE, TOMBSTONE ROSE   VINE

Evergreen to deciduous vine grows vigorously to 10 to 25 feet. 'Lutea' blankets plants with double pale yellow flowers in spring. 'Alba Plena' has double white flowers. Adapted to harsh, sunny, desert climates. Most at home in large-scale landscapes where it can spread out. Low to moderate water use. Native to China. Hardy to 10°F.

Rosmarinus officinalis, ROSEMARY   SHRUB OR GROUND COVER

'Lockwood deForest', dwarf rosemary, makes an excellent ground cover. Light blue flowers are profuse in early spring. Plant in full sun in soil with good drainage. Use on banks for attractive, drape-and-trail effect. Accepts no traffic. Spreads 4 to 8 feet and remains less than 2 feet high. 'Prostratus' also remains low to the ground. Many new varieties are becoming available, some with broader leaves, such as 'Miss Jessup', and others with brighter-colored flowers such as 'Collingwood Ingram'. Low to moderate water use. Native to the Mediterranean. Hardy to 10°F.

Rudbeckia hirta, BLACK-EYED SUSAN   PERENNIAL

Large, showy, yellow-orange flowers are excellent for cutting. They bloom all summer and into fall. Plants grow to 3 feet or more high. Plant in full sun in almost any soil spring to late fall. Cut back after bloom period. Cold hardy.

Ruellia brittoniana 'Katie', DWARF RUELLIA   GROUND COVER

This dwarf herbaceous plant grows to just 10 to 12 inches high, spreading by underground runners. Blue, bell-shaped flowers to 2 inches across bloom summer into fall, set off by 4- to 6-inch medium green leaves. Can be used in containers, as a ground cover or as a filler beneath taller plants. Hardy to 28°F.

Ruellia peninsularis, BAJA RUELLIA   SHRUB

An evergreen shrub to 3 feet high, putting out a profusion of purple flowers in late spring and summer. Combine with yellow-flowering *Encelia farinosa* and

Below left: Rhus lancea, African sumac, is a dense, evergreen tree with a slightly weeping growth habit. Trees reach 20 to 25 feet high and are wide-spreading—to 40 feet or more. Reddish stems and shiny, medium green leaves are borne in three slender leaflets.

Below: Rosmarinus officinalis, rosemary, is available in a wide range of forms and leaf textures. Prostrate varieties are excellent as bank and ground covers. Flowers in shades of blue flowers are profuse in early spring and attract bees.

Above: Not all *Saliva greggii* flowers are red or scarlet. A white-flowering form, 'White', is also available.

Above right: *Ruellia peninsularis*, Baja ruellia, is an upright, evergreen shrub to 3 feet high. It produces a profusion of purple flowers in late spring and summer.

red-flowering *Salvia greggii* for striking color combinations. Adapts well to heat, wind and reflected sun. Moderate water use. Plants seldom need pruning except to thin old growth to renew them. Hardy to mid-20s°F.

Russian sage—*see Perovskia atriplicifolia*

Sago palm—*see Cycas revoluta*

Saguaro cactus—*see Carnegiea gigantea*

St. John's bread tree—*see Ceratonia siliqua*

Salvia clevelandii, CHAPARRAL SAGE   SHRUB

Native to California's rugged coastal chaparral region, and surprisingly well adapted to low-elevation desert areas. Most plants reach 4 feet high and 5 feet or more wide. Fragrant blue flowers develop in whorls on stems in spring. Deadhead old flower stems in summer after bloom period has passed to renew growth. Well-drained soil recommended. Gray-green foliage blends well with many desert natives. It produces a pleasant musky fragrance when brushed by, and often scents the air after a vigorous rain. Low water use. Hardy to 20°F.

Salvia farinacea, MEALY CUP SAGE   PERENNIAL

Grows 1-1/2 to 2 feet high with an equal spread. Violet-blue flower spikes bloom for a long period through summer. Effective planted in masses. Best in full sun. Moderate water use. Native to New Mexico and Texas. Hardy to 24°F.

Salvia greggii, RED SALVIA, AUTUMN SAGE   SHRUB

Evergreen shrub to 3 feet high and as wide. Effective when planted in masses, the scarlet red flower spikes attract hummingbirds. 'White' is evergreen to 3 to 4 feet high with elongated white flowers. Finches enjoy the seed. Plant in full sun to partial shade; afternoon shade appreciated in low-elevation deserts. Low to moderate water requirement. Prune old flowering wood after flowering ceases to create new flush of growth. Native to Texas and Mexico. Hardy to 0°F.

Salvia leucantha, MEXICAN BUSH SAGE   SHRUB

Evergreen shrub to 2 to 4 feet high with an often greater spread. Casual, graceful growth habit is well-suited to a natural garden design. Long, slender, velvety purple spikes with small white flowers bloom late summer well into fall, sometimes winter. Moderate water requirement. Cut back plants after flowering in late winter for fresh growth in spring. Native to Mexico. Hardy to 24°F.

Salvia X superba, BLUE QUEEN SAGE   PERENNIAL

Compact plant to 12 inches high produces deep blue flower spikes from early summer until frost. Attractive when planted in masses. Best in full sun location. Moderate water use. Cold tender.

Scarlet flax—*see Linum grandiflorum 'Rubrum'*

Schinus molle, CALIFORNIA PEPPER TREE   TREE

Medium-sized, 30- to 40-foot evergreen tree. Round-headed form with graceful, weeping branches and feathery, bright green foliage. Rose-colored clusters of small berries hang on branches in fall. Low to moderate water use, depending on soil type. Branches of older trees are prone to breakage in strong winds. Native to Peruvian Andes. Hardy to 20°F.

Sea lavender—*see Limonium perezii*

Shasta daisy—*see Chrysanthemum X superbum*

Shrimp plant—*see Justicia brandegeana*

Senna species, Cassia, Senna

Note: Many species within this genus were formerly named *Cassia*. Be aware that many nurseries will have these plants labeled as *Cassia*.

This group of shrubs are star performers for the arid West producing yellow fragrant flowers in abundance from late winter into the spring months. They are low water users once they're established, and thrive in full sun. Plants develop to 5 to 6 feet high or more, with an equal spread. Foliage color and type varies with each species. All *Senna* species can be controlled by natural thinning and topping. Remove seed pods after flowering for a neater appearance. In addi-

Below, from left, a selection of *Salvia*s: *Salvia greggii,* red salvia, is an excellent small shrub that flowers almost continuously. Also see photo, page 124.
Salvia leucantha, Mexican bush sage, grows to 4 feet high with purple flowers in fall.
Salvia clevelandii, chaparral sage, grows to 4 feet high. Fragrant blue flowers cover plants in spring.

Above: *Senna* species flowers are profuse, and among the first to bloom in early spring.

Above right: *Senna* X *artemisioides artemisioides* (*Cassia artemisioides*), feathery cassia, in combination with *Dasylirion wheeleri.* It grows as a large shrub with gray-green, feathery leaves. and bright yellow flowers

tion, they can be toxic. Most are native to Australia, with a few exceptions. Plant in well-drained soil. Hardy to 20°F to 25°F.

Senna artemisioides X artemisioides, FEATHERY CASSIA SHRUB

(Cassia artemisioides). Large plant form makes a fine background for tall perennials or dwarf shrubs. The gray-green, feathery leaves blend perfectly with the yellow flowers that appear late winter and spring. Prune in cool weather following flowering to keep plants in proportion.

Senna polyantha, GOLDMAN'S SENNA SHRUB

(Cassia goldmanii). One of several yellow-flowering *Senna* (*Cassia*) species. It grows 4 to 5 feet high with an equal spread. Produces an interesting foliage pattern as new, bronze-colored leaves emerge then turn dark green. Slow growth rate keeps the plant in proportion with most home landscapes. It is deciduous so combining with evergreen *Senna* (*Cassia*) or *Leucophyllum* species will help disguise the bare branches. Prune in a natural form after summer flowering or while deciduous in winter. Native to Baja California.

Senna artemisioides subsp. filifolia, BUSHY SENNA SHRUB

(Cassia nemophila). This evergreen *Senna* has a refreshing, refined appearance. Yellow flowers that come in late winter and spring are followed by brown seed pods. Grows 4 to 8 feet high with an equal spread. Space 8 to 10 feet apart to allow the plant to grow naturally, which will also yield the most profuse flowers. Remove brown seed pods with a light natural pruning or knock them off. More hardy to cold than *Senna artemisioides.*

Senna artemisioides subsp. petiolaris, DESERT CASSIA SHRUB

(Cassia phyllodinea). Gray-green, sicklelike leaves shimmer in the wind. In late winter to spring, yellow flowers literally cover the plant. Evergreen, with mature size of 6 feet high with equal spread. Growth is more compact so heavy

shearing or pruning is not usually required. Prune when flowering has ceased in late winter or early spring while weather remains cool. Cold hardy to 22°F.

Senna wislizenii, SHRUBBY SENNA   SHRUB

(Cassia wislizenii). Stiff, gray-green foliage is deciduous. Bright yellow flower clusters bloom June to September (rather than February) against a background of dark, gray-green, 1-inch leaves. Spring growth has tinge of bronze that creates a striking effect. Grows 6 feet high and 8 feet wide. This is a tough plant that tolerates salinity, alkalinity, some flooding and even neglect. Early growth is slow, but after a season or two plants develop more vigor. Native to Mexico.

Silene armeria, CATCHFLY   WILDFLOWER

Pink to lavender flowers are borne in tight clusters on small bushy plants to 2 feet high. The individual flower petals are deeply notched. Most prolific bloom occurs in summer, when most annual wildflowers are long past their bloom period. Accepts full sun to partial shade in almost any soil. Moderate water use.

Simmondsia chinensis, JOJOBA   SHRUB

A distinctive shrub native to the Sonoran Desert, growing 4 to 8 feet high with an equal spread. Gray-green, leathery evergreen leaves are dense, producing a mounding growth habit well adapted to informal as well as formal designs. Use as a foundation plant, hedge or background shrub. Male and female flowers are borne on different plants, so both must be present for the female to produce the seeds, which have many commercial uses. Little or no pruning required. Plant in well-drained soil. Hardy to 15°F.

Silk floss tree—*see Chorisia speciosa*

Silk oak—*see Grevillea robusta*

Silk tree—*see Albizia julibrissin*

Silver bush morning glory—*see Convolvulus cneorum*

Silver dollar gum—*see Eucalyptus cinerea*

Silver lace vine—*see Polygonum auberti*

Snapdragon—*see Antirrhinum majus*

Above: *Simmondsia chinensis,* jojoba, is a distinctive, native desert shrub, growing 4 to 8 feet high with an equal spread. Gray-green, leathery, evergreen leaves are dense, producing a mounding growth habit suited to informal as well as formal designs.

Above left: *Senna wislizenii (Cassia wislizenii),* shrubby senna, is upright in form with stiff, gray-green foliage. Bright yellow flower clusters bloom June to September (rather than February as most *Sennas*) against a background of dark, gray-green, 1-inch leaves.

Snow-in-summer—*see Cerastium tomentosum*

Soaptree yucca—*see Yucca elata*

Society garlic—*see Tulbaghia violacea*

Soleirolia soleirolii, BABY'S TEARS   GROUND COVER

A light green, mossy mat 3 to 6 inches high for shade only; will not tolerate sun. Becomes a luxuriant small-area cover in a sheltered courtyard among ferns and other lush shade plants. Plant 12 inches apart for ground cover. Ideal between stepping stones or pavers. No traffic. High water use. Hardy to 32°F.

Sophora secundiflora, TEXAS MTN. LAUREL   SHRUB OR TREE

Large evergreen shrub or small tree to 10 to 15 feet high and 8 to 10 feet wide. Clusters of purple flowers that look much like those of wisteria have a delightful fragrance. Often grown as a large shrub or trim up lower branches to develop into a small tree. Red seeds inside the attractive, grayish white seed pods are poisonous. Plants have overall great tolerance for desert climates. Accepts almost any well-drained soil. Low water use. Restrained, compact growth requires minimal pruning. Native to Texas. Hardy to 10°F.

South African daisy—*see Gazania species*

Southern live oak—*see Quercus virginiana*

Spanish bayonet—*see Yucca aloifolia*

Star jasmine—*see Trachelospermum jasminoides*

Stock—*see Matthiola incana*

Sweet alyssum—*see Lobularia maritima*

Sweet pea—*see Lathyrus odoratus*

Tagetes erecta, MARIGOLD   ANNUAL

A valuable summer color plant in the Coachella Valley. Wide range of flower forms in yellows and oranges. Dwarf, 8- to 12-inch types are ideal in borders. Taller 18-inch varieties look best behind low border shrubs. Plant March

Below and below right: *Sophora secundiflora,* Texas mountain laurel, becomes a large evergreen shrub or small tree to 15 feet high and to 10 feet wide. Clusters of purple flowers (as shown) look much like those of wisteria and have a delightful fragrance. Often grown as a large shrub or trim up lower branches to develop into a small tree.

through April, spacing plants 8 to 12 inches apart. Remove flowers that are past prime for more flower production. Keep plants growing continuously with regular water and fertilizer—any slow down will reduce flower production. Well-prepared soil with good drainage allows plants to develop strong roots.

Tagetes lemmonii, MOUNTAIN MARIGOLD   SHRUB

This mounding shrub to 3 to 4 feet high can be recognized by the golden yellow, daisylike flowers that develop in late fall. If not frost damaged, flowering may continue into winter. Finely divided light green foliage is strongly aromatic and should be used in the background of planters. Cutting foliage back about half in early summer helps develop sturdy growth to support flowers. Prefers partial sun. Typically not bothered by insects or diseases. Native to southeastern Arizona. Hardy to 20°F.

Tagetes lucida, LICORICE MARIGOLD   SHRUB

A fall bloomer with flowers that are similar to mountain marigold but growth habit is more compact at 3 to 4 feet high. Leaves emit a scent of anise and are often used to flavor sun tea, or dried and used in hot tea. Moderate water use during summer, accepts low water the remainder of the year. Tolerates some sun but foliage tends to burn in hot-summer regions, so best with partial shade. midsummer pruning controls growth and helps produce stronger stems to support flowers. May go winter-dormant. Hardy to 20°F.

Tecoma stans, YELLOW TRUMPET FLOWER   SHRUB

(Stenolobium stans). Large, vigorous plant useful as shrub, espalier or background. In warm microclimates with time and training, it can become a small tree with a potential to reach 15 to 20 feet high. Yellow clusters of trumpet-shaped flowers adorn the plant from June to February. Provide full sun and heat, with moderate water. Prune to control the vigorous growth. Native to Mexico. Hardy to 28°F.

Tecoma 'Orange Jubilee' has a similar plant form but produces an abundance of bright orange tubular flowers.

Below: Leaves of *Tagetes lucida,* licorice marigold, produce an anise scent and can be used to flavor teas. Yellow flowers bloom in fall on compact plants to 4 feet high.

Below left: *Tagetes lemmonii,* mountain marigold, grows as a mounding shrub to 3 to 4 feet high. Golden yellow, daisylike flowers bloom in late fall. If winters are mild, flowering may continue into spring. Finely divided light green foliage is strongly aromatic to the point of becoming pungent, so locate plants accordingly.

Top: *Tecoma stans,* yellow trumpet flower, is a large, vigorous plant useful as shrub, espalier or background. Located in a warm microclimate (and with time and training), it can become a small tree with a potential to reach 15 to 20 feet high.

Above: *Tecoma* 'Orange Jubilee' has a similar form as *Tecoma stans* but the tubular flowers are bright orange.

Tecomaria capensis, CAPE HONEYSUCKLE   SHRUB OR VINE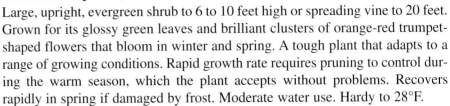

Large, upright, evergreen shrub to 6 to 10 feet high or spreading vine to 20 feet. Grown for its glossy green leaves and brilliant clusters of orange-red trumpet-shaped flowers that bloom in winter and spring. A tough plant that adapts to a range of growing conditions. Rapid growth rate requires pruning to control during the warm season, which the plant accepts without problems. Recovers rapidly in spring if damaged by frost. Moderate water use. Hardy to 28°F.

Teucrium chamaedrys, GERMANDER   GROUND COVER

A landscape herb grown for its bright green, mintlike foliage. 'Prostratum' is rapid-spreading, forming a thick cover 8 to 10 inches high. No traffic. Plants root deeply and make an excellent soil binder. Plant 12 to 15 inches apart. Spikes of attractive, rosy lavender flowers bloom in spring and summer. Plants love heat and accept sun to partial shade. Drought tolerant and cold hardy.

Texas bluebonnet—*see Lupinus texensis*

Texas ebony—*see Pithecellobium flexicaule*

Texas mountain laurel—*see Sophora secundiflora*

Texas olive—*see Cordia boissieri*

Texas ranger—*see Leucophyllum species*

Thymus praecox, MOTHER OF THYME   GROUND COVER

(T. serphyllum). This aromatic, creeping herb grows to just 6 inches high. Lavender-blue flower spikes rise 3 inches above a solid carpet of green foliage. Blooms over a long period late spring and summer. Plant 10 inches apart for ground cover. Accepts some traffic. Best in morning sun-afternoon shade location. Moderate water use. Cold hardy.

Tidy tips—*see Layia platyglossa*

Toadflax—*see Linaria maroccana*

Trachelospermum jasminoides, STAR JASMINE   VINE, SHRUB

(Rhynchospermum jasminoides). Strong-growing shrub or evergreen vine with lustrous, deep green, leathery foliage. Admired for its masses of white, highly perfumed, star-shaped flowers, which bloom most heavily in spring. Versatile uses include espalier, pillar support vine or ground cover. Needs support such as a trellis on which to climb. Full sun to partial shade, although best on east or north exposures. Native to China. Moderate water use. Cold hardy.

Transvaal daisy—*see Gerbera jamesonii*

Treasure flower—*see Gazania splendens*

Trumpet vine—*see Campsis radicans*

Tulbaghia violacea, SOCIETY GARLIC   PERENNIAL

Rosy lavender flowers bloom in large clusters in spring and summer; their long-term beauty help make up for the plant's garlic scent. Flowers bloom on tall stems well above leaves, and foliage develops into large clumps. Excellent for containers or planter boxes. Grow in well-drained soil. To renew growth, cut back in early spring. Hardy to 20°F.

Turpentine bush—*see Ericameria laricifolia*

Ulmus parvifolia, ELM   TREE

A superior cultivar, 'Drake', has rich, dark green leaves on sweeping branches. More upright than a regular evergreen elm. Becomes an attractive, round-headed small shade tree to 25 to 35 feet high. Moderate water use. Hardy to 20°F.

Verbena hybrids, VERBENA   ANNUAL

Colorful annual border plants, low growing to 8 to 12 inches high. Space 10 to 12 inches apart in a sunny location. Perennial ground cover types are discussed below. Available in a range of flower colors, including white, red, pink, blue and purple. After flowering, trim spent blooms for regrowth. Plant in fall to get a jump on producing late winter-spring flowers. Low to moderate water use.

Verbena peruviana, PERUVIAN VERBENA   GROUND COVER

This perennial puts on spectacular displays of brilliant, crimson-red or pink flowers spring through fall. Forms a low, dense, evergreen cover of dark green foliage to 4 to 16 inches high. Plant in full sun, 18 inches apart for ground cover. Accepts no traffic. 'Lipstick' is evergreen in warm climates to 8 to 10 inches and to 2 feet wide with purple flowers. 'Red' is low growing, retains its foliage in warm climates. 'St. Paul' is similar with pink flowers. All make great ground covers. Full sun. Moderate water use. Hardy to 25°F.

Verbena rigida, SANDPAPER VERBENA   PERENNIAL

(Verbena venosa). A vigorous perennial to 12 to 20 inches high with predominant dark green and rough-toothed leaves. Stems support lilac to purple-blue flowers in clusters summer and fall. Like most verbenas, plants perform better if their leaves remain dry. Irrigate with drip system instead of overhead spray. Plant 1-1/2 to 2 feet apart in well-drained soil. Full sun. Hardy to 0°F.

Verbena tenuisecta, MOSS VERBENA   GROUND COVER

A hardy verbena that tolerates extremes of heat and cold. Set off by attractive, medium green, feathery leaves, the blue, purple or violet flowers bloom the year-round in warm climates. Grows 12 to 15 inches high, with runners rooting as they spread. Plant 18 inches apart for solid cover. Accepts no traffic. Prefers sunny locations, accepting almost any soil. Hardy to 25°F.

Below left: *Ulmus parvifolia* is an elm tree adapted to grow in the Coachella Valley. 'Drake' is a superior cultivar, with rich, dark green leaves on sweeping branches. Becomes an attractive, round-headed, small shade tree to 25 to 35 feet high.

Below: *Teucrium chamaedrys*, germander, is a landscape herb grown for its bright green, mintlike foliage. Here it combines with gray artemisia and yellow coreopsis.

Viburnum suspensum, SANDANKWA VIBURNUM   SHRUB

Showy, evergreen shrub 3 to 6 feet high. Large, oval, shiny green leaves cover slender rough branches. Fragrant rose-tinted white flowers bloom in spring. Avoid full sun; plant in location that receives some shade or eastern exposure. Moderate water use. Hardy to 18°F.

Viburnum tinus 'Robustrum', ROUNDLEAF VIBURNUM   SHRUB

A dense-growing evergreen shrub to 6 to 12 feet high. Luxuriant deep green foliage is the background for large quantities of striking white flowers blushed with pink during fall and winter. Tends to develop mildew in heavy shade; locate in partial shade and out of afternoon sun. Native to the Mediterranean. Hardy to 5°F.

Vigna caracalla, GIANT SNAIL VINE   VINE

(Phaseolus gigantea). Vigorous, quick-covering vine, with a foliage effect similar to the vegetable pole bean. Masses of slightly fragrant, showy, lavender flowers bloom in large clusters through the year. Excellent for wire fences and banks. Full sun. If cold kills top growth, cut to ground level. Plants will regrow the following spring. Moderate to high water use. Cold tender.

Vinca major, PERIWINKLE   GROUND COVER

An excellent, easy-care plant useful for covering large banks and steep slopes. Grows to 1-1/2 feet high, with deep roots that bind the soil. Runners root as they spread. Vigorous, glossy green foliage is background for star-shaped blue flowers that bloom spring and summer. Best with shade or partial shade. Accepts no traffic. Plant 1-1/2 to 2 feet apart for ground cover. Cold hardy.

Vinca minor, DWARF RUNNING MYRTLE   GROUND COVER

Similar to *Vinca major* but more refined to 10 inches high. Creates a lush, evergreen cover that is dense enough to prevent weed growth. Blue flowers bloom in early spring and again in the fall. Accepts clipping if a more groomed

Below and below right: *Verbena* species are among the most colorful low-water use ground covers for desert regions.

Far left: *Vinca major* makes a suitable large-area ground cover for shady and partially shaded locations. The bright blue flowers bloom spring and summer.

Left: *Vitex agnus-castus,* chaste tree, is a deciduous shrub or tree. Grows 15 to 25 feet high, with dense, gray-green leaves. Blue or white flowers bloom in summer.

appearance is desired. Tolerates light traffic. Plant 12 to 18 inches apart for ground cover. Preferred exposure is partial shade. Can be grown successfully in a range of conditions. Extremely cold hardy.

Vinca rosea—see Catharanthus roseus

Viola cornuta, VIOLA, HORNED VIOLET ANNUAL

Blooms well in sunny to partially shaded locations. Flower colors come in white, blue, yellow and apricot. At home as a low, 6- to 9-inch border along walks, in front of mixed flower plantings and in containers. Solid colors planted in masses make colorful patterns. Plant 9 to 12 inches apart October to February. Profuse flowering until heat arrives in late spring. Moderate moisture requirement. Accepts temperatures as low as 28°F.

Viola X wittrockiana, PANSY ANNUAL

Reliable annual for winter and spring color. Many selections available, in a wide range of flower colors. Grows 6 to 8 inches high. Plant from October into February, spacing plants 8 to 10 inches apart. Enrich soil with blood meal before planting, and feed monthly with balanced fertilizer. Best in a warm microclimate. Remove spent blooms often for more flowers. Cut back plants lightly March to April to renew growth and to help extend bloom period. Use as a border or foreground for taller annuals or perennials. Moderate water use.

Vitex agnus-castus, CHASTE TREE SHRUB OR TREE

Deciduous shrub or tree, 15 to 25 feet high, with dense, gray-green foliage. Blue or white flower spikes bloom in summer. Prefers full sun. Low water use. Native to southern Europe. Cold hardy.

Vitis vinifera, GRAPE VINE

Deciduous, clinging vine with lush, heart-shaped medium green leaves. Vigorous growth to 10 to 20 feets, supplying cooling summer shade. Needs support for vine and fruit. Prune canes in winter. Watch for grape leaf skeletonizers in summer. These black and yellow caterpillars arrive in hordes to quickly strip leaves. Moderate water use. Cold hardy.

Yucca elata, soaptree yucca, is a large accent with refined 1/2-inch leaves. White flowers bloom in summer on tall spikes. Slow growing from 6 to 20 feet high.

Wallflower—*see Cheiranthus cheri*

Washingtonia filifera, CALIFORNIA FAN PALM   FAN PALM

This is the only palm native to California, growing naturally in Palm Canyon and other canyons in the Coachella Valley. Trunks can become massive, often reaching 3-1/2 feet in diameter. Large fronds are borne on long leaf stems; the leaves are fringed with coarse white hairs. Accepts the desert heat. Slower growing than *Washingtonia robusta*, following, attaining a mature height of 35 to 40 feet. Provide deep watering. Hardy to 20°F.

Washingtonia robusta, MEXICAN FAN PALM   FAN PALM

(Washingtonia gracilis). A native of Baja California. Similar to California fan palm, but trunk is more slender, usually 15 to 18 inches in diameter. Faster growth compared to *Washingtonia filifera*. Fronds are smaller with shorter stems and fewer filaments. Mexican fan palm becomes a skyline tree, reaching 50 to 75 feet high. Group only with own species. Most effective in clumps of plants that are of staggered heights. Provide deep watering. Hardy to 25°F.

Weeping fig—*see Ficus benjamina*

Willow-leafed jasmine—*see Cestrum parqui*

Wisteria floribunda, JAPANESE WISTERIA   VINE

'Longissima Alba' is impressive with its pure white flowers that cascade in spikes to 4 feet long. 'Royal Purple' attracts attention when its long, violet-purple flower clusters bloom in spring. Bright green foliage is deciduous. Twining, woody growth to 25 feet. Cold hardy.

Wisteria sinensis, CHINESE WISTERIA   VINE

Deciduous, with medium green foliage. Twining vine needs support to grow; reaches up to 10 to 30 feet long. Purple or white flower clusters bloom in spring. Full sun. Moderate water use. Cold hardy.

Woolly butterfly bush—*see Buddleia marrubifolia*

Woolly yarrow—*see Achillea tomentosa*

Xylosma congestum, XYLOSMA   SHRUB

(X. senticosom). Versatile, medium-sized evergreen shrub grows 6 to 10 feet high. Also useful as multiple-trunk tree, espalier or clipped hedge or screen. Arching branches on upright habit. New foliage has reddish tint, which then matures into glossy light green. Easy to control, accepts trimming well. Sun or partial shade exposure. Native to China. Hardy to 20°F.

Yellow trumpet flower—*see Tecoma stans*

Yellow yucca—see *Hesperaloe parviflora*

Yesterday, today and tomorrow—*see Brunfelsia pauciflora 'Exima'*

Yew podocarpus—*see Podocarpus macrophyllus*

Yucca aloifolia, SPANISH BAYONET   ACCENT

Evergreen, smooth leaf margins, sharp spike at tip, 3 to 10 feet high, white clusters of flowers bloom on 2-foot stalks. Low water use. Hardy to 15°F.

Yucca brevifolia, JOSHUA TREE   ACCENT

Evergreen, branching gray to dull green, 20 to 30 feet high. Clusters of greenish white flowers bloom in summer. Best performance in Mojave Desert climate. Low water use. Hardy to 10°F.

Yucca elata, SOAPTREE YUCCA   ACCENT

Refined 1/2-inch leaves. White flowers bloom in summer on tall spikes. Slow growing from 6 to 20 feet high. Plant in well-drained soil in full sun. Accepts drought. Native to Arizona. Cold hardy.

Yucca recurvifolia, PENDULOUS YUCCA   ACCENT

Plant grows rapidly to 6 feet high. Dark gray-green leaves to 3 feet long have soft tips. Clusters of white lilylike flowers bloom on tall spikes in summer. Do not overwater. Hardy to 20°F. Native to southeast U.S. and Mexico.

Yucca, red—see *Hesperaloe parviflora*

Yucca whipplei, OUR LORD'S CANDLE   ACCENT

Gray to green leaves have sharp spikes. They are thick and rigid, and several planted together make a good barrier. Plant is trunkless to 3 feet high. White flowers bloom in summer atop spikes 8 to 10 feet high. Native to California and Baja California. Hardy to 20°F.

Zauschneria californica, CALIFORNIA FUSCHIA   PERENNIAL

Upright stems 8 to 12 inches high form a mat composed of small gray to green leaves. Bright orange-red or white tubular flowers are borne in clusters at ends of stems early summer through winter; they are loved by hummingbirds. An aggressive grower, can become invasive with regular water. Many selected forms available. Hardy to 32°F.

Zinnia elegans, ZINNIA   ANNUAL

One of the best annuals for summer color. Plant as late as April for flowers beginning in June. Flowers come in a range of bright colors, and are large—up to 6 inches across. Dwarf types grow as low as 6 inches; taller types can be as much as 3 feet high. Space taller varieties 12 to 15 inches apart; dwarf types 8 to 12 inches apart. Dwarf types are excellent border plants. Plant zinnias in rich soil in a sunny location. Flood-irrigate or use drip irrigation. Overhead irrigation can encourages mildew. If it must be used, irrigate in early morning so leaves will dry in the sun.

Below left: *Washingtonia robusta*, Mexican fan palm, is similar to *Washingtonia filifera*, California fan palm, but trunk is more slender, usually 15 to 18 inches in diameter. Mexican fan palm eventually becomes a skyline tree, reaching 50 to 75 feet high, so plant with care in residential areas.

Below: *Zauschneria californica*, California fuschia, is upright with stems 8 to 12 inches high. Forms a mat composed of small gray to green leaves. Bright orange-red or white tubular flowers are borne in clusters at ends of stems early summer through winter.

Special Gardens, Special Plants

MANY GARDENERS ENJOY GROWING DIFFERENT PLANTS. Mild winters and ample sunshine of the Coachella Valley allow a wide range of plants and specialized gardens to be grown successfully. In this chapter, you'll find detailed information on some particular gardens and plants that may capture your interest. The following provides the basic information you need to select and grow roses, citrus, fruits and berries, vegetables, lawns, and flowers, including annuals and wildflowers. You'll learn how to handle specific kinds of garden situations, such as landscaping around pools and patios, creating a wildlife habitat in your own back yard, and how to grow many types of plants successfully in containers. In addition, you'll find a detailed guide on how to give your old garden a facelift, including ways to update your landscape with new, easier-to-grow, water-efficient plants.

Small Gardens and Landscapes

Even if your garden space is limited, and you live in a mobile home, townhome or on a small home lot, it is just as feasible to enjoy plants and gardens as for a home on a large city lot. Many of the same trees, shrubs, vines, ground covers, annuals and perennials that grow success-fully in large-scale garden areas are compatible in smaller planting loca-tions, as long as mature plant sizes are accounted for. In some instances dwarf plants are available that are identical to their full-size counter-parts. They are often better choices in small-space situations. Those who live on a small lot can enjoy a wide range of plants and gardens. The list is long and includes small lawns, shade and flowering trees, citrus, native and introduced shrubs and ground covers, vines, rose gardens, strawberry beds, vegetable gardens, annuals and perennial flowers in containers, hanging baskets, bird baths, fountains, hedges for wind-breaks, cacti and succulents, as well as boulders and crushed gravel as a ground cover.

Left: Special gardens include container gardens. These petunias, Johnny jump-ups and California poppies put on a spectacular springtime show.

Above: Several kinds of citrus can be grown successfuly in the Coachella Valley.

Planning a Small-Scale Landscape

Due to the smaller areas, gardening solutions are more creative. It is difficult for first-time desert residents to develop plans of action for new mobile home and town-home landscapes due to extremes in climate, soils and unfamiliar plant materials. When you get the urge to landscape your small-space lot, it's best to follow basic guidelines on planning a landscape.

❑ Begin by preparing a plan that shows location of walks, patios and driveway slabs. These should be in place before landscaping begins. Also show on the plan any existing trees and shrubs.

❑ If you are interested in growing vegetables or flowers, consider constructing narrow raised beds to provide a seating ledge so useful in planting, weeding and harvesting. If there is ample room on the street side to create low mounds, install a few boulders to set the stage for ground covers or accent plants.

❑ In addition to walks and patios, there may be a need to construct walls for privacy or as a windbreak. Adequate drainage is important to move excess water off the property as rapidly as possible. Make the soil level along hardscape areas 2 inches below grade.

❑ Visit retail nurseries and botanical gardens for plant ideas. Consider plants for their seasonal color, beauty, hardiness to cold, ultimate height and spread and water requirements. Study trees, in particular, for their mature height, spread, root structure and water needs. They must be adapted to smaller garden areas.

❑ Plan an irrigation system and layout after you determine plant locations. Drip irrigation with automatic valves will save water and reduce your water bill. See pages 32 to 41.

Mark the locations of trees, shrubs, vines and ground cover areas with stakes. A garden hose works well to show the outline of planting beds. Install the mainline of irrigation system before planting so you will be able to water plants immediately.

❑ See page 18 for step-by-step planting guidelines. Allow adequate space between plants and hardscapes. Take into account their full mature growth even if plantings appears sparse. You can always add annuals and perennials as temporary filler for a year or two until trees and shrubs begin to assert themselves.

Giving your Old Landscape a Facelift

If your garden is more than ten years old, it's probably time to retrofit irrigation systems. It's an opportunity to install new, colorful, water-efficient plants to reduce water use and maintenance costs.

If you have a front lawn, consider replacing it with interesting, natural-shaped contours and mounds of raked earth or mulch planted with water-efficient flowering shrubs, perennials and ground covers. Add your own dry creek (see page 149), some boulders and a few accent plants. Now your once common monochromatic grass yard is a visual feast for the eye. And it will use about half the water as the lawn.

You can also choose to *reduce* lawn size. Bordering it with a clean edge can enhance the look of your landscape and give it a finished appearance. The contrast of rich green grass against light-colored mulch such as decomposed granite or soil can be attractive.

Since your old landscape was installed, nurseries have introduced many new dry-climate shrubs, trees, accent plants, ground covers and perennials. Most are water-

Salvia greggii (red flowers), bright green *Myoporum parvifolium* and pink-flowering *Verbena* species combine to become a simple, water-conserving landscape.

Wildflowers such as red-flowering *Linum grandiflorum* 'Rubrum' add color with native and adapted shrubs.

efficient plants with a long flowering season in a wide range of colors and growth habits. Ornamental grasses as well come in a range of sizes and colors to create flowing patterns. Vertical accent plants, cacti and succulents add their own brand of new visual impact. See *Plants for Desert Success,* pages 43 to 135, for an array of choices.

First, Inventory the Site

Planning for a landscape facelift requires a review of the site and existing problems, then developing a theme or plan—including a budget—before beginning work.

To develop a complete review, it may be worth the services of an experienced landscape designer or landscape architect. He or she can define the scope of work, develop a time frame and prepare budgets for each phase.

Ask Some Questions—What is the condition of trees on site, including their spread and height? Are they rubbing against the roof overhang, and are roots uplifting walks or walls?

Are surface tree roots creating problems when mowing the lawns?

Are trees irrigated by deep watering drips or bubblers?

Are trees well-adapted to the desert environment?

Have any trees been lost to wind damage, frost or to age? Are replacements needed?

Are there extremely large date palms or fan palms on site that could cause property or personal damage as a result of storms?

Is there an ongoing program or schedule to prune and thin interior growth of shade trees?

Are shrubs and ground covers so old and woody that continual pruning has all but eliminated flowering?

Do old roots fill the soil in planting beds, reducing available space for short-term color plants?

Are there any plants on site you just don't like?

Some Solutions—Remove tired evergreen shrubs and replant with small flowering shrubs and perennials. Small shrubs, also called subshrubs, are more dwarf and produce more flowers over a longer period. Perennials can often take the place of annuals. They produce colorful flowers and are less costly than planting and replanting large beds of annuals several times a year. They are also strong options to older evergreen plants, renewing and invigorating a landscape. In addition, they require less pruning and produce less debris.

Replace or reduce the size of large lawns with graceful, flowing plantings. Add in decomposed granite, accent plants and low-profile ground covers to create a new, fresh look and also reduces water use. A well-constructed edging contains the lawn and gives definition to lawn and planting beds. Use pressure-treated wood, heartwood of cedar, redwood or cypress for edging or headers for the lawn border. When in direct contact with

Windmill palm, *Trachycarpus fortunei,* and beds of annuals surround a small, well-bordered lawn in this Palm Desert landscape.

the ground, they last much longer than pine or fir. If the lawn is curved use benderboard, strips of wood about 3/8-inch thick and 4 inches wide. Other choices are metal and plastic edging and concrete borders.

Limiting the lawn perimeter and avoiding small, narrow sections makes it easier to irrigate and maintain, greatly reducing maintenance and trimming.

Replace old irrigation heads with more water-conservative equipment. If necessary, re-space heads to eliminate overspray onto walks and paving. Review all equipment to make sure that there are no large leaks in line or with valve components. Check efficiency of automatic control equipment. They may be outdated and improved models may save money and time. Irrigation, including how to upgrade and maintain an existing system, is discussed on pages 38 to 41.

Landscaping Near Pools and Patios

Select plants for use around pools and patios with an eye for low maintenance. They should be relatively free of leaf drop or debris, although almost all plants produce some litter. Once you control foliage debris and wind- blown sand, a pool-side landscape can become low maintenance. A landscape around a pool is most appealing if plants with dramatic qualities are selected to enhance the setting.

Palms, both feather and fan leaves; ground-hugging junipers; annuals including petunias, phlox and verbena; and ground covers such as gazanias, rosemary and prostrate natal plum are good choices. All have foliage and forms that are at home around a pool.

Plants must also be able to tolerate heat, intense sun and reflected light. Drainage to move pool splash water away from planted areas is essential. The use of gravel, rock or paving helps reduce movement of sand or soil around a pool. Night lighting on palms and sword-leaf

plants enhances any landscape. Play of light reflections on stems and water add to the beauty.

Selecting trees for landscaping around a swimming pool is difficult, because few are litter proof. Most favored are palms with feather and fan leaves to create accents and shade. For a palm with character, *Washingtonia filifera,* California fan palm, grows slowly to 35 to 40 feet, with a massive 3-1/2-foot diameter trunk. *Washingtonia robusta,* Mexican fan palm, has a slender 18-inch trunk that reaches 50 to 75 feet high. Caution: It is a skyline tree and should only be used in large-scale garden settings. Both are attractive oasis plants, especially when the same species are used in clusters. Both are relatively hardy to frost.

For smaller gardens and for close up viewing, consider *Chamaerops humilis,* Mediterranean fan palm. It is typically multi-trunked to 8 to 12 feet high. Growth is slow in youth as pups (young offshoot plants) fill in around the base. Later on growth may develop more vertically.

When selecting shrubs or ground covers, choose plants with a sword-leaf form. As mentioned, avoid those known to produce volumes of leaf and flower litter. Likewise, avoid bristly or thorny plants around pool areas, due to the potential for injury. Plants to avoid include oleanders, bougainvilleas, pyracanthas, upright junipers, yuccas and cactus. If shade trees or citrus (a favorite) are desired, locate them on the downwind side and at least 25 to 35 feet away from the pool's edge.

Ornamental Pools and Fountains
The cooling sight and relaxing sound of water are themes common to most ornamental pools with bold rock groupings, which also relate to the surrounding natural desert. Vertical plants such as *Muhlenbergia rigens,* dwarf muhley; *Pennisetum setaceum* 'Rubrum',

Palms are ideal plants near pools. They create a tropical mood and are generally litter-free.

A poolside planter features colorful annuals with upright rosemary as a living centerpiece.

Bordering a lawn with a clean edge helps give your landscape a finished appearance. This entrance to a Palm Desert home is enhanced with colorful annuals and perennials.

purple fountain grass; *Dietes vegeta,* butterfly iris and *Hemerocallis* hybrids, daylily, become grassy accents among rock groupings. For fillers between boulders, add fascinating gray foliage of *Artemesia schmidtiana* 'Silver Mound', angel's hair; *Salvia farinacae,* mealy cup sage (violet-blue flower spikes) and *Salvia greggii,* red salvia. All are sun-loving, low-water users and blend well with other desert plants. Include dwarfish *Bougainvillea* shrub forms, such as 'La Jolla' or 'Temple Fire'. They add a lush, colorful, subtropical mood, with branches draping naturally over rocks.

Cacti and succulents can used among rocks and boulders to provide miniature desert scenes for close-up viewing. Set them back from walkways and the pool desk area so visitors won't be injured.

Patios

The intimacy of a large or small patio merits close attention to detail when selecting and placing plants. In many desert gardens, the walled patio area can create privacy in a mini-oasis setting.

Espaliered plants and color plants in containers add special interest. Small planters filled with flowering annuals and perennials add bright, gem-like effects. Bonsai plants are ideal in small areas, as are prostrate junipers and other coniferous plants. Select plants closest to seating and gathering areas for long-term interest.

Choose those that have textures and colors that will hold up well when viewed up close.

Special materials that can help define a patio area include Mexican beach pebbles around the bases of shrubs and vines, lava rock boulders, fountains, low voltage lighting, bird baths and hanging basket plants. Flowering vines also enhance to the scene.

Install bubblers or drip heads for watering. An automatic clock for an irrigation system takes the worry out of when and how much to water. Complete soil preparation prior to planting improves growing conditions, which is helpful when there is limited space for plant roots, typical in small-space planters and garden areas.

Small Lawns for Landscapes

Reducing an existing lawn area or making new lawns smaller than in the past helps curtail water use. This is a becoming more popular in new landscape designs. Even a small lawn provides an important surface for play and visual relief from the earth tones of the desert. If you do have a lawn or are planning one for a new landscape, ask your nursery or sod grower about the current crop of water-conserving grasses and how to maintain them.

In the Coachella Valley, the most common and easiest-to-grow grasses are the permanent, warm-season Bermudagrasses. They are seeded (common Bermuda only) or sodded (hybrids only, such as the 'Tif' series).

Hybrid Bermuda provides a close knit carpet that wears well. Its seed is sterile, so it must be planted from sod or stolons. Hybrids are fast becoming the favorites, due to their finer texture and richer color. And, unlike common Bermuda, it does not reseed and become a weedy, invasive nuisance in other plantings.

Many other types of grasses have been tested and tried, but, to date, few show much promise. Buffalograss from Texas and northern Mexico may have the potential of becoming a high-quality warm-season turf with better winter color than Bermuda, eliminating the need for overseeding in winter. However, it is not yet commonly available.

Overseeding a Winter-dormant Lawn

Bermuda, a warm-season grass, turns brown with cold temperatures, a time when cool-season grasses thrive. Sowing cool-season grass seed over a dormant Bermudagrass lawn, called *overseeding,* allows the gardener to have a green, thriving lawn all year-round.

One of the main gardening events in the low desert is the exercise of overseeding Bermuda lawns with ryegrass. Thousands of acres of lawns around homes, in parks and on golf courses are renovated to get them ready for overseeding. This occurs at a specific time when soil temperatures are 72°F to 78°F, usually October 1 to October 15. This is also the time that annuals, perennials and bulbs are planted for winter and spring color.

Annual ryegrass and perennial ryegrass are the most common cool-season grasses used for overseeding. Annual rye grows rapidly, however, its lush growth demands more frequent mowing. Grass leaves tend to be weaker and a lighter green color. It is less expensive than perennial rye.

Perennial rye grass has greater vigor and develops more sturdy, spreading growth. Its greater cost is worth the difference in expense. Germination period for both types is generally 3 to 10 days, depending on moisture coverage.

Other grasses such as rough-stalked bluegrass and bentgrass are used on golf greens for putting surfaces. Each of these fine-bladed grasses require much more maintenance than the rye grasses. Ask your nursery about the finer points of selecting a grass that will work best for your lawn situation.

Overseeding, step by step

❏ Check irrigation system to see if each sprinkler head is operating properly. It is necessary to have uniform coverage of the area. (See page 37 to 38 for methods.)
❏ Stop watering the Bermuda turf area 7 to 10 days before final mowing. But be certain nearby trees and plants continue to receive water as required.

❏ Use proper mowing equipment to *scalp* grass to about 3/8-inch high. It may take several cuttings to get to this height, but it is necessary so the ryegrass seed will make good contact with the soil.
❏ Remove debris generated from the mowing and preparation operation from the lawn area. Haul it away or add it to your compost pile.
❏ Moisten lawn before seeding.
❏ Apply seed at the rate recommended by the grower. Use a calibrated spreader to apply seed evenly.
❏ After seeding, apply a light layer of organic material as a top dressing. This helps ensure good seed-to-soil contact and keeps seed moist. Chase birds away. (You'll probably have to do this often throughout the process.)
❏ The seed and soil surface must be kept continually moist. Avoid puddling by watering lightly but frequently. This may require irrigating two to three time per day, for periods of only three to five minutes. For example, you may want to water midmorning, noon and midafternoon. As seedlings begin to grow, gradually reduce frequency of irrigation and increase length of time.
❏ After grass has germinated and is at the two- to four-leaf stage, apply a complete lawn fertilizer. It should contain nitrogen, phosphorus and potassium. Apply at recommended rates; excess fertilizers can cause seedling diseases.
❏ Mow grass for the first time after it reaches 2 inches high. Sharpen the mower blade so young grass plants are not pulled from the soil or shredded.

Container Gardening

Container plants on your desert patio, at the entrance to your home or around the pool deck can play a personal or even sentimental part in your gardening. In these areas you can showcase your favorite plants, enjoying them at close range. These include plants that offer interesting structure such as bonsai plants, as well as colorful annuals, bulbs and fragrant flowering shrubs.

Upright shrubs in containers can function as screens or as a way to divide a garden or outdoor area. Or select a plant to complement a special container.

The portable container garden can move with you from one home to another, and, if placed on casters, containers can be moved according to the weather or the season. Move them out of the range of extremes in cold weather in winter, or into a shaded location as the heat and sun intensity increases in the summer.

Select containers that can handle problems associated with our desert heat. Other factors include planting in a soil mix that drains well; providing adequate moisture and regular nutrients; proper exposure (shade, partial shade or sun); and attention to details such as supplying supports or repotting at the right stage of growth.

Container Choices

Containers can be porous, which allows evaporation of moisture through the sides. Porous materials include unglazed clay, terra cotta or wood. Wood containers dry out rapidly. Care must be taken that these types do not lose moisture too rapidly during warm periods of the year. However, if you water plants regularly, porous containers are more forgiving than non-porous ones.

Non-porous containers include those made of porcelain, glazed ceramic and plastic. They require careful attention to avoid overwatering because moisture does not evaporate through the sides so it remains in the soil longer. In almost all situations saucers or trays are necessary to prevent stains on decking or patio floors. Drainage holes are also required for all containers.

Soil mix ingredients that are satisfactory for long term growing include one-third ground bark or composted planter mix, one-third coarse sand, and one-third garden soil. Blend all three into a loose, friable mixture and moisten before you plant. Many brands of ready-to-use packaged mixes are available at nurseries.

Leave space at the top of the container—one to three inches—depending on the size of the container and plant type. This allows room for each watering. Water should flow through the soil mix on new plants as well as saturating the root ball of established plants with each irrigation.

If water seems to flow out of the container bottom too rapidly, there may be soil shrinkage due to excessive root growth. Water is not penetrating the rootball, but merely moving around and down the sides, doing little good. When this occurs, it's time to replant with fresh soil in a larger container.

Keep soil moist, not wet. It is sometimes helpful to place a 1- to 2-inch layer of pea gravel or Mexican beach pebbles on the soil surface. This prevents crusting, reduces water splash and improves appearance.

Nutrients must be furnished more frequently in containers than for plants in the ground. Measure and apply carefully according to label directions. Liquid types of organic fertilizers work best. Moisten soil prior to application and water it in. Don't overdo it thinking "a little more" will help. Overfertilizing will kill plants.

Location of your containers is entirely dependent on the need of sun or shade for each type of plant. If containers are mobile, you can move them to protect from frost, wind and reflected heat and sunlight.

Choice Plants for Containers

Some of the most satisfactory candidates for containers include sago and pygmy palms, camellias, gardenias and azaleas, citrus, junipers, lantana, geraniums, perennials and annuals; many kinds of herbs; ornamental grasses such as *Ophiopogon gigantea;* giant bulbs such as tulips, daffodils, hyacinths and ornamental ficus; araliads and bonsai plants.

Cacti and succulents are a special part of the Southwest, and the majority are highly adapted to con-

The portable container garden can move with you from one home to another. These containers are filled with colorful annuals and perennials, including white sweet alyssum, pansies and *Asparagus* 'Myers'.

Roses can bloom for 9 to 10 months when adapted varieties are grown and by following the right cultural program. These beautiful roses greet visitors to this Palm Desert home.

tainer culture. Most have fascinating shapes, textures and colors, making it easy to collect them. Containers in groupings is an excellent way to show off favorites. A few to consider are *Euphorbia millii,* crown of thorns; *Euphorbia tirucalli,* pencil bush; *Echinocactus grusonii,* golden barrel and *Hesperaloe parviflora,* red yucca. *Aloe vera* is a favorite to have close by to treat minor cuts and burns.

Roses in the Desert

Although they are thirsty plants, the long flowering season of roses place them high on the list for a place in desert gardens. Many old-time varieties continue to find favor, while hybridizers increase the number of new forms, colors and types of roses available each year.

If you find the many categories of roses confusing, here is a quick primer that will help you choose varieties that are right for you and your garden.

Floribundas—Noted for their prolific clustering flowering habit, available in many bright colors. Growth is dwarf and compact, typically reaching 18 to 30 inches high. Their best use is as low hedges and as a foreground to hybrid tea and grandiflora roses.

Hybrid tea roses—Generally grow taller—2-1/2 to 5 feet high. Many are noted for the great number of petals, others for their fragrance, some for their brilliance and robust, mildew-resistant foliage. Flowers generally bloom in spring and fall. Coachella Valley gardeners

that adhere to a regular pruning, fertilizing and watering program can enjoy roses for 9 to 10 months.

Grandiflora roses—These were developed by hybridizers from a breeding program between floribunda and hybrid tea roses. Grandifloras often show the most desirable traits of both parents, plus are vigorous plants, growing 5 to 6 feet high. Flowers have many petals that are produced in clusters on long vigorous stems. They can be grown alone or as background plants in hybrid tea beds. Space plants 4 to 5 feet apart.

Climbing roses—These perform best in an east exposure. Provide support such as a wall or sturdy trellis.

Tree roses—Generally don't do well with intense sun on their tall stems. Protect from afternoon sun and wrap stems to prevent sunburn.

Local nurseries are excellent sources for current and adaptable varieties for specific areas of the valley.

Cultural Requirements for Roses

Location and planting—Plant in full or morning sun. Avoid locations receiving reflected sun or heat, such as the west side of buildings or walls. Always keep the bud union above ground and plant so it faces to the northeast, helping prevent sunburn. Space floribunda and hybrid tea plants 2-1/2 to 3 feet apart. Space grandifloras 4 to 5 feet apart.

Watering—Keep soil moist (but not wet) at all times. Use bubblers placed at the drip line. Apply water at ground level in basins, soaking the root area. Avoid overhead applications of water in evening hours, especially in late spring and summer. This can create conditions that encourage mildew. Sprinkle-irrigate only in early morning hours.

Mulching—Keep roots cool by applying a 2- to 4-inch mulch of organic materials such as composted manures.

Fertilization—Apply first applications of a basic rose fertilizer on mature plants in February. Make the next application after flowers reach bud stage. Apply fertilizer once again each time buds begin to form. Fertilizing during August and September will stimulate plants into producing a fall burst of bloom.

Chlorosis control—Prevent the development of chlorosis by applying chelate materials the first signs of yellowing leaves. This is most often done in late spring and every two months through the growing season until the condition is corrected.

Insect control—Watch for signs of aphids in early spring to late March. These tiny pests suck juices of new shoots and tender buds. Blasting them with water spray from a garden hose helps to a degree, but complete control can be achieved using an insecticide. Control scale infestations during the dormant season by applying a dormant oil spray. Follow all product label directions.

Pruning—Avoid pruning plants through the summer months. The foliage will protect interior stems from the intense sun. Prune January to early February—no later than February 15. Remove suckers from below bud union. (They grow from the rootstock and have a different appearance from flowering stems.) Cut dead wood back to healthy stems and remove small, twiggy growth. Reduce height of main stems by about half to encourage vigorous new growth.

Fruit and Vegetable Gardens

Fruits and vegetables grown in Coachella Valley are harvested and shipped throughout the world. Growing conditions are most favorable in the low-elevation deserts during fall, through winter and into spring. Planting in spring and caring for food-producing plants for a summer harvest is much more difficult, due to the extreme high temperatures. It can be done, but it can also be a battle, combating nature.

If you are a beginning gardener or new to the desert, consider a fall garden. Planting at this time is more likely to result in harvests that will be tasty and abundant. But keep in mind, however, that even winter-grown garden crops require irrigation on a regular basis from seed-sowing time right up until harvest.

The time to begin planting is generally September 15. Follow with new plantings every 3 to 4 weeks for successive harvests until February. Fruits and vegetables that can be grown successfully in the Coachella Valley include beets, carrots, endive, leeks, head lettuce, leaf lettuce, green onions, radishes, spinach, onions, potatoes, peanuts, tomatoes, sweet corn, squash, asparagus, turnips, melons, broccoli, Brussels sprouts, cabbage, chard and mustard.

Winter vegetable gardens are usually more successful than summer gardens because plants avoid intense heat. This planting of assorted lettuce varieties is not only bountiful but highly attractive.

It is possible to grow many vegetables in containers, in small plots or in borders along a wall or fence. An east, south or west exposure is acceptable, as long as vegetables receive at least six hours of sun.

Prepare soil well in advance of planting. Moisten soil to 1-1/2 to 2 feet deep. Add organic materials and mix thoroughly into top 12 inches. Remove stones, weeds and debris and grade to create a smooth, ready-to-plant seed bed. Consider a raised bed garden surrounded by a low wall. You can sit and work garden areas to irrigate, thin seedlings, remove weeds and harvest crops.

Planting Seeds for a Winter Garden

If sowing seeds directly into the garden, be aware that each vegetable has a preferred planting depth. You'll find directions on seed packets. Don't plant too deep.

After planting seeds, tamp the soil firmly. Water by sprinkling with a fine-mist sprinkler or hose attachment so soil is not washed away. Continue to sprinkle soil lightly on a regular basis until seeds germinate and seedlings produce three or four leaves. Now you can begin watering with a soaker hose or garden hose, flooding the planting bed at the base of plants. Check the soil for moisture several times a week. Dig down at least 6 inches deep and feel if the soil is moist. Any dry period can slow down or interrupt the growth process and reduce or destroy crops.

Planting a Summer Garden

Some good-tasting summer vegetables are also good-looking, and can be mixed into flowerbeds or grown in containers. These including warm-season varieties such as eggplant, sweet or bell peppers, chili peppers and chard.

Set out young plants in packs or 4-inch pots after all danger of frost has passed. They are usually available at your nursery, ready to plant. Just a few plants will produce enough harvests for most home gardens. Succession plant—planting new seeds or setting out young plants every three weeks or so, will extend harvests and avoid having an overabundance of produce to harvest all at one time.

Deciduous Fruit Trees

Figs—Picturesque fig trees such as the 'Mission', 'Brown Turkey' and 'Kadota' varieties thrive in the heat, and will grow in almost any soil. In addition, they are attractive trees in the landscape.

Peaches and Nectarines—Low-chill varieties of peaches such as 'Blazing Gold', 'Gold Dust', 'Desert Gold' and 'Babcock' ripen early and produce reasonable crops. Old favorites such as 'Elberta', 'Hale Heaven' or 'J. H. Hale', which excel in colder regions, are just not adapted to our desert climate. Also consider 'Party News Four Stars' peach. It produces highly colored, red freestone fruit with white flesh in mid-season. Prune to remove two of every three branches formed the previous year for improved fruit production.

Dwarf 'Bonanza Peach' eventually grows to only 6 feet high. It produces yellow-fleshed freestone fruit with a bland flavor early in the season. Its mature size is suited to border areas. Or grow in a large container; a half whiskey barrel is ideal.

Adapted nectarine varieties with low-chilling requirements include early fruiting 'Desert Dawn', 'Gold Mine' and 'Sunred'.

Pomegranates—Pomegranates have been grown in low-elevation deserts for centuries and in all kinds of soils, even alkaline. Long hedge rows of pomegranates are common in citrus and grape orchards from Indio to the Salton Sea.

'Wonderful' is generally grown as a large shrub to 10 feet high and as wide. Giant, red, burnished fruit appear in markets in the fall months. Regular and deep water are important for crop production. Selectively prune one-third of the previous years growth each winter is necessary or trees become too twiggy.

Avoid planting in lawn areas because trees need deep watering. Full sun is important. Bare-root trees are generally available and can be planted in December, January and February. Trees are available in containers for planting the rest of the year.

Citrus

Citrus trees are abundant in their offerings to desert gardeners, with evergreen foliage, fragrant flowers in season and decorative, tasty fruit. High heat required by most citrus is easily met in Coachella Valley. Full flavor and juiciness develop better here than almost anywhere.

Planting New Trees

Citrus plants need deep, well-drained soil. In frost-free areas they can be planted any time. Wait to plant in spring after danger of frost has passed in colder parts of the valley.

When planting more than one tree in an average-sized garden, space grapefruit 20 feet apart; other citrus 15 feet apart. Plant in the warmest location available—in full sun or with some afternoon shade. Avoid planting in lawns. A step-by-step planting guide can be found on page 18.

Irrigation

Build a basin around newly planted plants at least 4 feet in diameter with sides about 6 inches high. Be sure the rootball is being thoroughly moistened. Fill basin and soak soil well at least twice a week from March to May. Soak about three times a week June through September. Water every 10 to 12 days during the winter months.

Sun Protection

Wrap tree trunks with tree wraps or paint trunk with white latex paint diluted with water (50-50 solution) on exposed areas of the trunk to prevent sunburn.

Mature Tree Care

Irrigating properly helps prevent gummosis, a bark disease. After trees are established, maintain a dry area about 12 inches in diameter area around the trunk. Slightly raise the soil level so that the basin tapers down and away from the trunk, causing water to move away.

Contine to expand the basin so that it is slightly wider as the spread of branches. In sandy soils, water trees every 8 to 10 days March through May. Water twice a week June through September. Water every 10 to 14 days October through February.

Trees in lawns require deep watering and grow best without spray from lawn sprinklers hitting them. Typical shallow lawn irrigation to a few inches deep is not adequate for citrus. Green scum on the basin surface may indicate excess moisture. Check moisture depth every two weeks or so by digging down 18 inches with a shovel or use a soil probe. This is a long metal rod that can be pushed into the soil. It penetrates as deeply as the moisture, stopping when it reaches dry soil.

Avoid digging or cultivating around the basins of trees, which disturbs surface roots. Mulch, if applied, should be kept well away the trunk. Don't allow weeds or Bermudagrass to grow beneath trees.

Fertilization

Make the first application of complete citrus fertilizer in February to help set blossoms. Follow with one application per month until September. Apply fertilizer according to the fertilizer label. If trees are in lawns, it may be helpful to add a bit more to compensate for the competition. Spread fertilizer evenly across the watering basin, and water thoroughly after applying.

Pruning Citrus

Remove all dead wood, crossed limbs and control haphazard growth from the tree. Pull off (rather than cutting) suckers that grow below the bud union. Low-hanging branches around the perimeter of the tree should not be removed. They help the tree shade itself, preventing sunburn of the bark. If the tree is pruned, exposing the trunk, whitewash or wrap trunk to protect it.

Lemons often require more pruning than other citrus due to their rapid and sometimes rampant growth. Heavy pruning may reduce the number of lemons produced, but it can improve size and quality of fruit. Lemon trees may be pruned to fit a garden or kept at 8 to 12 feet to make it easier to pick fruit.

Fruit Drop

Some immature fruit can be expected to drop after blossoms fall and until fruit is 1/2-inch in diameter. Excess fruit drop can be caused by lack of moisture or fertility, overfertilization, excessive pruning, sudden change in temperature, freezing, poor soil drainage and insect pests. Avoid these by irrigating carefully, keep pruning to a minimum, control pests and fertilize on schedule. (See gardening calendar, pages 24 to 27.)

'Valencia' orange is one of the easiest citrus to grow. Its flavor is sweet, and fruit will hold well on the tree for months.

'Rio Red' grapefruit thrives in the valley's intense heat.

Frost Damage

Prune a frost-damaged tree only after new growth develops. After a severe freeze, die-back may continue into late spring and summer. If the tree is heavily damaged, remove the fruit. Limit water to the needs of the tree. fertilize frost-damaged trees lightly until they recover.

Harvesting Fruit

Remove fruit by cutting them from the stem rather than pulling. The rind must not be cut or split if the fruit is to be stored. Harvested fruit keeps best at 60°F. Wrapping in plastic reduces withering if the air is dry. Most citrus fruit can be left on the tree for long periods, but not too long or they become over-ripe. Frost-damaged fruit feels hard and the segments inside are often dry.

Mulching

Mulch materials—bark, planter mix, peat moss and gravel, to name a few, should be applied over the basin area to keep roots cool, reduce water loss through evaporation and to suppress weed growth. A 3-inch layer will keep roots 8°F to 10°F cooler. Keep mulch away from trunk to reduce gummosis disease.

Pest and Disease Control

Aphids are common citrus pests, sucking plant juices. The most important period to spray for them is just prior to or at the first flush of new growth—late February to early March. If ripe fruit are on the trees, pick enough to last at least three weeks before applying any insecticide. A second application may be necessary three weeks later. Most important, use only products labeled for use on citrus, and follow all directions. Thrip insects generally arrive with hot weather and can be controlled with insecticides. Timing of application is important.

Gummosis is a bark disease, evidenced by scaly bark and flow of sap, most often at the base of the tree. It develops in poorly drained soils and when wet soils remain in contact with bark. Affected trunks can be treated by removing scaly bark and dressing the area with one teaspoon of potassium permanganate to a pint of water. Soil and moisture must be kept away from the wound.

Iron Chlorosis—This is not a disease but a nutrient deficiency. When veins remain a dark green and the rest of the leaf turns a pale yellow, it is a good indication the plant is not able to absorb the iron it needs. This can be treated by applying iron sulfate at the rate of a pound per inch of trunk diameter measured three feet above the ground. Chelates (see glossary, page xx), act more quickly and can be applied as a foliar spray or to the soil. Chlorotic condition also can be caused by excess water, lack of other nutrients or excess alkalinity.

Annuals that bloom in winter and early spring brighten the landscape.

Gardening with Annuals

The vibrant colors of flowering annuals, lined up in the nursery, tempt us all. Each variety looks appealing and we want to take them all home to add to our gardens. But for the best results, design planting areas for flower color before purchasing plants. Here are a few tips to get you started.

Curved planting beds are relaxed and are generally more appealing than square patterns. Arrange color combinations to please the eye and to complement surrounding colors of walls, interior arrangements and nearby landscape plants.

Color helps create a mood: red, orange, and yellow are warm, exciting colors. Blue, green, and violet are cool, calm colors. White can be used in masses, in borders or as guidelines along walks and drives. Flower colors in gray-green, gray-blue, soft mauve, dull violet and dusty pink create a quiet, restful effect.

Getting Ready to Plant

To prepare for planting, pre-moisten beds to 12 inches deep. Add organic soil amendments and turn under 4 to 6 inches deep. Do this several weeks before planting.

(It's not necessary to add soil amendments if planting desert natives.) Provide adequate irrigation and prepare for seeding or setting out transplants.

Planting at the right season can make a difference in success or failure. Most ideal temperatures for planting winter and spring annuals are when night air temperatures range between 40°F to 60°F, and daytime air temperatures are in the 60°F to 80°F range. Daytime temperatures in the upper soil area is ideal at 50°F. These conditions generally occur from mid-October through November.

New plantings quickly become stressed due to strong, drying winds or sudden heat, so water new plants carefully. In fast-draining sandy soil, moisture must be supplied continually for plants to grow. Neglect will cause hardening of tissues and loss of plant health or life.

Annuals and perennials complement each other and can create long-lasting shows of color. Cultural needs are similar except that once established, perennials generally use less water. Most annuals tend to be overwatered. If fungus has been a problem in the past, use a fungicide before planting.

Soil-borne organisms can cause considerable trouble, plaguing new plantings of petunias and vincas, especially if they have been planted in the same location year after year. Prevent by removing leaf debris from planting beds, discard dead or dying plants and keep plants growing vigorously at all times. Rotate plantings. In other words, don't always grow the same kind of plant in the same bed. Try something new each planting season. Contact your nursery for current disease control products and practices.

Adding a Dry Creek to your Landscape

Many landscape projects, large and small, benefit from the addition of a dry creek bed. A dry creek bed becomes a landscape feature, simulating those common in the arroyos of our local foothills. It can be used to reduce turf areas, provide a means for drainage and create the backbone and setting of a natural habitat. Properly placed, flowering accent plants, small shrubs, ground covers and wildflowers complement natural patterns of pebbles, rocks and boulders.

Begin by creating a meandering swale 1-1/2 to 2 feet deep and 3 to 5 feet wide. Line the bottom and sides with 3- to 6-inch stones bolstered with clusters of 2- to 3-foot diameter boulders along edges. Bury rocks and boulders about one-third to one-quarter of their depth for a more natural effect.

Adding wildflowers in such natural areas will provide color for long periods and complement other plantings. Native plants to enhance the garden could include

A dry creek bed can be used to reduce turf areas, provide an avenue for drainage and create the backbone and setting of a natural, colorful scene.

Penstemon species are excellent perennial wildflowers, with abundant spring flowers.

Wildflowers such as golden *Eschscholzia californica,* California poppy, and bright blue California bluebells, *Phacelia campanularia,* combine with purple *Verbena* species. Many wildflowers reseed, coming back year after year.

ground covers such as *Baccharis* 'Centennial', prostrate coyote brush, *Dalea greggii,* prostrate indigo bush, and small shrubs such as *Encelia farinosa,* brittle bush, *Justicia californica,* chuperosa, and *Ericameria laricifolia,* turpentine bush. These are great companions, both for their foliage and seasonal color.

In a mature garden, existing trees and shrubs can continue to be an integral part of the scene. A dry creek bed can help the landscape "flow together," stimulating and creating a new, exciting look.

Wildflowers

Many wildflowers are included in the Plants for Desert Success chapter, pages 43 to 136. Follow some simple guidelines for preparation and planting to be successful with this large group of plants.

Any large or small garden area in a sunny location is a candidate for wildflowers. Wildflowers native to the desert are, by nature, better equipped to cope with your landscape needs than water-demanding species introduced from other parts of the world.

Fall, winter and early spring are natural periods for seeding spring-blooming species. Summer-flowering varieties can be planted during the spring. Locate in areas where there is ample sun. Select a seed mix or individual species to match your climate, elevation and availability of moisture. Seed mixtures typically contain six or more species to ensure a long season and a variety of color. A 1-ounce packet of seed will cover approximately 200 square feet.

Prepare planting area by moistening the soil to 12 inches deep. Remove weeds and debris prior to cultivation. Rake lightly to create a seed bed.

Broadcast seed with a hand-held fertilizer spreader or by hand. Most wildflower seed is very small. Mixing it with fine dry sand will enable more even distribution, and allow you to see where seed is being applied. Don't plant seeds too deep. Most wildflowers do best with 1/8-inch coverage of soil; read the packet to be sure.

After seeding, rake soil lightly in a cross pattern to cover seed. Water lightly with a fine mist attachment on the hose. Avoid washing soil or applying so much water at one time that it creates runoff. Water planted areas regularly (perhaps once a twice each day during warm temperatures) until seedlings appear. After sprouting, space out watering to every 7 to 14 days, depending on moisture content of soil. Pull weeds as they appear.

Fertilization is seldom necessary. Wildflowers generally do well in soils having low fertility.

Germination periods vary considerably for different wildflowers according to soil and air temperatures. Some may sprout in two weeks, others take four to six weeks or longer. Adequate deep moisture is essential. Temperatures 30°F or colder often delay germination.

Plants for Wildlife Habitats in the Coachella Valley

TREES FOR SHADE AND RESTING
Acacia smallii, sweet acacia
Cercidium floridum, blue palo verde
Prosopis species, mesquite
Olneya tesota, ironwood tree
Chilopsis linearis, desert willow

SHRUBS FOR NECTAR, FOOD AND SHELTER
Anisacanthus species, desert honeysuckle
Asclepias tuberosa, butterfly bush
Cleome isomeris, bladderpod
Calliandra species, fairy duster
Encelia farinosa, brittle bush
Larrea tridentata, creosote bush
Juniperus species, juniper
Justicia californica, chuparosa
Rosmarinus species, rosemary
Ligustrum species, privet
Zauschneria californica, California fuchsia

WILDFLOWERS FOR NECTAR
Baileya multiradiata, desert marigold
Aquilegia species, columbines
Heuchera species, coral bells
Kniphofia uvaria, red hot poker
Coreopsis species, coreopsis
Penstemon species, penstemon, bearded tongue
Salvia species, sage

VINES
Tecomeria capensis, cape honeysuckle
Campsis radicans, trumpet flower

CACTI AND SUCCULENTS
Fouquieria splendens, ocotillo
Hesperaloe parviflora, red yucca
Opuntia species, prickly pear
Cholla species, cholla
Echinocactus species, barrel cactus

Hummingbirds are common and welcome visitors to the wildlife garden.

After plants complete their flowering cycle and set seed, cut to 4 to 6 inches high and remove debris. Some fallen seed will have been eaten by birds or otherwise lost. To ensure another season of color, reseed with roughly half as much as the original planting. Spring seeding for summer annuals will require additional moisture. Perennial species will usually continue into the following year.

Creating a Wildlife Habitat

A well-established wildlife habitat in a corner of your landscape can become an invitation to many kinds of birds, animals, butterflies and other creatures that live in the desert environment.

Water, nectar, seeds, shelter in the form of low-growing trees and shrubs are important ingredients. Windbreaks can also become hospitable shelters. It become a remarkable discovery that no matter how distant our urban areas are removed from nature, wildlife will discover your garden when you create a suitable habitat. It is then that you will discover the magic and mysteries of nature so rich in our desert land.

If possible, include plants indigenous to the desert. Locate in a quiet part of the garden where trees and plants can grow as they will. Unpruned (or lightly pruned) forms provide the food and shelter wildlife require. Plants that grow naturally, with branches reaching to the ground, are preferred. Their density will create safe places for hiding, resting and nesting.

Water is a necessary element in a wildlife habitat. A water source can be as simple as a dripping faucet, a small, shallow fountain or a water dish.

Wildflowers and perennials with deep-throated, brightly colored flowers full of nectar are essential to attract hummingbirds and butterflies. Wildflowers and grasses that produce seeds become dependable food sources for seed-eating birds such as dove and quail.

Hummingbirds hone in to enjoy the nectar of brightly colored flowers. They pollinate with each visit. Butterflies and bees also visit to enjoy the nectar.

A bird feeder or two may be fine to interest small birds, yet avoid broadcasting grerat quantities of grain on the ground. This often attracts too many larger birds, which can stress the habitat and bird population.

As the garden ages the soil becomes home for earthworms, lizards, desert pocket mice and other soil-related animals and insects. They help to develop a balanced food cycle for all the residents. And when you create the right environment, roadrunners, quail and doves help keep snails, slugs and other pests under control.

The list on this page provides some recommended plants to help establish your wildlife habitat.

Glossary

Acid, Acidic [soil]—Having a pH value below 7. See pH.

Air Layering—Method of propagation. Portion of stem is induced to root by enclosing it in a rooting medium while attached to the parent plant.

Alkaline [soil]—A pH value above 7. See pH.

Alluvial [soil, slopes]—Areas of "young," rocky soils, typically at the bases of mountains.

Alternate [leaves]—Borne singly at each node, on either side of a stem.

Angiosperm—Any plant that has its seeds enclosed in an ovary.

Annual—Plant that completes its life cycle in one season.

Anther—Part of a stamen that produces pollen, usually borne on a filament.

Apex—Tip or growing point of an organ such as a leaf or shoot.

Aquatic—Plant that grows in water.

Architectural—Plants that have strong and often spectacular shapes.

Backfill—Soil that is returned to planting hole to fill in around rootball of plant.

Bare root—Plants that are sold and planted without soil around their roots, which occurs when they are dormant. Roses and certain deciduous fruit trees are examples.

Beneficial Insects—Insects that prey and feed on insect pests that attack garden plants.

Biennial—Plant that completes its life cycle in two years, usually flowering and fruiting the second year.

Blow Sand—Sand that is blown into an area, propelled by strong winds. Can damage plants and property if wind velocity is too high.

Bolt—To produce flowers and seed prematurely, such as bolt to seed. Occurs most often when plants are set out too late in the year or when unseasonably hot weather accelerates their growth.

Bract—Modified leaves that can take on the appearance of flowers. Bracts are usually green but can be conspicuous and colorful. An example is bougainvillea.

Bud—Rudimentary or condensed shoot containing embryonic leaves and or flowers.

Caliche—Soil condition found in some areas of the Southwest. A deposit of calcium carbonate beneath the soil surface.

Chlorosis—Nutrient deficiency in plants. Shows itself when leaves take on a yellowish cast. Iron chlorosis is common in the Southwest U.S.

CIMIS—California Irrigation Management Information System. Computer-generated information from weather stations across the state record and disseminate data to help determine a plant's water need.

Compost—Mixture of decomposed vegetative matter, useful for amending soil, mulching and fertilizing.

Controller (irrigation system)—Regulates of when and how much water is applied via an irrigation system.

Crown—The "heart" of a plant, where roots and stems join. Important to position most plants with the crown slightly above soil level when planting to prevent rot.

Cultivar—Cultivated variety of a plant, rather than a variety that occurs naturally in the wild. Designated in this book with single quotation marks.

Cuttings—Portions of stem or root, sometimes called "slips," that can be induced to form roots and develop into new plants.

Deadheading—Removing flower heads after they are past prime, which can encourage more flowers.

Deciduous—Losing leaves or other plant parts during dormant season of year. Plant almost appears to die but regrows the next season.

Division—Propagation by dividing a clump into several parts, often while plant is dormant.

Dormant, Dormancy—Alive but not actively growing.

Drainage (soil)—Water movement through the soil, in regard to plant roots. Sandy soils are fast-draining; clay soils drain slowly.

Drip Irrigation—System in which water is delivered (dripped) to plants at their root zones via emitters (see next column.)

Dripline—Imaginary area around a tree that marks its widest growth. So called because rain tends to fall from the tree to the ground at its drip line.

Drought Tolerant—Inherent ability of a plant to survive without water for long periods of time.

Emitter—Irrigation equipment that is part of a drip system. Allows water to be applied slowly to plant roots in controlled increments, such as 1-gallon, 2-gallon or 5-gallon.

Establish—When, after planting, a plant passes the shock of transplanting and produces good root and top growth. Plants are sometimes considered "established" after living and growing through one summer season.

Evapotranspiration (ET)—Evaporation of moisture from a leaf's surface. The ET rate for a given plant is the amount of moisture it needs to sustain itself.

Evergreen—Plants that have green leaves throughout the year.

Family—A biological classification. All members of a plant family share certain characteristics that are not found in other families. See Genus.

Feeder Roots—Roots that absorb moisture and nutrients for a plant, typically located at the perimeter of a plant at its dripline.

Floret—Small, individual flower in the flowerheads of the Compositae family, or a cluster of flowers.

Flower—Reproductive unit of an angiosperm. The basic flower forms are single, with one row of usually 4 to 6 petals; semidouble, with more petals, usually in two rows; double, with many petals in several rows and few or no stamens; fully double, usually rounded in shape, with densely packed petals and with stamens obscured.

Foliage—A plant's leaves.

Genus—Most important subdivision of a plant or animal family, designated by the first word in the botanical name. In *Salvia elegans,* (pineapple sage), Salvia is the genus, elegans is the species. See the listing, Species.

Growing Season—Days between last frost and first frost. In the Coachella Valley it is approximately 330 days.

Habit (growth, flowering)—The natural form or tendencies of a plant. For example, compact, upright or spreading growth habit.

Harden Off—To gradually adjust (harden) plants to colder temperatures. Common when plants from a nursery greenhouse are brought home.

Hardpan—See Caliche.

Hardy, Cold Hardy—Describes a plant's resistance to, or tolerance of, frost or freezing temperatures (as in "hardy to 20F"). The word does not mean tough, pest resistant or disease resistant. See Tender.

Heading—also called Topping. Removing limbs and branches at arbitrary height, which ruins the tree's form.

Herbaceous—In a general sense, plants having non-woody tissues.

Humus—Soft, moist, dark brown to black content of soil, mostly derived from decaying plant matter.

Hybrid—Offspring of genetically different parents, usually produced accidentally or artificially in cultivation, rarely occurring in the wild.

Hydrozoning—Grouping and placing plants in a landscape according to water requirement. Typical zones are high, moderate and low.

Leach, Leaching—The washing action of rainfall or irrigation water to move nutrients or salts from the upper layers of soil where plant roots are located.

Leader—In a single-trunk shrub or tree, the central, upward-growing stem.

Loam (soil)—Well-structured, fertile soil that is moisture retentive and well drained.

Microclimate—A small climate that differs from a surrounding large climate zone. Can be as small as a cool north exposure compared to a warm south exposure.

Mulch—A layer of matter applied to the soil around a plant's root zone to conserve moisture, protect the roots from frost, reduce weed growth and enrich the soil.

Native Plant—A plant that grows in the wild in a given region.

Naturalize—Plants that spread on their own to grow in an area. For example, wildflowers can reseed to naturalize in a given location.

Organic Matter—Materials blended into soil to improve plant growth. Compost, peat moss and ground bark are examples.

Overseed (lawn)—As warm-season grasses such as Bermuda go dormant and turn brown in winter, cool-season grasses such as annual or perennial rye are seeded over the lawn.

Perennial—Living for at least three seasons, normally flowering every year. May die down during the winter season.

Petiole—In botany, the stalk to which a leaf is attached.

pH, pH Scale—A measure of soil acidity or alkalinity. 0-6.9 is acid; 7 is neutral, 7.1-14 is alkaline.

Rhizome—Underground stem that lives for more than one season.

Runner—Horizontally spreading, usually slender stem that forms roots at nodes. Often confused with stolon.

Runoff—When rainfall or irrigation is too great for the soil to absorb and water is wasted as it "runs off."

Self-Seed, Self-Sow—Dropping or freely distributing its seed, from which new plants grow the following season.

Species—Plants having certain differences from other plants within the same genus. The second word in a plant's Latin name. See Genus.

Sprig—Small, 2- to 3-inch twig or section of stem and leaves cut from the tip of a plant.

Stolon—Stem that creeps along the surface of the ground, taking root at intervals and forming new plants where it roots.

Sucker—Plant growth that appears different from other stems and branches in a grafted plant. Sucker growth originates at the rootstock, not the desired grafted part of the plant.

Tender, Cold Tender—Susceptible to cold temperature damage, as contrasted to Hardy.

Topiary—Technique of shaping shrubs and trees into formalized shapes, often in geometric or animal forms.

Transitional Garden—Plants with low to moderate water needs that blend with and make the transition between a high-water oasis garden and low-water plants on the landscape perimeter.

Tuber—Thick underground stem, from which a plant grows. Similar to a rhizome but is usually shorter and thicker.

Umbel—Flower cluster sometimes resembling an umbrella supported by pedicels (small stems) that seem to rise from the same point.

Variegated—Marked with patches or streaks of different colors.

Variety—Naturally occurring variation of a species. Sometimes abbreviated as var.

Windbreak—Planting of trees and shrubs to block, filter or deflect the wind.

Windthrow—Plant, usually a tree, uprooted by strong winds.

Xeriscape—A method of landscaping that uses common-sense plant selection and maintenance principles to save water while enhancing our surroundings .

Resources

In addition to this book, there are many other resources and reference materials, several of which are listed here. Videotapes and CD-ROMs add visual elements to the educational process. For example, Coachella Valley Water District supplements this publication with a localized version of a CD-ROM, *Desert Landscaping: Plants for a Water-Scarce Environment*, published by the Water Resources Research Center of the University of Arizona.

These and many of the following may be purchased in the Living Desert gift shop in Palm Desert, and other specialty stores, bookstores and nurseries. This book and *Desert Landscaping* CD-ROM are available directly from the Coachella Valley Water District.

This publication can be viewed on-line at Coachella Valley Water District's internet site: www.cvwd.org. In fact, it was available long before this print version. Searches for "desert landscaping" and "water conservation" could lead you to new web sites for more information.

Books

Beautiful Gardens: A Guide to over 80 Botanical Gardens, Arboretums and More in Southern California and the Southwest. Eric A. Johnson and Scott Millard, Ironwood Press, Tucson, Ariz.

California Native Trees and Shrubs, Lee W. Lentz and John Dourley, Rancho Santa Ana Botanical Garden, Claremont, Calif.

Citrus, Lance Walheim, Ironwood Press, Tucson, Ariz.

Coping with Soil Salinity, Sam Aslan, U.S. Department of Agriculture Consolidated Farm Service Agency, Indio, Calif., field office

Desert Accent Plants; Desert Bird Gardening; Desert Butterfly Gardening; Desert Grasses; Desert Ground Covers & Vines; Desert Shrubs; Desert Trees; and Desert Wildflowers are booklets available from Arizona Native Plant Society, Tucson, Ariz.

Desert Gardener's Calendar, George Brookbank, University of Arizona Press, Tucson

Desert Landscape Architecture, John Krieg, CRC Press, Tampa, Fla

Desert Landscaping, George Brookbank, University of Arizona Press, Tucson

Gardening in the Desert, Mary Irish, University of Arizona Press, Tucson

Gardening in Dry Climates, Scott Millard, Ortho Books, (Meredith Books), Des Moines, Iowa

How to Grow The Wildflowers, Eric A. Johnson and Scott Millard, Ironwood Press, Tucson, Ariz.

Landscape Plants for Dry Regions, Warren Jones and Charles Sacamano, Fisher Books, Tucson, Ariz.

Landscape Plants for Western Regions, Bob Perry, Land Design Publishing, San Dimas, Calif.

The Low-Water Flower Gardener, Eric A. Johnson and Scott Millard, Ironwood Press, Tucson, Ariz.

Low-Water Use Plants, Carol Schuler, Fisher Books, Tucson, Ariz.

Native Texas Plants, Sally Wasowski and Andy Wasowski, Gulf Publishing, Houston, Tex.

Natural by Design, Judith Phillips, Museum of New Mexico Press. Santa Fe, New Mexico

Natural History of the Sonoran Desert, Steve Phillips, editor, Arizona-Sonora Desert Museum Press, Tucson, Ariz.

Plants for Dry Climates, Mary Rose Duffield and Warren D. Jones, Fisher Books, Tucson, Ariz.

Plants for Natural Gardens, Judith Phillips, Museum of New Mexico Press, Santa Fe, New Mexico

Pruning, Planting & Care: Johnson's Guide to Gardening, Eric A. Johnson, Ironwood Press, Tucson, Ariz.

Saline and Alkali Soils, Agriculture Handbook 60, U.S. Department of Agriculture, Washington D.C.

Southwestern Landscaping with Native Plants, Judith Phillips, Museum of New Mexico Press, Santa Fe, New Mexico

Sunset Western Garden Book, Sunset Publishing, Menlo Park, Calif.

Taylor's Guide to Gardening in the Southwest, Houghton Mifflin Co., Boston, Mass.

Turfgrass Water Conservation, Victor A. Gibeault and Stephen T. Cockerham, University of California, Division of Agricultural and Natural Resources, Berkeley, Calif.

Waterwise Gardening, Sunset Publishing, Menlo Park, Calif.

Videos and CD ROMs

Desert Landscaping: Plants for a Water-Scarce Environment, Coachella Valley Edition: CD-ROM, Water Resources Research Center, University of Arizona, Tucson, Ariz.

Drought Survival Guide: video, Sunset Publishing, Menlo Park, Calif.

Efficient Water Management in the Landscape: video, San Luis Video Publishing, San Luis Obispo, Calif.

Landscape Irrigation Maintenance and Troubleshooting: video, San Luis Video Publishing, San Luis Obispo, Calif.

Micro Irrigation Management: video, Richard J. Soltys Productions, Coachella Valley Resource Conservation District, Indio, Calif.

Micro Irrigation Uniformity and Efficiency: video, Richard J. Soltys Productions, Coachella Valley Resource Conservation District, Indio, Calif.

Public Gardens

Arboretums and botanic gardens play important roles in the study of arid-climate plants. Each offers valuable information and ideas on plant selection, landscaping and water conservation, particularly for the surrounding area. Note that the information regarding these gardens is subject to change. Phone ahead to be certain of hours of operation.

COACHELLA VALLEY GARDENS

Coachella Valley Water District
Avenue 52 at Hwy 111
Coachella, CA 92236
(760) 398-2651
Demonstration gardens are available for public viewing at headquarters (address above) and CVWD's domestic water facility at Hovley Lane and Water Way in Palm Desert.

Desert Water Agency
1200 S. Gene Autry Trail
Palm Springs, CA 92264
(760) 323-4971
Serving Palm Springs proper, DWA houses water-efficient demonstration gardens at its headquarters and nearby water-recycling facility.

College of the Desert Arboretum
43-500 Monterey Avenue
Palm Desert, CA 92260
(760) 773-2561
The landscaping on this 160 acre campus is designed to suggest appropriate plants for the public and landscape industry. Six pie-shaped areas on campus repre-sent the flora of a continent or geographic region. Also on site are specialty gardens such as palms, flowering perennials, succulents and grasses. A volunteer program provides an opportunity to learn propagation, culture of nursery stock and botanical labeling.

Living Desert
47-900 Portola Avenue
Palm Desert, CA 92260
(760) 346-5694
Coachella Valley gardeners have easy access to Living Desert where new horticultural and landscape plant displays are created regularly to offer a variety of ideas for home use. Here, local Sonoran Desert plants can be viewed with species from Australia, Africa, South America and Asia. Educational programs and tours supplement the exhibits. Located 1-1/2 miles south of Highway 111. Open 9 a.m. to 5 p.m. daily. Entrance fee.

ARIZONA GARDENS

Arizona-Sonora Desert Museum
2021 North Kinney Road
Tucson, AZ 85743
(520) 883-2702 for recorded information
(520) 883-1380
Located 14 miles west of downtown Tucson. Head west from I-10 on Speedway through Gates Pass, then north on Kinney Road to the Museum entrance.

Over 15 developed acres on a total of 186 acres, including natural habitat zoo, walk-in aviary, demonstration gardens, earth science exhibits and more. Over 300 plant species and 200 live animal species.

Open daily 8:30 a.m. to 5 p.m. from mid-September to mid-March. Open 7:30 a.m. to 6 p.m. from mid March to mid-September. No tickets sold one hour before closing. Entrance fee; children under 6 free with an adult.

Desert Botanical Garden
1201 North Galvin Parkway
Phoenix, AZ 85008
(602) 941-1225
Located 8 miles east of the center of metropolitan Phoenix. From I-10 take east Van Buren Street to north Galvin Parkway. From Scottsdale Road to McDowell Road, then west on Galvin Parkway.

145 acres of landscaped ground. October through April is most comfortable time to visit. May through September is usually quite hot. Touring time is one to three hours.

Open daily 9 a.m. to sunset. Open at 8 a.m. during July and August. Closed Christmas Day. Entrance fee.

Boyce Thompson Southwestern Arboretum
37615 Highway 60
Superior, AZ 85273
(520) 689-2811 for recorded information
(520) 689-2723
Located 60 miles east of Phoenix on Highway 60, 3 miles west of Superior.

Over 35 acres and two miles of nature trails that represent plants and gardens adapted to live in the Sonoran Desert of Arizona.

Open daily 8 to 5 p.m. Closed Christmas Day. Entrance fee. Children under 5 free with an adult. Picnic facilities available.

Tohono Chul Park
7366 North Paseo del Norte
Tucson, AZ 85704
(520) 575-8468 for recorded information
(520) 742-6455
From I-10, take Ina Road exit east to North Paseo del Norte. Go north a short distance and turn east into the garden entrance.

Over 400 plant species on 49 acres of demonstration gardens and nature trails, including several patios, ramadas and special gardens. Features two well-stocked gift shops.

Park open daily all year 7 a.m. to sunset. Donation suggested.

Tucson Botanical Gardens
2150 North Alvernon Way
Tucson, AZ 85712
(520) 326-9255 for recorded information
(520) 326-9255
Located in central Tucson, on North Alvernon Way just south of Grant Road. Take I-10 exit east on Grant, travel to Alvernon, then head south a short distance to garden entrance.

More than 5 acres of gardens and displays, with over 400 plant species. Many specialty gardens, including Xeriscape.

Open daily 8:30 a.m. to 4:30 p.m. Closed July 4, Thanksgiving, Christmas Eve, Christmas Day, New Year's Day.

Entrance fee required. Children 5 and under are free.

CALIFORNIA GARDENS

Landscapes Southern California Style Western Municipal Water District
450 Alessandro Blvd.
Riverside, CA 92508
(909) 780-4177
A 1-acre, water-wise demonstration garden designed for self-guided tours. Shows how to save water, time and money in the landscape.

Open daily (except holidays) 10 a.m. to 4 p.m. No entrance fee.

Los Angeles State & County Arboretum
301 North Baldwin Ave.
Arcadia, CA 91007-2697
(818) 446-8251 or
(213) 681-8411
Located 20 miles east of downtown Los Angeles. From the 210 Freeway, take the Baldwin Avenue exit south about 1 mile to entrance.

Over 127 acres of landscaped grounds demonstration gardens, plant collections and historic buildings.

Open daily 9 a.m. to 4:30 p.m. Closed Christmas Day. Entrance fee required.

Rancho Santa Ana Botanic Garden
1500 North College Avenue
Claremont, CA 91711
(714) 625-8767
Located 30 miles east of Los Angeles. From I-10 take Indian Hill Boulevard exit north to Foothill Boulevard. Travel east to College Avenue. Go north on North College Avenue to the garden entrance.

86 acres of native California plants, including more than 2,800 species.

Open daily 8a.m. to 5 p.m. Closed July 4th, Thanksgiving Day, Christmas Day and New Year's Day. No entrance fee.

Santa Barbara Botanic Garden
1212 Mission Canyon Rd.
Santa Barbara, CA 93105
(805) 563-2521 for recorded information.
(805) 682-4726
Over 65 acres of display gardens and preserve of California native plants, grouped by geographical regions of the state. Although this is a coastal region, the limited water resources of Santa Barbara make it a resource to learn more about water conservation. Open each day 8 a.m. to sunset.
Entrance fee required.

Theodore Payne Foundation for Wildflowers and Native Plants
10459 Tuxford Street,
Sun Valley, CA 91352
(818) 768-1802
(818) 768-3533
Wildflower Hotline from March to May Northwest of Glendale off I-5. Take the Sunland Boulevard exit north to Tuxford Street. Turn right on Tuxford to entrance, which is marked with a small sign.

The Theodore Payne Foundation is a learning and information center and nursery for 800 plant species, including rare and endangered plants.

Open 8:30 a.m. to 4:30 p.m. Wednesday to Saturday. 11a.m. to 4:30 p.m. Sunday. Summer hours vary: Call ahead. Closed major holidays. No entrance fee.
www.theodorepayne.org

UCR Botanic Gardens University of California, Riverside campus
Riverside, CA 92521
(714) 787-4650
From I-215/State Highway 60, exit Martin Luther King Blvd. and head west. Turn north on Canyon Crest Ave. to enter the University. At Campus Drive turn east and follow the signs to the gardens.

Open daily 8 to 5 p.m. Closed July 4th, Thanksgiving, Christmas and New Year's Day. No entrance fee but contributions appreciated.

NEVADA GARDENS

Desert Demonstration Garden
3701 Alta Drive
Las Vegas, NV 89153
(702) 258-3205
From I-15 take the West Charleston Boulevard off ramp. Proceed west on Charleston then right on Valley View, and right again on Alta Drive to entrance.

A garden dedicated to water conservation. Founded by the Las Vegas Kiwanis Club, rededicated by Las Vegas Water District and University of Nevada Cooperative Extension Service.

Open Monday to Friday 8 to 6 p.m. Open Saturdays 8 to 12 p.m. Closed New Year's Day, Washington's Birthday, Memorial Day, July 4th, Labor Day, Nevada Day (October 31st), Veteran's Day, Thanksgiving (Thursday and Friday), and Christmas Day.
No entrance fee.

Ethel M® Chocolates Botanical Cactus Garden
2 Cactus Garden Drive
Henderson, NV 89014
(702) 458-8864
Located 5 miles from I-15 and Las Vegas Boulevard. Take Tropicana Boulevard east to Mountain Vista, go south to Sunset Way (adjacent to the Ethel M Chocolate Factory on Cactus Garden Drive in the Green Valley Business Park). Follow signs to garden entrance.

A beautiful, 4-acre display of colorful, well-maintained desert shrubs, trees and exotic cacti and succulents.

Open daily 8:30 a.m. to 7:00 p.m.

No entrance fee.

University of Nevada Las Vegas Arboretum
4505 Maryland Parkway
Las Vegas, NV 89154
(702) 739-3392
Travel two miles east of I-15 and Las Vegas Boulevard on Tropicana Avenue to Swenson Avenue, turn north to Harmon Avenue. Entrance to garden is off Harmon Avenue. Parking areas located north of Barrick Museum of Natural History at the end of Harmon.

A unique, on-campus arboretum and Xeriscape demonstration garden.

Open daily—does not close.
No entrance fee.

Museum hours are Monday to Friday 9 a.m. to 4:45 p.m.; Saturday 10 a.m. to 4:45 p.m.

Index
GARDENING TERMS

Index

Plants